Practical Video Game Bots

Automating Game Processes using C++, Python, and AutoIt

Ilya Shpigor

APress®

Practical Video Game Bots: Automating Game Processes using C++, Python, and AutoIt

Ilya Shpigor
St. Petersburg, c.St-Peterburg, Russia

ISBN-13 (pbk): 978-1-4842-3735-9   ISBN-13 (electronic): 978-1-4842-3736-6
https://doi.org/10.1007/978-1-4842-3736-6

Library of Congress Control Number: 2018954729

Managing Director, Apress Media LLC: Welmoed Spahr
Acquisitions Editor: Steve Anglin
Development Editor: Matthew Moodie
Coordinating Editor: Mark Powers

Cover designed by eStudioCalamar

Cover image designed by Freepik (www.freepik.com)

Distributed to the book trade worldwide by Springer Science+Business Media New York, 233 Spring Street, 6th Floor, New York, NY 10013. Phone 1-800-SPRINGER, fax (201) 348-4505, e-mail orders-ny@springer-sbm. com, or visit www.springeronline.com. Apress Media, LLC is a California LLC and the sole member (owner) is Springer Science + Business Media Finance Inc (SSBM Finance Inc). SSBM Finance Inc is a **Delaware** corporation.

For information on translations, please e-mail editorial@apress.com; for reprint, paperback, or audio rights, please email bookpermissions@springernature.com.

Apress titles may be purchased in bulk for academic, corporate, or promotional use. eBook versions and licenses are also available for most titles. For more information, reference our Print and eBook Bulk Sales web page at http://www.apress.com/bulk-sales.

Any source code or other supplementary material referenced by the author in this book is available to readers on GitHub via the book's product page, located at www.apress.com/9781484237359. For more detailed information, please visit http://www.apress.com/source-code.

Printed on acid-free paper

Table of Contents

About the Author

Ilya Shpigor is a software developer and open source enthusiast. He has significant experience in such domains as Embedded Systems, Information Security, and Real-Time Computing.

Ilya currently works in the automotive industry. He develops security systems for Ethernet networks in cars. Before that, he developed intrusion detection systems, flight simulators, and control systems for sea ships. Also, he has participated in the Wine open source project and ALT Linux distribution.

Ilya is interested in automating routine tasks and researching the capacities of different programming languages to solve specific problems. In his free time, he explores software vulnerabilities and AI approaches.

About the Technical Reviewer

Massimo Nardone has more than 24 years of experience in Security, Web/Mobile Development, Cloud, and IT Architecture. His true IT passions are Security and Android.

He has been programming and teaching how to program with Android, Perl, PHP, Java, VB, Python, C/C++, and MySQL for more than 20 years.

He holds a Master of Science degree in Computing Science from the University of Salerno, Italy.

He has worked as a Project Manager, Software Engineer, Research Engineer, Chief Security Architect, Information Security Manager, PCI/SCADA Auditor, and Senior Lead IT Security/Cloud/SCADA Architect for many years.

His technical skills include Security, Android, Cloud, Java, MySQL, Drupal, Cobol, Perl, Web and Mobile development, MongoDB, D3, Joomla, Couchbase, C/C++, WebGL, Python, Pro Rails, Django CMS, Jekyll, Scratch, etc.

He has worked as a visiting lecturer and supervisor for exercises at the Networking Laboratory of the Helsinki University of Technology (Aalto University). He holds four international patents (PKI, SIP, SAML, and Proxy areas).

He currently works as Chief Information Security Officer (CISO) for Cargotec Oyj and is a member of the ISACA Finland Chapter Board.

Massimo has reviewed more than 45 IT books for different publishing companies and is the coauthor of *Pro Android Games* (Apress, 2015), *Pro JPA 2 in Java EE 8* (Apress, 2018), and *Beginning EJB in Java EE 8* (Apress, 2018).

Acknowledgments

A special thank you to Svetlana Zalogina, who reviewed the first chapters of this book and provided many style recommendations. Also, I would like to thank Danila Bogdanov and Emil Shaykhilislamov, who pointed out my mistakes and gave me advice on how to cover the game bot topic better. Thanks to Ruslan Piasetskyi, who explained to me some subtleties of the cryptography domain.

Preface

This is not a guide on how to cheat and violate rules in video games. This is a book about approaches to automating a game process and protecting it against automation.

We will consider applications that play video games in your place; they are named bots. You will find here a classification of such applications by their internal mechanics. The book covers most methods and technologies that are used by bot developers. Also, the various approaches of anticheating systems are considered here.

This book provides solutions and useful advices for such topics as process automation, reverse engineering, encryption, and network applications. Modern bots use technologies in all these domains.

Introduction

Sometimes when you play your favorite video game, you can find yourself repeating simple actions. Perhaps this process reminds you of working with old manual machines. You would mount a piece of metal, press the button to launch the drill, pull the lever down, and so forth. But wait a minute. We live in the 21st century, and long before us people have learned ways to automate simple, monotonous actions. These thoughts occurred to me while I was playing my favorite video game.

After that, I decided to start looking for ways to automate my game process. I have visited plenty of forums and websites. Most of the applications for game automation that I found contained malicious software. Some of them were virus-free, but they did not work at all. During my searches, people with strange nicknames suggested that I buy these black magic applications that should solve all my problems. But it seems pretty weird to buy something from an anonymous person over the Internet without any guarantees. Further, I realized why bot developers prefer to hide their names. Thus, my searches failed.

My next step was an attempt to implement a bot myself. But I faced a shortage of systematic documentation about the topic, despite the fact that bot applications often solve difficult algorithmic tasks and are based on several information technology domains. The situation looked very strange, because this kind of software can be very complex, and moreover, bot development has a long history. Enthusiasts and professional software developers found a lot of solutions and approaches to effectively solving this task. Why didn't anybody care about sharing this kind of information?

This book is an attempt to overcome this information vacuum around the topic of bot development. You will find a bot classification here that I developed from my experience and research. We will consider the internal mechanisms of different kinds of bots and will try to write simple prototypes. You will learn about tools for bot development as well as anticheating systems for preventing usage of the bots.

The book will be interesting to all players who want to discover a new sense and approach to the game process. It will also be useful for players who do not care about bot application internals but just want to buy one and use it. You will learn about the available kinds of bots and which exploitation issues you may face. I hope everybody will find something interesting and new in this book.

CHAPTER 1

Overview of Bots

This chapter provides necessary information about video game applications and bots for them. The working scheme of a typical game application is described here in detail. We will consider bot classification according to the ways of interacting with a game. It will be convenient to use this classification throughout the book for simplifying the discussion of the topic. This chapter begins with a brief overview of game bots' purposes and the tasks that bots can solve.

Purpose of Bots

"What kind of tasks do video game bots solve?" This is the question you will ask when you hear about video game bots for the first time. We can make a step backward and look at the history and reasons for inventing bots.

The first mention of bots appears in first-person shooter (FPS) games. The problem arises when people start to compete in the "player-versus-player" mode, which is also known as the "deathmatch." Sometimes players wanted to practice alone without human opponents, or they just did not have any chance to connect with other players. A deathmatch game differs significantly from the single-player mode. When you play single-player mode, you pass through the game world level by level and fight against enemies. These enemies just stay somewhere and attack you when you come too close. The primitive artificial intelligence (AI) algorithms can easily solve this task. The AI in a deathmatch should behave in a much more complicated way. It should move around the game level, pick up weapons and ammo, decide when it will be favorable to attack a player or to retreat for recovery, and do many other things. In other words, it should behave or at least look like a human player. This kind of AI was named a "bot."

Video game evolution brings new kinds of tasks. Massively multiplayer online role-playing games (MMORPGs) were becoming more and more popular in conjunction with increasing Internet penetration. This new genre has a lot in common with the

© Ilya Shpigor 2018
I. Shpigor, *Practical Video Game Bots*, https://doi.org/10.1007/978-1-4842-3736-6_1

classic role-playing game (RPG), but now a game process became more stretched in time because of the large number of players participating and interacting. Also, the MMORPG developers intend to keep players' interest in a game as long as possible. These traits of the new genre lead to increasing the time for a player's character development. Now you should spend weeks or months performing quests and extracting resources. All these things are required to achieve a character level that is high enough to compete with other players. The main attraction of most MMORPG games is this kind of competition with human opponents.

Most of the players consider the process of character development as very monotonous, having a vast number of repetitious actions. At some point, they start looking for ways to automate this tedious task. Some MMORPG developers provide tools to create plug-ins with trivial automation. But usually, you do not have it, and even you have it, you need much more. Workarounds, which are unintended by developers, are required to extend MMORPG functionality appropriately. The game developers do not get any benefit from this kind of feature. Even worse, players spend less time in the game and make fewer in-game purchases. Thus, developers would frequently prohibit any workarounds. These custom applications and plug-ins for game automation were named MMORPG bots. Perhaps this name is because of the imitation of player behavior, which looks very similar to the FPS game bots.

The automation of the game process is not the only task that has appeared with the new genre of online games. Some players compete with others so enthusiastically that they start looking for ways to avoid game rules, which allows them to get significant advantages over opponents. These advantages can be showing extra information about game state, changing characteristics of the game characters, immediately receiving the necessary resources, and so forth. Applications for achieving these goals are called "cheats," "hacks," and sometimes "bots." This naming can create confusion. Cheating in the games is not the same as automating the game process. I would prefer to distinguish the "cheat" name from the "bot" name. In this book, "bot" will mean automating actions.

You have seen that game bots can solve various tasks. Players can use them for training their skills before competitions with other players in FPS and other electronic sports disciplines. Also, bots can boost the development of the player character in multiplayer online games. Finally, bots can give an advantage over other players by affecting a game process.

Game Application

Before we start our investigation of bot internals, we should consider how a typical video game application works. There are many genres of video games. All of them differ, but the same architecture and principles are used to develop them.

Let us consider a typical online game application. You can find its logical elements on Figure 1-1.

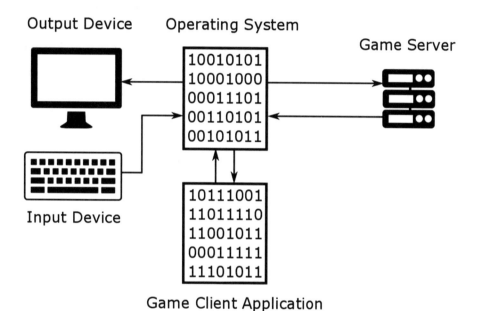

Figure 1-1. *Elements of a typical online game application*

When you launch the game on your computer, you start a new **computing processes**. Each of them has a separate **memory sandbox** that has been allocated by **operating system** (OS). The memory is only one type of the resources which are provided to launched processes by OS. Another resource consists of devices like the monitor, keyboard, mouse, network adapter, and so forth. The CPU is just a special device that does the actual execution of the launched process.

You may ask, "Why do we need OS instead of launching the game directly on the hardware?" The OS system provides a platform to develop applications. Without OS, each software company would need to invent its own way to work with all the required devices, which is a lot of work. It is much easier to take already available device drivers, which are provided by OS.

Now we come back to our game application scheme. You can see several arrows there. They match to the data transfers that are performed by OS to serve the launched process.

OS handles commands from the process to display some pictures on the screen or to send a packet to a server through the network adapter. Also, OS responds to notify the process about device events. For example, when you do a keypress or when the game server sends a packet, the OS immediately reports the game process about it. OS performs all these tasks using drivers and system libraries. They are combined in the block with the "Operating System" name in the scheme for simplification purposes.

Now we will consider an algorithm for processing one player's action. We will use the scheme to follow the elements that participate in this processing. For example, you want to move a player character. You press an arrow key on the keyboard to do it. Then these steps will be done as a reaction to your press:

1. **Input Device → Operating System**

   A keyboard driver notifies OS through the **interrupt** mechanism that the arrow key has been pressed.

2. **Operating System → Game Client Application**

   OS handles the keyboard driver event. Then, OS notifies the game process about the keyboard event. Usually, this notification will be received by the process whose window has an active state at the moment. Let us assume that this is the game application.

3. **Game Client Application**

   The game process receives the keyboard event notification from OS. The process updates the state of game objects in its own memory according to the new character position.

4. **Game Client Application → Operating System**

   The game process should notify the game server about a new state. The process commands OS to send a packet via its network library. The packet contains information about the new character position. The library asks a network adapter driver to send the packet.

5. **Operating System → Game Server**

   The game server receives the network packet from the client host.
   Then, it validates the new character position according to the
   game rules. If this validation succeeds, the server sends a network
   packet to the client host with confirmation for updated data.

6. **Operating System → Game Client Application**

   OS notifies the game process about the confirmation packet from
   the game server. The process reads packet data via the network
   library of the OS. The library again uses the driver to read data.

7. **Game Client Application**

   The game process extracts the server's confirmation from the
   received network packet. If the confirmation fails, the character
   position is kept unchanged. Otherwise, the new position will be
   assigned to the character object.

8. **Game Client Application → Operating System**

   The game process requires OS to update a picture on the screen
   according to the new character position.

9. **Operating System → Output Device**

   OS requires a graphics library like OpenGL or DirectX to draw a
   new picture on the screen. The library performs calculations for
   the new picture and draws it using a video driver.

We considered everything that is needed to move a player character.

The algorithm is kept unchanged for almost all other player actions. It does not
matter if you play with a keyboard, mouse, joystick, or steer. The algorithm can slightly
vary when a server confirmation is not required (for example, when a player opens
a menu). Also, it differs when server-side events happen. In this case, the algorithm
contains the steps from number 6 to 9. The game server notifies a client that something
was changed. The game process updates the state of game objects and commands OS to
refresh a screen picture.

The considered scheme is valid for most modern popular online games. The specific
game genre (like RPG, real-time strategy, shooter, sports, etc.) is not important in this
case. All of them use similar mechanisms and **client-server architecture**.

If we talk about a single mode game without connection with other players, our scheme differs. Figure 1-2 shows this case. There is no game server element. All player actions and game events affect the memory of the game process only. The state of all game objects is stored on a local PC.

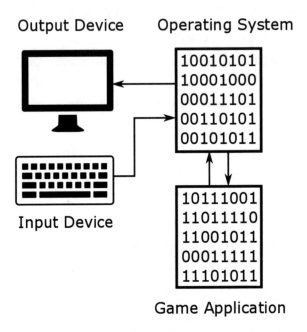

Figure 1-2. *Elements of a typical single mode game application*

The game state (like player's position, ammo, hit points, etc.) is stored on both the server side and the client side in the case of online games. But server-side information has a higher priority than the client-side one. Therefore, if the states of game objects differ, the server-side variant is chosen as the original. Thus, the game server controls the correctness of the game state. In the case of a single-player game, neither side controls this correctness.

Single-player and online games have the same interaction algorithm with the OS resources via drivers and system libraries.

Types of Bots

To become familiar with game bots, we should consider their types. There are two general approaches to classify bots: community and developer classifications. Let us examine them.

Community Classification

If you try to find information about video game bots on the Internet, you definitely will come face-to-face with the words "in-game" and "out-game." These are two types of bots that are commonly used and well known in the gamer community. Let us consider these types and understand them better.

In-game bots receive their name because they integrate into a game process as Figure 1-3 shows. Some techniques allow one process to access the memory sandbox of another one. Therefore, you can manipulate the game data (for example, read and write them). In-game bots use these exact techniques.

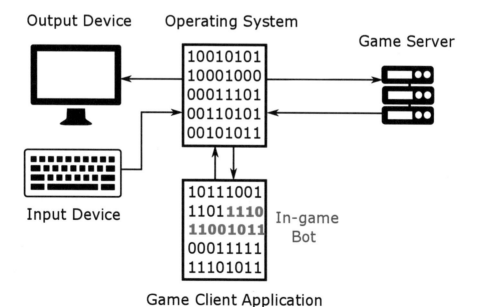

Figure 1-3. *The in-game bot*

Out-game bots use another approach and work separately from the game process, as seen in Figure 1-4. They do not touch the memory sandbox of the game process. Instead, they rely on the capabilities of the OS for interaction between processes or network hosts (like a game client and server). There are two groups of out-game bots.

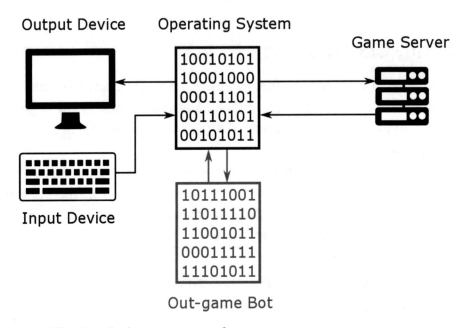

Figure 1-4.   *The stand-alone out-game bot*

The first group substitutes for the whole game process. You do not need a game application at all. The bot will interact with the game server instead. The most challenging task with this approach is to mislead the game server and force it to believe that it is communicating with the real game process.

The second group of out-game bots works with a game process in a parallel manner. These bots can gather information about the state of the game objects and notify the game process about the simulated player actions via the OS libraries. Figure 1-5 shows how they work.

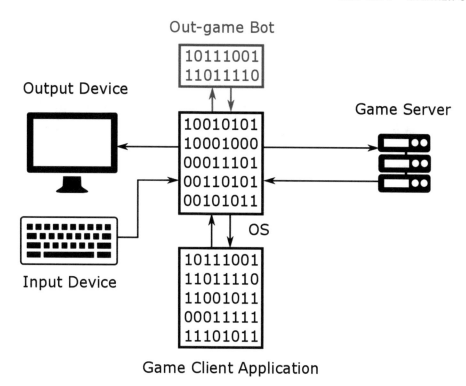

Figure 1-5. *The parallel launched out-game bot*

Also, you will certainly see discussion of the "clicker" type of bots. This type is a particular case of the second out-game bots group. Clicker bots send the keyboard and mouse event notifications to the game process through the OS libraries or drivers.

Developer Classification

The community classification is quite convenient for users of the bots. When you learn which type you have (in-game or out-game), you can easily understand its application capabilities and use cases. The problem is that the classification does not reflect which techniques a bot uses internally. So, developers need extra information.

We can avoid this lack of information if we choose another basis for classifying the bot. Instead of considering how they are used, we can focus on how they work. For example, does the bot capture the game data directly from memory or does it intercept network packets? This kind of information can be a basis for the classification.

Now we will consider points in our game process scheme where a bot can capture a game state. The red crosses mark these points on Figure 1-6.

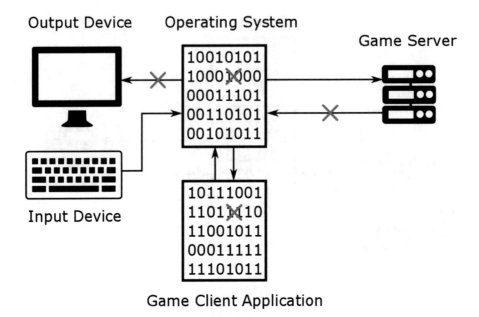

Figure 1-6. *Data capture points in a game*

Here is a list of the data capture points:

- **Output Devices**

  It is possible to capture data from output devices like a monitor or an audio card. We can do this via OS libraries. For example, when game objects are drawn on the screen, they have specific colors. Similar game events are often accompanied by particular sounds, which are produced by an audio card and speakers. You can compare these captured colors and sounds with the predefined values. Then you can conclude the current game state.

- **Operating System**

  You can replace or modify some OS libraries or drivers. Then you can trace interactions between the game process and OS. Another way is to launch the game application in a virtual machine (VM) or OS emulator (like Wine or other). Emulators often have advanced logging features, which give you detailed information about each action of the game process.

- **Game Server**

  You can capture the network packets that the server sends to the game process. They contain pieces of information about the game state. When you gather all the pieces together, you get the whole picture.

- **Game Client Application**

  You can get access to the memory sandbox of the game process and read the game state there. OS libraries provide the functions to do this.

The primary purpose of any bot is to make game actions. So, the bot should do it in a way that the game server confirms as legal. The Figure 1-7 illustrates points where a bot can embed this data.

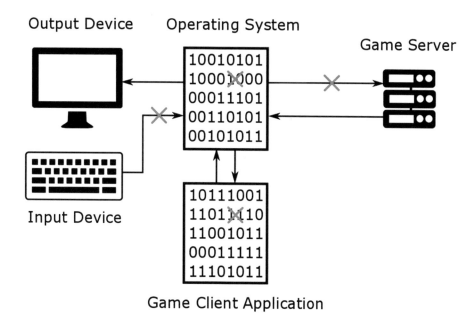

Figure 1-7. *Points of a game allowing data embedding*

Here is a list of the data embedding points:

- **Input Device**

  Any input device is a legal source of user actions from the OS point of view. Therefore, you can use your own device, which can substitute for or emulate standard input devices like a mouse or a keyboard. For example, you can use an Arduino board, which emulates a keyboard input and can be controlled by a bot.

- **Operating System**

  Again, you can modify some components of the OS. For example, you can change a keyboard driver and notify the OS about keypresses when a bot needs it. In this case, the OS cannot distinguish whether the keyboard event happened or the bot embedded it. Also, the interprocess communication OS features allow you to simulate keyboard events for the specific process.

- **Game Server**

  The bot can send network packets with required actions directly to the game server via OS library and a network adapter. It can be performed in the same way as the game process does. The game server can distinguish legal and simulated packets only if it uses special security techniques (for example encryption).

- **Game Client Application**

  You can embed the simulated player actions and a new game state directly into the memory of a game process. Thus, the process will consider that the player performed these actions and report to the server about them.

Bot Comparison

Table 1-1 summarizes the community and developer bot classifications. Columns and rows match to techniques of capturing and embedding game data. The developer classification dictates them. You can see that the community classification (names in the cells) distinguish only a few variants of all possible bot variants.

Table 1-1. *Matching of the Community and Developer Classifications*

	Network capture	Memory capture	Output device capture	OS capture
Network embedding	Out-game	-	-	-
Memory embedding	-	In-game	-	-
Input device embedding	-	-	-	-
OS embedding	-	-	Clicker	-

Why does the community classification not cover all variants of bots? These three combinations of capturing and embedding data techniques provide the most beneficial results. It does not mean that these three types are the most reliable and efficient. Each of them has its own advantages and disadvantages. Let us consider them.

There are several parameters which we can use to estimate bots:

- How much effort does it cost to implement and support the bot?

- How reliable is the bot (i.e., mistake free) when it plays instead of a human?

- How difficult is it for the game developers to detect a bot?

It is evident that each type of bot has own strengths and weaknesses.

Clicker bots are the easiest to implement and support. However, they provide the less-reliable results and are error-prone. In most cases, it is challenging for anticheat protection systems to detect these bots.

Out-game bots are the most difficult to implement and support. They can be detected easily. Their strength is that they produce the most reliable results when used.

In-game bots are the middle variant between out-game and clicker types. They are much more complicated for implementation than clickers but a little bit easier than the out-game type. They can be detected, but it can be more difficult than for out-game bots, and their results are almost as reliable.

Let us take a step forward and consider why we get these results. We should estimate each technique of capturing and embedding data from our three-question (implementation, reliability, and protection) point of view.

- **Network**

  Network packet analysis is one of the most difficult methods to capture data. You should implement the communication protocol between the game client and the server. Obviously, official documentation for this protocol is not available for anyone except the game developers. Usually, when you develop a bot, you have examples of the captured network packets only. In most cases, these packets are encrypted, and sometimes there is no way to decrypt it unambiguously. On the other hand, this method provides the most precise and complete information about the game state because you get it directly from a server. The game client does not modify or filter it yet.

- **Memory**

  Memory analysis is the second hardest method to capture game data. Game developers distribute their applications in binary code. This is a result of **compiler** execution over the source code (which is human-readable text). There is no way to turn the compiler's work back unambiguously and get the source code from the binary. Moreover, protection systems can make it harder to understand the algorithms and data structures of the game application. However, this method provides almost the same comprehensive information about the game state as capturing the network packets. Patching the process memory is a very dangerous method of embedding data because of the possibility of crashing the process.

- **Output Device**

  Capturing the output device data is one of the simplest techniques to get the game state. However, the method provides less-reliable results. For example, algorithms of the image analysis make mistakes very often. The effectiveness of this method depends on the game features.

- **Input Device**

  Embedding data with an emulator of a real input device is an effective way to avoid some types of anticheat protections. But you need to buy a device itself and to write a firmware for it. It makes sense to use this method only when you want to avoid specific protection system. This method works as effectively as embedding data on the OS level.

- **OS**

  Capturing data with the features of OS libraries is a universal and very reliable method. There are a few open source projects (graphics.stanford.edu/~mdfisher/D3D9Interceptor.html) which allow wrapping the system libraries by the third-party libraries. The game process will interact with these wrappers instead of the real library. When tracing this interaction, you will get information about the game process actions. Embedding data with the OS system libraries is a simple method for implementation. However, bot applications that use this method can be easily detected by the protection systems.

In sum, we can conclude that the community classification covers the most effective and simplest-to-implement combinations of techniques to capture and embed game data. However, this classification does not consider ineffective and rarely used combinations. This will be the classification used most throughout this book. The developer classification will be used in rare cases when it is essential to emphasize the implementation details.

Summary

From this chapter, we got basic knowledge about bots and their types. We have considered the solutions that they use. Now you can quickly distinguish in-game, out-game, and clicker bots. Moreover, you can guess how they behave and which advantages and disadvantages they have.

CHAPTER 2

Clicker Bots

First, we will consider clicker bots, which require minimum effort for development. This chapter covers commonly used developer tools and techniques to embed game data on the OS level and capture game data on output devices. An appropriate example will demonstrate each considered approach. We will write a small clicker bot for the MMORPG game Lineage 2. It will help us to gain a good understanding of the pros and cons of this type of bot. Finally, we will consider techniques which allow anticheat protection systems to catch clicker bots.

Developer Tools

When you start to develop software, it is very probable that you face tasks which somebody has already solved. It can happen that others have already made tools that fit your purposes perfectly. Therefore, the best thing that you can do before starting development is to consider existing programming languages, frameworks, and libraries. In the best case, you will just take existing solutions and integrate them together to get required functionality. It is critical to not get stuck on using only your familiar tools. You will solve a task with them, but it can require much more effort than you will spend using a more appropriate tool.

This section gives you an overview of a few tools that work well for clicker bot development. But of course, you can always find (buy) something better or create the required software on your own. Choosing the right tool is always important.

© Ilya Shpigor 2018
I. Shpigor, *Practical Video Game Bots*, https://doi.org/10.1007/978-1-4842-3736-6_2

Programming Language

AutoIt (`www.autoitscript.com`) is one of the most popular scripting programming languages for writing clicker bots. It has a lot of features that assist development of automation scripts:

- Easy-to-learn syntax.

- Detailed online documentation and community-based support forums.

- Smooth integration with **WinAPI** (OS) functions and third-party libraries.

- Built-in source code editor.

AutoIt is an excellent tool to start studying programming from scratch. We will use it for this chapter's examples. But if you already have experience with another language (like C++, C#, Python, etc.) and want to use it, you can easily rewrite the examples. We will consider WinAPI functions that you can call to achieve the required functionality.

AutoHotKey (ahkscript.org) is a second most popular scripting language for writing clicker bots. It has most of the AutoIt features but its syntax is a little bit strange compared to other commonly used languages. You can implement some things faster and more efficiently with AutoHotKey than with AutoIt. But AutoHotKey may be slightly more challenging to learn.

There are a lot of examples and guides about the development of game bots with both AutoIt and AutoHotKey on the Internet. Thus, you are free to choose a tool that you prefer.

Image Processing Libraries

AutoIt itself has several image processing functions. But the following two third-party libraries significantly extend them.

The **ImageSearch** (`www.autoitscript.com/forum/topic/148005-imagesearch-usage-explanation`) library allows you to search a specified image in the game window. Thus, your bot can easily find a required game object to interact with it.

The **FastFind** (`www.autoitscript.com/forum/topic/126430-advanced-pixel-search-library`) library provides advanced methods for searching a specific pixel combinations in the game window. For example, you can ask the library to find the nearest pixel of a given color to the point. It helps to detect game objects when we cannot apply ImageSearch library (for example in the case of 3D objects).

Image Analysis Tool

The possibility to check image parameters (like pixel color or pixel coordinates) is beneficial for debugging clicker bots. It helps you to check if image processing algorithms work correctly.

There are plenty of tools that allow you to take the color of pixels from the screen and to get the current coordinates of a mouse cursor. You can easily find these tools with Google. I use the **ColorPix** (colorpix.en.softonic.com) application, which solves my tasks well.

Source Code Editors

The AutoIt language is distributed with the customized version of **SciTE** editor. It is an excellent editor for programming and debugging AutoIt scripts. But more universal editors like **Notepad++** (notepad-plus-plus.org) can be more suitable if you prefer another programming language (like Python or AutoHotKey). **Visual Studio Community** (`www.visualstudio.com/vs/visual-studio-express`) is the best choice if your language is C++ or C#.

API Hooking

We will develop example applications using high-level AutoIt language. The language encapsulates calls of WinAPI functions in the simplified interface, but it is necessary to know which of the internals of AutoIt has used WinAPI functions. This allows you to understand algorithms better and to fix bugs. Moreover, when you know the exact WinAPI function which is called, you can interact with it directly using your favorite programming language.

There are a lot of tools that provide WinAPI call hooking. I use the freeware **API Monitor v2** (`www.rohitab.com/apimonitor`) application. It has the following features:

- Filter all hooked calls.

- Gather information about the process.

- Decode input and output parameters called functions.

- View process memory.

A full list of features is available on the developer's website.

OS-Level Data Embedding

The primary goal of any OS is to manage software and hardware resources and to provide access to them for working processes. Memory, CPU, and peripheral devices are examples of the hardware resources. Examples of the software resources are synchronization primitives and algorithms, which are implemented in system libraries.

You can launch all examples of this book in Windows, so we will imply Windows each time we mention "OS" throughout the book.

Figure 2-1 illustrates how OS provides access to its resources. Every working process can ask Windows to do an action (like the creation of a new window, drawing a line on the screen, sending a packet via a network, allocating memory, etc.). All actions are implemented in subroutines. Subroutines, which solve tasks from one domain, are gathered into separate system libraries. You can see *kernel32.dll*, *gdi32.dll*, and other system libraries in the scheme.

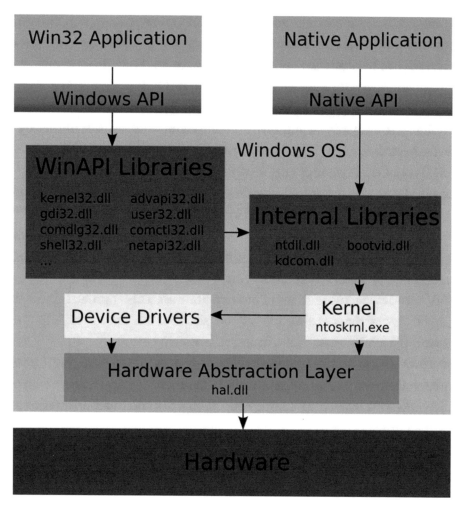

Figure 2-1. *Access to the Windows resources via system API*

The way a process can call an OS subroutine is strictly defined, well documented, and kept unchanged. We can compare this interaction with the agreement. If the process fits the preconditions of a subroutine call, OS promises to provide the expected result. The agreement is named **Windows Application Programming Interface** (API) or Windows API (WinAPI).

The software is a thing that is very flexible and easy to change. For example, each Windows update changes OS internals (for example, in some library). Also, consider that these internals are interconnected (libraries use each other's subroutines). So, even a tiny change can have a significant impact on the overall system. The same story happens to the game application. In this sea of changes, only one thing can keep everything working, and this is a reliable interface. Thus, WinAPI allows you to keep the system in a consistent state and provides compatibility between new applications and OS versions.

You can see two types of the applications in Figure 2-1. The **Win32 application** is a process that interacts with a subset of Windows libraries through WinAPI. Win32 is a historical name which appears in the first 32-bit version of Windows (Windows NT). The libraries, which are available through WinAPI (also known as **WinAPI libraries**), provide **high-level subroutines**. The "high-level" terminology indicates that these subroutines operate with complex abstractions like a window, control, file, and so forth.

The second kind of process consists of **native applications**. They interact with underlying internal Windows libraries and **kernel** through **Native API**. These libraries become available during the system boot when other components of OS are unavailable. Also, the libraries provide low-level subroutines, which operate with simple abstractions like memory page, process, thread, and so on.

WinAPI libraries use subroutines of internal libraries. This approach allows them to get complex abstractions as a combination of simple ones. The internal libraries use kernel functions, which are available through the system calls.

Drivers provide a simplified representation of devices for the overlying libraries. This representation includes a set of subroutines which perform typical actions with a device. These subroutines are available for both WinAPI libraries and internal libraries through functions of a kernel.

Hardware Abstraction Layer (HAL) is a library that provides an abstract representation of physical hardware. The primary goal of this level is to simplify launching Windows on new hardware platforms. HAL contains subroutines with hardware-specific implementation for both device drivers and kernel. These subroutines allow developers to work with different hardware in the same way. The interface of these subroutines is kept unchanged. Also, the interface does not depend on the underlying hardware. Therefore, developers can minimize the changes in their source code to port Windows on new platforms.

Now, you have a general overview of how you can access the OS resources.

Keystroke Simulation

Now we will consider ways to simulate keypresses. It is the most straightforward approach to allowing a bot to control a game application.

Keystroke in Active Window

Let us consider the AutoIt features for performing a keystroke. The list of available functions includes the Send function (`www.autoitscript.com/autoit3/docs/functions.htm`).

We will apply this function and write a test script, which presses the "a" key in running Notepad window.

The script performs the following algorithm:

1. Find a Notepad window.

2. Switch to the Notepad window.

3. Simulate the "a" keypress.

The script can find the Notepad window with the `WinGetHandle` function. Its first parameter can be either a title or a class of the target window. The return value is the **handle** of the window. The handle is an abstract reference to some OS resource or object. Most AutoIt and WinAPI functions can find the real object by this reference.

The most reliable way is to specify the class of Notepad window. We can know it in the following way:

1. Open the `C:\Program Files (X86)\AutoIt3\Au3Info.exe` application. The installation path of AutoIt can be different in your case.

2. Drag and drop the "Finder Tool" icon to the Notepad window.

3. You get the result illustrated in Figure 2-2.

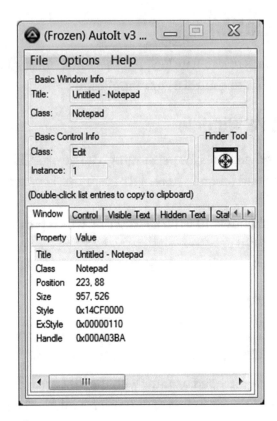

Figure 2-2. *Finder tool*

The "Basic Window Info" panel contains a window class name. It is "Notepad".

The *Send.au3* script in Listing 2-1 implements the described keypressing algorithm through the *Send* function call.

Listing 2-1. The *Send.au3* Script

```
$hWnd = WinGetHandle("[CLASS:Notepad]")
WinActivate($hWnd)
Send("a")
```

In the first line, we get the Notepad window handle via the *WinGetHandle* function. The second line activates and switches the input focus to the required window with the *WinActivate* function. The last line simulates the "a" keypress. You can just put this code snippet into the file named *Send.au3* and launch it by double-clicking.

AutoIt Send Function Internals

The Send AutoIt function is just a wrapper around the WinAPI subroutine. Let us find this WinAPI function. We can use API Monitor to hook all calls, which are done by the *Send.au3* script.

These are steps to attach API Monitor to the launched process and hook its system function calls:

1. Launch the API Monitor 32-bit application.

2. Select the "API Filter" panel by mouse click. Press the *Ctrl+F* hotkey and find the "Keyboard and Mouse Input" check box. Activate this check box.

3. Press the *Ctrl+M* hotkey to open the "Monitor New Process" dialog.

4. Choose the `C:\Program Files (x86)\AutoIt3\AutoIt3.exe` application in the "Process" field and click "OK".

5. Choose the *Send.au3* script in the opened "Run Script" dialog. The script starts working on this action.

6. Find the 'a' text (with single quotes) in the "Summary" panel of the API Monitor application.

You will get a result like that shown in Figure 2-3. *VkKeyScanW* is a function that explicitly receives the "a" character as a parameter. However, if we check the WinAPI documentation, we know that this subroutine does not perform a keypress simulation. *VkKeyScanW* and also the `MapVirtualKeyW` function are used to prepare input parameters for the `SendInput` call, which finally performs keypress simulation.

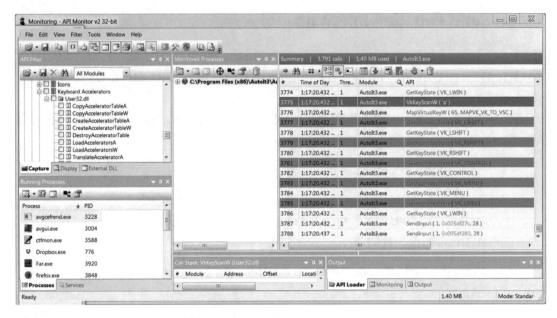

Figure 2-3. *Hooking WinAPI calls with API Monitor*

Now we will implement the AutoIt script, which presses the "a" key in the Notepad window and interacts with WinAPI functions directly. We will rewrite the third line only, which is a response to the keypress simulation. High-level *WinGetHandle* and *WinActivate* AutoIt functions will be kept.

The *SendInput.au3* script in Listing 2-2 simulates keypress via WinAPI directly.

Listing 2-2. The SendInput.au3 Script

```
$hWnd = WinGetHandle("[CLASS:Notepad]")
WinActivate($hWnd)

Const $KEYEVENTF_UNICODE = 4
Const $INPUT_KEYBOARD = 1
Const $iInputSize = 28

Const $tagKEYBDINPUT = _
    'word wVk;' & _
    'word wScan;' & _
    'dword dwFlags;' & _
    'dword time;' & _
    'ulong_ptr dwExtraInfo'
```

```
Const $tagINPUT = _
    'dword type;' & _
    $tagKEYBDINPUT & _
    ';dword pad;'

$tINPUTs = DllStructCreate($tagINPUT)
$pINPUTs = DllStructGetPtr($tINPUTs)
$iINPUTs = 1
$Key = AscW('a')

DllStructSetData($tINPUTs, 1, $INPUT_KEYBOARD)
DllStructSetData($tINPUTs, 3, $Key)
DllStructSetData($tINPUTs, 4, $KEYEVENTF_UNICODE)

DllCall('user32.dll', 'uint', 'SendInput', 'uint', $iINPUTs, _
        'ptr', $pINPUTs, 'int', $iInputSize)
```

We do the *SendInput* call through the *DllCall* AutoIt function here. This function has the following parameters:

- *user32.dll* – this is a name of the library whose subroutine should be called.

- *uint* – this is a return type of the called function.

- *SendInput* – this is its name.

- *uint, $iINPUTs, ptr, $pINPUTs, int, $iInputSize* – these are type-parameter pairs for the function.

The first *iINPUTs* parameter of the *SendInput* is a number of **structures**, which are passed to the function. Each structure has the same *INPUT* type. Our script passes only one structure. Therefore, the *iINPUTs* variable equals to one.

The second *pINPUTs* parameter is a **pointer** to the array of *INPUT* structures. The array contains one element in our case. We use the *tagINPUT* variable to represent fields of the structure according to the WinAPI documentation. Only two fields of the structure are essential in our case. The first one has the *type* name, and the second one has the *KEYBDINPUT* type. You probably noticed that we have a situation of nested structures. The *INPUT* structure contains the *KEYBDINPUT* one. The *tagKEYBDINPUT* variable is used for representing fields of the *KEYBDINPUT* structure. We use the *tagINPUT* variable to create a structure in the script memory by *DllStructCreate* call. The next step is receiving the pointer of the created *INPUT* structure with the *DllStructGetPtr* function. The last step is writing actual data to the *INPUT* structure with the *DllStructSetData* function.

The third parameter of the *SendInput* function is the size of the single *INPUT* structure. It has a constant value, which equals to 28 bytes in our case:

```
dword + (word + word + dword + dword + ulong_ptr) + dword =
4 + (2 + 2 + 4 + 4 + 8) + 4 = 28
```

The question is why we need the last padding *dword* field in the *INPUT* structure. This is a definition of the *INPUT* structure:

```
typedef struct tagINPUT {
  DWORD type;
  union {
    MOUSEINPUT     mi;
    KEYBDINPUT     ki;
    HARDWAREINPUT hi;
  };
} INPUT, *PINPUT;
```

You can see the *union* C++ keyword here. This keyword means that only one of the specified structures is stored in the same memory area. Therefore, the amount of the reserved memory should be enough to store the biggest structure among the possible variants: *MOUSEINPUT*, *KEYBDINPUT*, or *HARDWAREINPUT*. The biggest structure is *MOUSEINPUT*. It has an additional *dword* field compared to *KEYBDINPUT* structure that is used in our case.

The *SendInput.au3* script demonstrates the benefits you get when using a high-level language such as AutoIt. It hides from you a lot of irrelevant implementation details. This approach allows you to operate with simple abstractions and functions. Moreover, your applications become shorter and clearer.

Keystroke in Inactive Window

The *Send* AutoIt function simulates a keystroke in the active window. It means that you cannot minimize or switch this window to a background. It is not suitable in some cases. AutoIt has a function called *ControlSend* that can help in this situation.

We can rewrite our *Send.au3* script to use the *ControlSend* function. You can find a result in Listing 2-3.

Listing 2-3. The `ControlSend.au3` Script

```
$hWnd = WinGetHandle("[CLASS:Notepad]")
ControlSend($hWnd, "", "Edit1", "a")
```

In the *ControlSend.au3* script, we should specify the control which receives the keystroke event. The control has an `"Edit1"` class in our case according to information from the Au3Info tool. Instead of the control's class, you can specify its name or ID.

We can use the API Monitor application to clarify the underlying WinAPI function, which is called by the *ControlSend* function. This WinAPI function is the *SetKeyboardState*. You can rewrite our *ControlSend.au3* script using the *SetKeyboardState* function directly for an exercise.

The *ControlSend.au3* script works well until we try to send keystrokes to the maximized DirectX window. The problem is that this kind of window does not have internal controls. Simulation of keystrokes works correctly if you just keep empty the *controlID* parameter of the *ControlSend* function.

The *ControlSendDirectx.au3* script in Listing 2-4 simulates the a keystroke in the inactive Warcraft III window:

Listing 2-4. The `ControlSendDirectx.au3` Script

```
$hWnd = WinGetHandle("Warcraft III")
ControlSend($hWnd, "", "", "a")
```

We use the "Warcraft III" title of the window here to get its handle. Discovering this title is tricky because sometimes it is impossible to change a fullscreen mode of the DirectX window. Tools like Au3Info do not give you any possibility to gather information from fullscreen windows. You can use an API Monitor application for this goal. Just move a mouse cursor on the desired process in the "Running Process" panel. You will see the window title as Figure 2-4 shows.

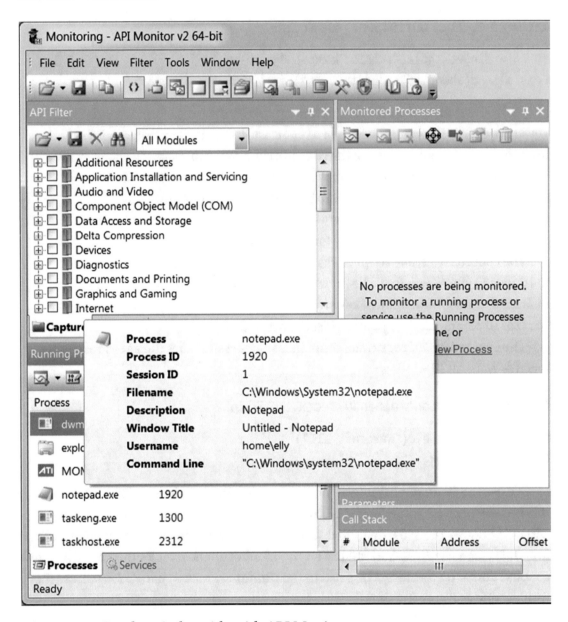

Figure 2-4. *Read a window title with API Monitor*

If you cannot find the required process in the "Running Process" panel, you can enable the administrator mode of the API Monitor application or launch another version of API Monitor (32 or 64 bit).

Some fullscreen windows have empty titles. You cannot select a window by a title text in this case. Another way to do it is to select a window by its class. Unfortunately, API Monitor does not provide information about a class of the window.

We can write a simple AutoIt script which solves this task, as demonstrated in Listing 2-5. The script shows you a message with a title text and class of the currently active window:

Listing 2-5. The GetWindowTitle.au3 Script

```
#include <WinAPI.au3>

Sleep(5 * 1000)
$handle = WinGetHandle('[Active]')
MsgBox(0, "", "Title   : " & WinGetTitle($handle) & @CRLF _
        & "Class : " & _WinAPI_GetClassName($handle))
```

The first line of the script contains the *include* keyword. It allows you to append a specified file to the current script. The *WinAPI.au3* file contains a definition of the *_WinAPI_GetClassName* function. The function provides a class of the specified window. There is a five-second delay after starting the script, which is done by the *Sleep* call. You should switch to the target fullscreen window during this delay. Then, a handle of the currently active window is saved into the *handle* variable. The last *MsgBox* call shows you a message with the results.

Mouse Simulation

Simulation of keystrokes is enough for controlling a player character in some games. However, most modern video games have complex controls: both keyboard and mouse actions are required. The AutoIt language has several functions that allow you to simulate typical mouse actions (like clicking, moving, and holding a pressed button). Now we will consider these functions.

Mouse Actions in Active Window

We will use the standard Microsoft Paint application to test our mouse simulation scripts. The *MouseClick.au3* script in Listing 2-6 simulates mouse click in the active Paint window:

Listing 2-6. The MouseClick.au3 Script

```
$hWnd = WinGetHandle("[CLASS:MSPaintApp]")
WinActivate($hWnd)
MouseClick("left", 250, 300)
```

You should launch the Paint application, switch to the "Brushes" tool, and launch the script. It draws a black dot at the point with coordinates x=250 and y=300. The ColorPix application will help you to check the correctness of the coordinates. The *MouseClick* AutoIt function is used here. It has the following parameters:

- Mouse button (left, right, middle, etc.).

- Click coordinates.

- A number of clicks.

- Move speed.

The *MouseClick* function uses the *mouse_event* WinAPI call internally.

You can specify coordinates of mouse actions in one of three possible modes. They are listed in Table 2-1.

Table 2-1. *Coordinate Modes of the mouse_event WinAPI Function*

Mode	Description
0	Relative coordinates to the active window.
1	Absolute screen coordinates. This mode is used by default.
2	Relative coordinates to the client area of the active window.

Figure 2-5 illustrates coordinate modes in the Notepad window example.

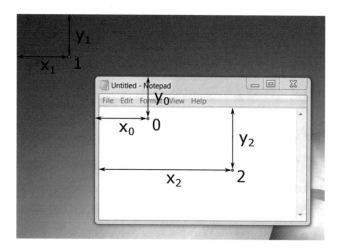

Figure 2-5. *Coordinate modes of the mouse_event WinAPI function*

Each titled number corresponds to the mouse coordinate mode. For example, the dot number "0" has coordinates relative to the active window. The "x" and "y" letters, which are indexed by "0", are the corresponding coordinates of this dot.

You can select a coordinate mode with the *MouseCoordMode* parameter of the *Opt* AutoIt function. Listing 2-7 shows the modified version of the *MouseClick.au3* script. It uses relative client area coordinates of the active window:

Listing 2-7. The Modified MouseClick.au3 Script

```
Opt("MouseCoordMode", 2)
$hWnd = WinGetHandle("[CLASS:MSPaintApp]")
WinActivate($hWnd)
MouseClick("left", 250, 300)
```

This script draws a black dot in the Paint window. Coordinates of this dot differ from the coordinates of the dot, which we have before the modification.

The mode with relative coordinates to the client area provides more precise positioning when simulating mouse actions. It is recommended to use this mode for clicker bots. This mode works well for both normal and fullscreen windows. However, it is difficult to check the correctness of your script with tools like ColorPix, since it works with absolute coordinates only.

Drag-and-drop is a common action in video games. AutoIt provides a *MouseClickDrag* function, which simulates this action. Listing 2-8 demonstrates how the *MouseClickDrag* function works:

Listing 2-8. The MouseClickDrag.au3 Script

```
$hWnd = WinGetHandle("[CLASS:MSPaintApp]")
WinActivate($hWnd)
MouseClickDrag("left", 250, 300, 400, 500)
```

When you launch the *MouseClickDrag*.au3 script, you see a drawn line in the Paint window. The line starts at the point with absolute coordinates equal to x=250 and y=300. The line ends at the point with coordinates x=400 and y=500. The *MouseClickDrag* AutoIt function uses the same *mouse_event* WinAPI function internally. Both *MouseClick* and *MouseClickDrag* AutoIt functions perform mouse actions in the currently active window.

Mouse Actions in Inactive Window

AutoIt provides the *ControlClick* function, which allows you to simulate a mouse click in an inactive window. Listing 2-9 demonstrates usage of this function.

Listing 2-9. The ControlClick.au3 Script

```
$hWnd = WinGetHandle("[CLASS:MSPaintApp]")
ControlClick($hWnd, "", "Afx:00000000FFC20000:81", "left", 1, 250, 300)
```

The *ControlClick.au3* script performs a mouse click in the inactive or minimized Paint window. The *ControlClick* function is very similar to *ControlSend* one. You should specify the control where the mouse click is simulated. The control of the Paint window, which is used for drawing, has the "Afx:00000000FFC20000:81" class according to information from the Au3Info tool.

If you pass the same coordinates as input parameters for both *MouseClick* and *ControlClick* functions, simulated mouse click actions have different coordinates. The coordinates, which are passed to the *ControlClick* function, are relative coordinates to the target control where the mouse click is performed. It means that simulation of a mouse click in our example occurs at the point with x=250 and y=300 coordinates, which are relative to the upper left corner of the control for drawing. However, the mode of the coordinates, which is passed to the *MouseClick* function, is defined by the *MouseCoordMode* AutoIt option.

The *ControlClick* AutoIt function performs two calls of the *PostMessageW* WinAPI function internally, as Figure 2-6 shows.

Module	Q API	Return Value
AutoIt3.exe	⌐GetClassNameW (0x0002048c, 0x006deb68, 256)	16
AutoIt3.exe	⌐GetClassNameW (0x0012043c, 0x006deb68, 256)	7
AutoIt3.exe	⌐GetClassNameW (0x00060472, 0x006deb68, 256)	9
AutoIt3.exe	⌐GetClassNameW (0x00090320, 0x006deb68, 256)	22
AutoIt3.exe	⌐GetClassNameW (0x00090434, 0x006deb68, 256)	11
AutoIt3.exe	⌐GetClassNameW (0x000204c0, 0x006deb68, 256)	22
AutoIt3.exe	GetWindowRect (0x000204c0, 0x006df728)	TRUE
AutoIt3.exe	PostMessageW (0x000204c0, WM_LBUTTONDOWN, 1, 19661050)	TRUE
AutoIt3.exe	PostMessageW (0x000204c0, WM_LBUTTONUP, 0, 19661050)	TRUE
AutoIt3.exe	QueryPerformanceCounter (0x006df730)	TRUE
AutoIt3.exe	QueryPerformanceFrequency (0x006df720)	TRUE
AutoIt3.exe	QueryPerformanceCounter (0x006df738)	TRUE
AutoIt3.exe	QueryPerformanceCounter (0x006df738)	TRUE
AutoIt3.exe	QueryPerformanceCounter (0x006df738)	TRUE
AutoIt3.exe	QueryPerformanceCounter (0x006df738)	TRUE

Figure 2-6. *Internal calls of the ControlClick AutoIt function*

The first call of the *PostMessageW* function has the *WM_LBUTTONDOWN* input parameter. This call allows us to simulate the mouse button down action. The second call has the *WM_LBUTTONUP* parameter to simulate the mouse button up action.

The *ControlClick* function works unreliably with minimized DirectX windows. Some applications I tested just ignore this mouse action simulation. Other applications process these actions only after activation of their windows. This means that minimized DirectX application hangs until it is restored to the normal mode again.

OS-Level Data Embedding Summary

We have considered AutoIt functions that allow us to simulate typical keyboard and mouse actions in a game window. There are two types of these functions. The first type allows us to simulate actions in an active window only. The second type of function works with both active and inactive (or minimized) windows. The primary drawback of the second type of function is low reliability. Therefore, it is recommended to use the first type of function for clicker bot development.

Output Device Capture

Now we will consider approaches to capture game data from the output devices. We will start with an investigation of features which Windows provides for applications to print their information on the screen. Then we will consider how we can intercept this application output.

Windows Graphics Device Interface

Graphics Device Interface (GDI) is a basic component of Windows OS. This component is responsible for representing graphical objects and transmitting them to output devices. All visual elements of typical application window are constructed using graphical objects. Examples of these objects are device contexts (DC), bitmaps, brushes, colors, and fonts.

The core concept of the GDI is DC. DC is an abstraction that allows developers to operate with graphical objects in a universal way: one which does not depend on the type of output device. Examples of output devices are display, printer, plotter, and so forth. Any operation which you do in DC is performed into memory. Then the result of these operations is sent to the output device.

You can see two DCs on Figure 2-7. They store the content of two windows. Also, there is a DC of the entire screen with a content of overall desktop. OS can gather this DC by combining DCs of all visible windows and desktop visual elements (like a taskbar). When the screen DC is ready, OS sends it to the display.

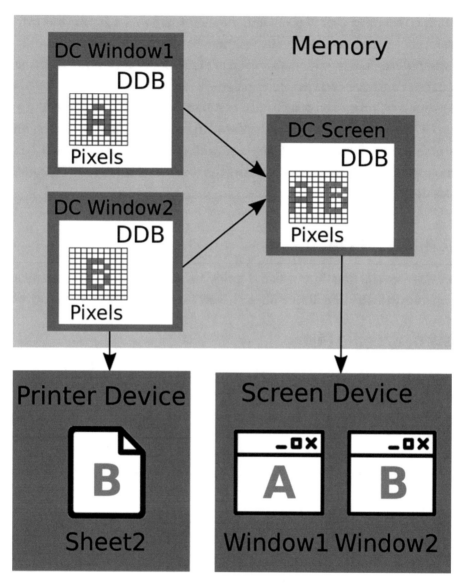

Figure 2-7. *Matching of graphical objects and devices*

Another case is when you want to print a document. OS needs a DC of the text editor window to send it to the printer. All other DCs are ignored in this case.

DC is a structure in memory. Developers can manipulate it only via WinAPI functions. Each DC contains a **Device Depended Bitmap** (DDB). The **bitmap** is an in-memory representation of a drawing surface. All manipulations with graphical objects in the DC affect its bitmap. Therefore, the bitmap contains a result of all performed operations.

The bitmap contains a set of pixels and metainformation. Each pixel has two parameters: coordinates and color. A two-dimensional array defines accordance of these parameters. Indexes of array elements match to pixel coordinates. A numeric value of the element defines the color code in a color palette, which is associated with the bitmap. The array should be processed pixel by pixel sequentially for analyzing the bitmap.

When DC is ready for the output, it is passed to the device-specific library. An example of the library for a screen device is *vga.dll*. The library transforms DC data to the representation of a device driver. It allows the driver to show screen DC content on the display device.

AutoIt Analysis Functions

AutoIt provides several functions which simplify analysis of a current screen picture. All of them operate with the GDI library objects. Now we will consider these functions.

Analysis of Specific Pixel

We will start with the task of getting a color of a specific pixel on the screen. To do this, we need to know its coordinates. There is a set of coordinate modes that AutoIt functions use for pixel analysis. This set is the same as the AutoIt mouse functions have, as shown in Table 2-2.

Table 2-2. *Coordinate Modes of the Pixel Analysis Functions*

Mode	Description
0	Relative coordinates to the specified window.
1	Absolute screen coordinates. This mode is used by default.
2	Relative coordinates to the client area of the specified window.

You can use the same *Opt* AutoIt function with the *PixelCoordMode* parameter to switch between the coordinate modes for pixel analysis. This is an example of enabling the mode of relative to the client area coordinates:

```
Opt("PixelCoordMode", 2)
```

The elementary AutoIt function to get pixel color is *PixelGetColor*. You should pass pixel coordinates to the function and get back the decimal code of its color. Listing 2-10 demonstrates the usage of this function.

Listing 2-10. The PixelGetColor.au3 Script

```
$color = PixelGetColor(200, 200)
MsgBox(0, "", "The hex color is" & Hex($color, 6))
```

The *PixelGetColor.au3* script reads a color of the pixel with absolute screen coordinates x=200 and y=200. Then, the *MsgBox* function shows the code of the color. After launching the script, I see the message "The text color is 0355BB".

The code 0355BB is a **hexadecimal representation** of the number. We use the *Hex* AutoIt function to transform a result of *PixelGetColor* from decimal to hexadecimal code. Color representation in hexadecimal is widespread; most graphical editors and tools use it.

If you switch to another window (it should cover coordinates x=200 and y=200) and relaunch the script again, you get another result. It means that the PixelGetColor function analyzes not just one specific window but the entire desktop picture instead.

Figure 2-8 shows WinAPI calls of the *PixelGetColor.au3* script.

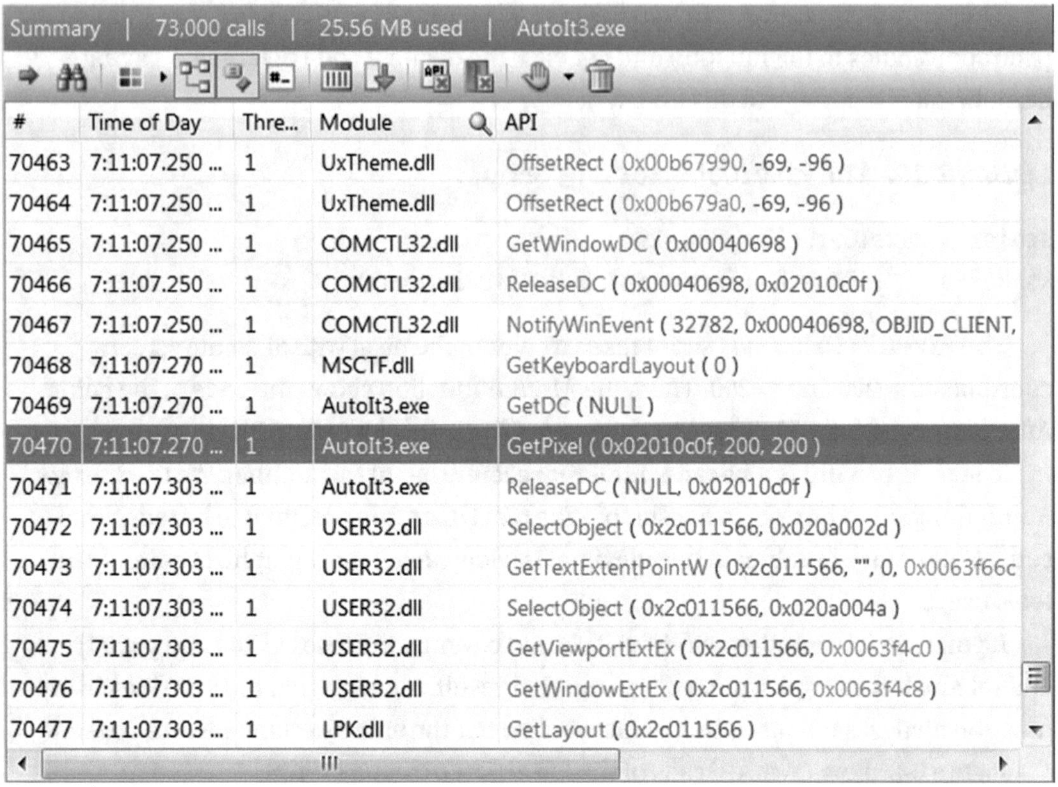

#	Time of Day	Thre...	Module	API
70463	7:11:07.250 ...	1	UxTheme.dll	OffsetRect (0x00b67990, -69, -96)
70464	7:11:07.250 ...	1	UxTheme.dll	OffsetRect (0x00b679a0, -69, -96)
70465	7:11:07.250 ...	1	COMCTL32.dll	GetWindowDC (0x00040698)
70466	7:11:07.250 ...	1	COMCTL32.dll	ReleaseDC (0x00040698, 0x02010c0f)
70467	7:11:07.250 ...	1	COMCTL32.dll	NotifyWinEvent (32782, 0x00040698, OBJID_CLIENT,
70468	7:11:07.270 ...	1	MSCTF.dll	GetKeyboardLayout (0)
70469	7:11:07.270 ...	1	AutoIt3.exe	GetDC (NULL)
70470	7:11:07.270 ...	1	AutoIt3.exe	GetPixel (0x02010c0f, 200, 200)
70471	7:11:07.303 ...	1	AutoIt3.exe	ReleaseDC (NULL, 0x02010c0f)
70472	7:11:07.303 ...	1	USER32.dll	SelectObject (0x2c011566, 0x020a002d)
70473	7:11:07.303 ...	1	USER32.dll	GetTextExtentPointW (0x2c011566, "", 0, 0x0063f66c
70474	7:11:07.303 ...	1	USER32.dll	SelectObject (0x2c011566, 0x020a004a)
70475	7:11:07.303 ...	1	USER32.dll	GetViewportExtEx (0x2c011566, 0x0063f4c0)
70476	7:11:07.303 ...	1	USER32.dll	GetWindowExtEx (0x2c011566, 0x0063f4c8)
70477	7:11:07.303 ...	1	LPK.dll	GetLayout (0x2c011566)

Summary | 73,000 calls | 25.56 MB used | AutoIt3.exe

Figure 2-8. *WinAPI calls of the* PixelGetColor.au3 *script*

You can see that the PixelGetColor function calls the GetPixel WinAPI function. Also, there is the GetDC call before the GetPixel one. The input parameter of the GetDC function equals to "NULL". This means that we select a desktop DC for further operations. We can change this behavior and specify the window, which should be analyzed. Thus, our script will be able to analyze inactive windows, which are overlapped by other ones.

We pass the window handle as the third parameter to the PixelGetColor function. Listing 2-11 shows how to do so.

Listing 2-11. The PixelGetColorWindow.au3 Script

```
$hWnd = WinGetHandle("[CLASS:MSPaintApp]")
$color = PixelGetColor(200, 200, $hWnd)
MsgBox(0, "", "The hex color is: " & Hex($color, 6))
```

The *PixelGetColorWindow.au3* script should analyze a pixel color in the Paint window even it is overlapped. The resulting value should be "FFFFFF" (white). This is a color of the empty canvas. Now you can try to overlap the Paint editor with another window which does not have a white color. The script returns another result in this case. That is not expected behavior because it should still return the white color.

Let us compare the behavior of the *PixelGetColorWindow.au3* and *PixelGetColor.au3* scripts with API Monitor. Their sequences of WinAPI calls look entirely the same. The "NULL" parameter is still passed to the *GetDC* WinAPI function. It looks like a bug of the *PixelGetColor* function implementation in the AutoIt v3.3.14.1 version. Probably, this will be fixed in the next AutoIt versions. However, we need a solution to analyze the pixel color of an overlapped window.

The issue with the *PixelGetColor* function happens because of the wrong *GetDC* call. We can repeat all WinAPI calls of the *PixelGetColor* function from the AutoIt script (see Listing 2-12). This allows us to pass the correct parameter to the *GetDC* call.

Listing 2-12. The GetPixel.au3 Script

```
#include <WinAPIGdi.au3>

$hWnd = WinGetHandle("[CLASS:MSPaintApp]")
$hDC = _WinAPI_GetDC($hWnd)
$color = _WinAPI_GetPixel($hDC, 200, 200)
MsgBox(0, "", "The hex color is:" & Hex($color, 6))
```

The *GetPixel.au3* script starts with the *include* keyword. It appends the *WinAPIGdi.au3* file into our script. This file provides *_WinAPI_GetDC* and *_WinAPI_GetPixel* wrappers to the corresponding WinAPI functions. If you launch the script, you always get the message with the white pixel color of the Paint canvas. This means that the result of the *GetPixel.au3* script does not depend on windows overlapping.

There is still one issue with the *GetPixel.au3* script. If you minimize the Paint window, the script returns a white color. This result looks correct. Now we change the Paint canvas color to red (for example), minimize the window again, and launch the scripts. It still returns the white color. If you restore the window in the normal mode, you get the red color.

Each window has a **client area**. All elements (like buttons or labels) of a window are placed there. Our issue happens because a client area of the minimized window has a size of zero. Therefore, a DC of the minimized window has an empty bitmap. The *GetPixel* WinAPI function returns white color in this case. Listing 2-13 shows how we can measure the window client area.

Listing 2-13. The GetClientRect.au3 Script

```
#include <WinAPI.au3>

$hWnd = WinGetHandle("[CLASS:MSPaintApp]")
$tRECT = _WinAPI_GetClientRect($hWnd)
MsgBox(0, "Rect", _
            "Left: " & DllStructGetData($tRECT, "Left") & @CRLF & _
            "Right: " & DllStructGetData($tRECT, "Right") & @CRLF & _
            "Top: " & DllStructGetData($tRECT, "Top") & @CRLF & _
            "Bottom: " & DllStructGetData($tRECT, "Bottom"))
```

Each of *Left*, *Right*, *Top*, and *Bottom* variables equals zero for a window in minimized mode. If you restore the window, you get a nonzero result.

This limitation can be critical if you want to execute a bot in one window and be able to work in another. There is a sophisticated solution to the issue. We can restore a minimized window in the transparent mode. Then we can copy a window client area to the memory DC and minimize the window again. The *PrintWindow* WinAPI call can do this copy operation. Now we have a full copy of the window client area and can analyze it with the *_WinAPI_GetPixel* function. This approach is described in details in the article (www.codeproject.com/Articles/20651/Capturing-Minimized-Window-A-Kid-s-Trick).

Analysis of Pixels Changing

We have considered a way to get the color of the specific pixel on the screen. However, when you analyze a real game window, you do not know the exact coordinates of the pixels in most cases. Because instead of a static picture we have a scene with many moving objects. Thus, we should find a way to process changes on the screen. AutoIt provides functions that can help us in this case.

Let us assume that we want to find a specific game object on the screen. We know the color of the object and want to get its coordinates. There is an inversion of the task, which can be solved by the *PixelGetColor* function.

The *PixelSearch* AutoIt function helps us to find a game object by its color. Listing 2-14 demonstrates the usage of this function.

Listing 2-14. The PixelSearch.au3 Script

```
$coord = PixelSearch(0, 207, 1000, 600, 0x000000)
If @error = 0 then
    MsgBox(0, "", "The black point coord: x = " & $coord[0] & " y = " &
$coord[1])
else
    MsgBox(0, "", "The black point not found")
endif
```

The *PixelSearch.au3* script searches a pixel with the 0x000000 (black) color inside a rectangular area between two points with coordinates x=0, y=207 and x=1000, y=600. Then it checks if any error happens during the *PixelSearch* execution. We use the special *@error* macro for this check. If there is no error, a message with the result appears.

You can use the Paint application again to test the script. You should just draw a black point on the white canvas. If you launch the script, you get coordinates of the black point. Please make sure that the Paint window is active and it is not overlapped when doing this test.

Now we will check WinAPI functions, which are called internally by the *PixelSearch* function. You should launch the *PixelSearch.au3* script from the API Monitor application. Then wait until script finishes and search the "0, 207" text in the "Summary" window. You will find the *StretchBlt* WinAPI call as shown in Figure 2-9.

#	Time of Day	Thre...	Module	Q	API	Return Value
48093	11:01:41.23...	1	COMCTL32.dll		ReleaseDC (0x000b0696, 0x06011022)	1
48094	11:01:41.23...	1	COMCTL32.dll		NotifyWinEvent (32782, 0x000b0696, OBJID_CLIENT, 0)	
48095	11:01:41.24...	1	MSCTF.dll		GetKeyboardLayout (0)	0x04090409
48096	11:01:41.25...	1	AutoIt3.exe		GetDC (NULL)	0x5a011146
48097	11:01:41.25...	1	AutoIt3.exe		CreateCompatibleBitmap (0x5a011146, 1001, 394)	0x69051de7
48098	11:01:41.25...	1	AutoIt3.exe		CreateCompatibleDC (0x5a011146)	0x72011dcd
48099	11:01:41.25...	1	AutoIt3.exe		SelectObject (0x72011dcd, 0x69051de7)	0x0185000f
48100	11:01:41.25...	1	AutoIt3.exe		StretchBlt (0x72011dcd, 0, 0, 1001, 394, 0x5a011146, 0, 207, 1001, 394, SRCCOPY)	TRUE
48101	11:01:41.32...	1	AutoIt3.exe		GetDIBits (0x72011dcd, 0x69051de7, 0, 0, NULL, 0x0069f2d8, DIB_RGB_COLORS)	1
48102	11:01:41.32...	1	AutoIt3.exe		GetDIBits (0x72011dcd, 0x69051de7, 0, 394, 0x04e50020, 0x0069f2d8, DIB_RGB_COLORS)	394
48103	11:01:41.32...	1	AutoIt3.exe		SelectObject (0x72011dcd, 0x0185000f)	0x69051de7
48104	11:01:41.32...	1	AutoIt3.exe		DeleteObject (0x69051de7)	TRUE
48105	11:01:41.32...	1	AutoIt3.exe		DeleteDC (0x72011dcd)	TRUE
48106	11:01:41.32...	1	AutoIt3.exe		ReleaseDC (NULL, 0x5a011146)	1
48107	11:01:41.32...	1	USER32.dll		SelectObject (0x5a011146, 0x020a002d)	0x038a002f

Figure 2-9. WinAPI calls of the `PixelSearch` function

The `StretchBlt` function copies a bitmap from the screen DC to the memory DC (which is also known as **compatible DC**). You can verify this fact easily. Compare the input parameters and returned values of the `GetDC`, `CreateCompatibleDC`, and `StretchBlt` calls in the API Monitor log. The result of the `GetDC` function (which has "NULL" input parameter) is used to create a compatible DC via the `CreateCompatibleDC` call. Then the `StretchBlt` function copies bitmaps.

The next step of the `PixelSearch` function is a `GetDIBits` call. It performs a conversion of pixels from the DDB format to the **Device Independent Bitmap** (DIB).

The DIB is the most convenient format for a picture analysis because it allows processing bitmap in the same way as a regular array. The next step of the `PixelSearch` function is to check the colors of the pixels in the DIB. WinAPI functions are not required to do this checking. It is a reason why we do not see any other WinAPI calls.

You can find the sample C++ implementation of the image capturing algorithm on MSDN (msdn.microsoft.com/en-us/library/dd183402%28v=VS.85%29.aspx). This implementation demonstrates two actions which we have considered:

- Copying a screen DC to the memory DC.

- DDB-to-DIB conversion.

The `PixelSearch` function receives a window handle input parameter. We can leave this value empty. The entire desktop is used for searching a pixel in this case. Otherwise, the function analyzes pixels of a specified window.

The *PixelSearchWindow.au3* script in Listing 2-15 demonstrates how to use the window handle parameter:

Listing 2-15. The PixelSearchWindow.au3 Script

```
$hWnd = WinGetHandle("[CLASS:MSPaintApp]")
$coord = PixelSearch(0, 207, 1000, 600, 0x000000, 0, 1, $hWnd)
If @error = 0 then
    MsgBox(0, "", "The black point coord: x = " & $coord[0] & " y = " & $coord[1])
else
    MsgBox(0, "", "The black point not found")
endif
```

According to the AutoIt documentation, our script should analyze the overlapped Paint window, but it does not work as expected. Again, we face the same bug as we have in the *PixelGetColor* function. The API Monitor log confirms that the *GetDC* function receives the "NULL" input parameter. Therefore, the *PixelSearch* function always processes a desktop DC. You can avoid the bug by using WinAPI functions directly. As an example of the solution, you can use the *GetPixel.au3* script. You should just call WinAPI functions in the same manner and repeat whole work of the *PixelSearch* function.

PixelChecksum is another AutoIt function which we can use to analyze dynamically changing pictures. Both *PixelGetColor* and *PixelSearch* functions gather information about one specific pixel. The *PixelChecksum* works differently. This function detects if something was changed inside the specified region of a screen. This kind of analysis can be useful when you implement bot reaction to game events.

Listing 2-16 shows a typical use case of the function:

Listing 2-16. The PixelChecksum.au3 Script

```
$checkSum = PixelChecksum(0, 0, 50, 50)

while $checkSum = PixelChecksum(0, 0, 50, 50)
    Sleep(100)
wend

MsgBox(0, "", "Something in the region has changed!")
```

The *PixelChecksum.au3* script reacts if something changes on a screen inside the region between two points with coordinates x=0, y=0 and x=50, y=50. You see that we call the *PixelChecksum* function two times. The first time, we calculate an initial value of the checksum. The second time, the function is called in a **while** loop every 100 milliseconds. The *Sleep* function stops the script execution for a specified amount of time. Our loop continues until the checksum value does not change. When that happens, the message notification appears.

Now we consider the internals of the *PixelChecksum* function. API Monitor shows us the same sequence of WinAPI calls as it is for the *PixelSearch* function. This means that AutoIt uses the same algorithm for both *PixelChecksum* and *PixelSearch* functions to get a DIB. However, the *PixelChecksum* has more steps. After receiving DIB, its checksum is calculated using the selected algorithm. You can choose either the **ADLER** or the **CRC32** algorithm for this calculation. They differ in speed and reliability. The CRC32 algorithm works slower, but it provides more reliable detection of pixel changes.

All considered, AutoIt functions can process pictures in fullscreen DirectX windows. So, you can use them for your bots.

Advanced Image Analysis Libraries

We have considered AutoIt functions for screen analysis. Now we will consider extra functions that are provided by third-party libraries.

FastFind Library

The **FastFind** library provides advanced functions for searching game objects on the screen. You can call the library functions from both AutoIt scripts and C++ applications. These are the steps to do it from an AutoIt script:

1. Create a project directory for your script (for example, with the name *FFDemo*).

2. Copy the *FastFind.au3* file from the FastFind archive to the *FFDemo* directory.

3. Copy either the *FastFind.dll* or the *FastFind64.dll* file from the archive to the *FFDemo* directory. You should use the *FastFind64.dll* file for the x64 Windows systems and *FastFind.dll* for the x32 case.

4. Include the *FastFind.au3* file in your script using the *include* keyword:

    ```
    #include "FastFind.au3"
    ```

Now you can call FastFind functions in the same manner as the regular AutoIt functions.

These are the steps to use the FastFind library from a C++ application:

1. Download a preferable C++ compiler. It can be **Visual Studio Community** from the Microsoft website or the **MinGW** environment (nuwen.net/mingw.html).

2. Install the C++ compiler.

3. Create a source file named *test.cpp* if you use the MinGW compiler. Create the "Win32 Console Application" project if you use Visual Studio IDE.

4. Listing 2-17 shows a content of the *test.cpp* source file.

Listing 2-17. The test.cpp Source File

```cpp
#include <iostream>

#define WIN32_LEAN_AND_MEAN
#include <windows.h>

using namespace std;

typedef LPCTSTR(CALLBACK* LPFNDLLFUNC1)(void);

HINSTANCE hDLL;                 // Handle to DLL
LPFNDLLFUNC1 lpfnDllFunc1;      // Function pointer
LPCTSTR uReturnVal;

int main()
{
    hDLL = LoadLibraryA("FastFind");
    if (hDLL != NULL)
    {
        lpfnDllFunc1 = (LPFNDLLFUNC1)GetProcAddress(hDLL,
```

```
            "FFVersion");
        if (!lpfnDllFunc1)
        {
            // handle the error
            FreeLibrary(hDLL);
            cout << "error" << endl;
            return 1;
        }
        else
        {
            // call the function
            uReturnVal = lpfnDllFunc1();
            cout << "version = " << uReturnVal << endl;
        }
    }
    return 0;
}
```

5. Copy the *FastFind.dll* file into the project directory. You should use the *FastFind64.dll* file only if you use a compiler version which produces the 64-bit binaries.

6. If you use MinGW, create the file named *Makefile*, which contains these two lines:

```
all:
    g++ test.cpp -o test.exe
```

7. Build the application with the *make* command for MinGW and the F7 hotkey for Visual Studio.

Now you get the executable file. If you launch it, you see the version of the FastFind library in the console output. This is an example of the output:

```
version = 2.2
```

We have used the **explicit library linking** (msdn.microsoft.com/en-us/library/784bt7z7.aspx) approach to communicate with the FastFind library. There is an alternative approach with the **implicit library linking** (msdn.microsoft.com/en-us/library/d14wsce5.aspx) name. You can also use the second approach to call FastFind

functions. However, there is one limitation in this case. You should use the same C++
compiler version that is used by the developer of the FastFind library.

Now we will consider possible tasks which we can solve with the FastFind library.
The first task is to search an area that contains the best number of pixels of a given color.
The *FFBestSpot* function solves this task. Let us consider an example.

You can see two models in the Figure 2-10 screenshot. The first one is the player
character, named "Zagstruk". The second model is a monster named "Wretched Archer".
We can use the *FFBestSpot* function to figure out the monster's screen coordinates.
To do so, we should choose an appropriate color for the pixels. The color of text labels
(you can see them under the models) is the best target for searching. These labels
remain unchanged even if the game scene changes. They do not depend on light effects
or camera scale. Therefore, searching their coordinates provides us the most reliable
results. The monster has an extra green text label, but a player does not. So, we can use
the green color for searching.

Figure 2-10. *Screenshot of famous MMORPG game Lineage 2*

In some cases, we do not have unchanged elements of the game interface (as the text labels in the Lineage 2 case). Then we can use the models as the search targets. In this case, an algorithm of the *FFBestSpot* function can make wrong decisions very often. It happens because the models are affected by shadows and light effects, and they can also rotate. This leads to a wide variation of model colors.

The *FFBestSpot.au3* script in Listing 2-18 searches the green text on the screen and displays a message with its coordinates:

Listing 2-18. The FFBestSpot.au3 Script

```
#include "FastFind.au3"

Sleep(5 * 1000)

const $sizeSearch = 80
const $minNbPixel = 50
const $optNbPixel = 200
const $posX = 700
const $posY = 380

$coords = FFBestSpot($sizeSearch, $minNbPixel, $optNbPixel, $posX, $posY,
0xA9E89C, 10)

if not @error then
    MsgBox(0, "Coords", $coords[0] & ", " & $coords[1])
else
    MsgBox(0, "Coords", "Match not found.")
endif
```

You can launch this script, switch to the window with the Lineage 2 screenshot, and get coordinates of the text. The script waits five seconds after launching, which gives you enough time to switch to the right window. The *FFBestSpot* function is called after the delay. Table 2-3 shows a list of parameters which are passed to the function.

Table 2-3. *List of the FFBestSpot Function Parameters*

Parameter	Description
sizeSearch	Width and height of the area to search
minNbPixel	Minimum number of pixels of a given color in the area
optNbPixel	An optimal number of pixels of a given color in the area
posX	x coordinate of a proximity position of the area
posY	y coordinate of a proximity position of the area
0xA9E89C	Pixel color in hexadecimal representation
10	Shade variation parameter from 0 to 255, which defines allowed deviation from the specified color for red, blue, and green color components

The *FFBestSpot* function returns an array of three elements when it succeeds and a zero value when it fails. The first two elements of the array are x and y coordinates of a found area. A third element is a number of matched pixels in the area. You can find detailed information about this function in the documentation for the FastFind library.

The *FFBestSpot* function is an effective option to search the interface elements like progress bars, icons, windows, and text. Even more, you can use it to search 2D models.

The second task that we can solve with the FastFind library is a localization of changes on the screen. The *FFLocalizeChanges* function provides an appropriate algorithm for this case. We can use the Notepad application to demonstrate how this function works.

The *FFLocalizeChanges.au3* script (see Listing 2-19) detects the coordinates of the new text, which you type in the Notepad window:

Listing 2-19. The FFLocalizeChanges.au3 Script

```
#include "FastFind.au3"

Sleep(5 * 1000)
FFSnapShot(0, 0, 0, 0, 0)

MsgBox(0, "Info", "Change a picture now")

Sleep(5 * 1000)
FFSnapShot(0, 0, 0, 0, 1)
```

```
$coords = FFLocalizeChanges(0, 1, 10)

if not @error then
    MsgBox(0, "Coords", "x1 = " & $coords[0] & ", y1 = " & $coords[1] & _
            " x2 = " & $coords[2] & ", y2 = " & $coords[3])
else
    MsgBox(0, "Coords", "Changes not found.")
endif
```

Here are the steps to launch the script:

1. Launch Notepad application and maximize its window.

2. Launch the *FFLocalizeChanges.au3* script.

3. Switch to Notepad window.

4. Wait until the "Change a picture now" message appears.

5. Type several symbols in the Notepad window. You have five seconds to do it.

6. Wait until a message with the coordinates of the added text appears.

Functions of the FastFind library operate with the **SnapShots** abstraction. The SnapShot is a copy of the screen in memory (it is very similar to DIB). When we use the *FFBestSpot* function, the SnapShot is made implicitly. However, we should make SnapShots explicitly when using the *FFLocalizeChanges* function. This function compares two SnapShots to find their differences.

Let us look at the *FFLocalizeChanges.au3* script. The *FFSnapShot* call makes the first SnapShot right after the sleep. This five-second delay is needed for switching the active window. We do the second SnapShot in the same way after showing the "Change a picture now" message.

Table 2-4 shows the input parameters of the *FFSnapShot* function.

Table 2-4. *List of the FFSnapShot Function Parameters*

Parameter	Description
0	x coordinate of the top-left SnapShot area corner.
0	y coordinate of the top-left SnapShot area corner.
0	x coordinate of the bottom-right SnapShot area corner.
0	y coordinate of the bottom-right SnapShot area corner. The whole screen is copied in case all coordinates are zeroed.
0 or 1	A number of the SnapShot slot. The maximum slot number is 1023.

The function does not have a return value.

When we have prepared two SnapShots, we can compare them with the *FFLocalizeChanges* function. Table 2-5 shows its input parameters.

Table 2-5. *List of the FFLocalizeChanges Function Parameters*

Parameter	Description
0	Slot number of the first SnapShot to compare
1	Slot number of the second SnapShot to compare
10	Shade variation parameter that works in the same way as for FFBestSpot function

A return value of the function is a five-element array. The first four elements of the array are the left, top, right, and bottom coordinates of the changed region. The last element is a number of the changed pixels.

The *FFLocalizeChanges* function is a useful alternative for the *PixelChecksum*. It is more reliable and provides more information about a detected change.

The functions of the FastFind library can work with overlapped windows. However, they do not work with minimized windows. Most of the functions have a window handle parameter, so you can specify the target window for analysis. Also, all functions work correctly with DirectX windows in the fullscreen mode.

ImageSearch Library

The **ImageSearch** library solves one specific task. It allows you to find a picture in the specified region of the screen. These are the steps to call library functions from the AutoIt script:

1. Create a project directory named *ImageSearchDemo* for example.

2. Copy the *ImageSearch.au3* file to the directory.

3. Copy the *ImageSearchDLL.dll* library to the directory.

4. Include the *ImageSearch.au3* file in your script:

```
#include "ImageSearch.au3"
```

Now you can call library functions.

If you want to use C++, you can use explicit library linking to access ImageSearch functions. This approach was described in the details for the FastFind library.

To demonstrate the capabilities of the ImageSearch library, we find a Notepad icon in its window title. First of all, you should prepare an image file with the icon. Our script will use it for searching. You should place the image file named *notepad-logo.bmp* to the project directory. You can use the Paint application to make a window screenshot and cut the icon. Figure 2-11 is an example of the result:

Figure 2-11. *The Notepad icon*

The *Search.au3* script in Listing 2-20 searches the icon:

Listing 2-20. The Search.au3 Script

```
#include <ImageSearch.au3>

Sleep(5 * 1000)

global $x = 0, $y = 0
$search = _ImageSearch('notepad-logo.bmp', 0, $x, $y, 20)
```

```
if $search = 1 then
    MsgBox(0, "Coords", $x & ", " & $y)
else
    MsgBox(0, "Coords", "Picture not found.")
endif
```

These are the steps to launch the script:

1. Launch the Notepad.

2. Launch the *Search.au3* script.

3. Switch to the Notepad window.

4. Wait for a message with the coordinates of the Notepad icon. This message should appear five seconds after starting the script.

If you face issues with usage of a current version of ImageSearch library, you can download a previous stable version (github.com/ellysh/ImageSearch). Table 2-6 shows input parameters of the *_ImageSearch* function.

Table 2-6. *List of the _ImageSearch Function Parameters*

Parameter	Description
notepad-logo.bmp	A path to the file with a picture for searching.
0	The flag to define which coordinates of the resulting picture should be returned. The 0 value matches the top-left coordinates of the picture. The 1 value matches the coordinates of the picture center.
x	Variable to write the resulting x coordinate.
y	Variable to write the resulting y coordinate.
20	Shade variation parameter. This parameter defines a possible color deviation from the specified picture.

The function returns the error code. If any error happens, it returns the zero value (otherwise nonzero).

The *_ImageSearch* function searches the specified picture in whole screen area. The ImageSearch library provides another function named *_ImageSearchArea*. It allows you to search a picture in the specified region of the screen.

The code snippet demonstrates the _ImageSearchArea_ call:

```
$search = _ImageSearchArea('notepad-logo.bmp', 0, 100, 150, 400, 450, $x,
$y, 20)
```

The function receives four extra parameters compared to the _ImageSearch_. These are coordinates of the top-left and bottom-right points of the screen region. The coordinates of these points equal to x1=100, y1=150 and x2=400, y2=450 in our example. The result of the function has the same meaning as the _ImageSearch_ function case.

Both functions of the ImageSearch library can search only a picture which is present on the screen at the moment. It means that the Notepad window should not be overlapped or minimized. Also, both functions work correctly with fullscreen DirectX windows.

The ImageSearch library is a reliable tool for searching static pictures in the game window. Examples of these pictures are elements of interface or 2D models.

Capturing Output Device Summary

We have considered AutoIt functions for analyzing specific pixels on the screen. Also, functions which detect a position of changes that have happened on the screen have been considered.

Basic features of the FastFind and ImageSearch libraries have been explored. The first provides an advanced function for pixel search. The second allows you to find a specific picture on the screen.

Example with Lineage 2

Now we will make a simple clicker bot for the famous MMORPG game Lineage 2. Thus, we will apply our new knowledge in practice.

Lineage 2 Overview

The gameplay of Lineage 2 is very typical for the RPG genre. A player should select one of the available characters before starting to play. Then he should do quests and hunt monsters to achieve new skills, extract resources, and buy new items. This process is known as **farming**. The player can communicate and cooperate with other players during the game. Other players can assist or hamper his farming. When several players want to get the same valuable resource (for example, an artifact or a castle), they should fight with each other. This competition aspect is the main attraction of the game, so players want to develop their character as fast as possible to reach the required level and start a competition.

The most straightforward way to improve a player character is hunting monsters. A player will get experience points to improve skills, gold to buy new items, and random resources after killing a monster. We focus on the automation of this process because it allows comprehensively developing a player character. Also, there are other ways to develop a character like trading, fishing, crafting new items, and completing quests.

Let us consider the game interface in Figure 2-12:

1. **Status Window** with the parameters of the player character. The most important of them are **health points** (HP) and **mana points** (MP).

2. **Target Window** with information of the selected monster. Here we can see the HP of the monster which is being attacked at the moment.

3. **Shortcut Panel** with icons of available actions and skills, which are attached to the hotkeys.

4. **Chat Window** for input game commands and chatting with other players.

Figure 2-12. *The interface of the Lineage 2 game*

Considering the interface in detail helps us to develop an algorithm of a clicker bot for interaction with the game. The game interface details are available on the wiki page (l2wiki.com/Game_Interface).

You can find a lot of Lineage 2 servers on the Internet. They differ by game version, additional gameplay features, and protection systems which are used to prevent usage of bots. The most reliable and efficient protection systems are used on official servers (`www.lineage2.eu`). Also, there are many private servers which use simpler protection algorithms. We will use the **Rpg-Club** (`www.rpg-club.com`) server in our example because the clicker bots work there well.

Bot Implementation

You can try to hunt several monsters to understand the game mechanics. You will notice that most of the time, you press almost the same buttons. Our next step is to write this algorithm as a sequence of actions which we should automate. This is my version of such algorithm:

1. Select a monster by left-clicking him. Another way to select a monster is typing a command in the chat window or using the macro with this command:

    `/target MonsterName`

2. The full list of the game commands and the manual for using macros are available on the official website (`www.lineage2.com/en/game/getting-started/how-to-play/macros-and-commands.php`).

3. Click the "attack" button on the Shortcut Panel. Another way to start attacking is pressing the F1 (by default) keyboard key.

4. Wait until a player character kills the monster.

5. Click the "pickup" button on the Shortcut Panel for picking up the monster's dropped items. You can also use a hotkey for this action.

This algorithm looks straightforward without any complex conditions. Let us write a script to automate it.

The Blind Bot

As a first try, we will just follow the steps of our monster-hunting algorithm. The bot will simulate a keystroke for each action in the list. We name it a blind bot because it just presses a button and does not "look" on the screen.

It will be helpful to consider a configuration of our Shortcut Panel before we start to write code. You should configure the panel as Figure 2-13 shows.

Figure 2-13. *Screenshot of the Shortcut Panel*

Table 2-7 describes each hotkey in detail.

Table 2-7. *List of Actions and Corresponding Hotkeys on the* Shortcut Panel

Hotkey	Command
F1	Attack the currently selected monster
F2	Use an offensive skill on the selected monster
F5	Use a health potion for restoring player's HP
F8	Pick up items near the player
F9	Macro with */target MonsterName* command to select a monster
F10	Select the nearest monster

Now it looks simple to associate hotkeys with algorithm steps and write code. The *BlindBot.au3* script (see Listing 2-21) implements all steps of our algorithm.

Listing 2-21. The BlindBot.au3 Script

```
#RequireAdmin

Sleep(2000)

while True
    Send("{F9}")
    Sleep(200)
    Send("{F1}")
    Sleep(5000)
    Send("{F8}")
    Sleep(1000)
wend
```

The first line of the script contains the *#RequireAdmin* keyword. This keyword permits interaction between the script and other applications which are launched with administrator privileges. You should be an administrator of your computer to launch some of the Lineage 2 clients. So, I recommend using *#RequireAdmin* in all your bot scripts.

The second action in the script is a two-second delay, which allows you to switch to the Lineage 2 window. The current version of the bot can work in the active game window only.

Then we have the infinite `while` loop where we gather all bot actions:

1. `Send("{F9}")` - select a monster by the macro, which is assigned to the F9 hotkey.

2. `Sleep(200)` – make a 200-millisecond delay. This is required for the game application to choose a monster and to draw a Target Window.

You should remember that all actions in the game window take nonzero time. Often this time is much less than a time of human reaction, and therefore it looks instantaneous.

---

3. `Send("{F1}")` - attack the selected monster.

4. `Sleep(5000)` – wait five seconds while the character reaches the monster and kills it.

5. `Send("{F8}")` – pick up one item.

6. `Sleep(1000)` – wait one second while the character picks up the item.

In this example, the sequence of bot actions is strictly defined. It means that every action succeeds only if the previous action was successful too. First of all, the bot should find the monster. Otherwise, all further actions have no effect. Then, the character should reach and kill the selected monster in five seconds. This time can vary. It depends on the distance to the monster. Finally, the monster can drop more than one item when defeated. Thus, our script works correctly only if all considered conditions are fulfilled. Otherwise, it makes mistakes.

You can launch the script and check how it works. You will see that the bot frequently works incorrectly because very often the conditions are violated. However, it is not a serious issue for our bot, because in general, it continues working anyway. The features of in-game */target* command and the attacking mechanism make the script sustainable. If the macro with the */target* command is pressed twice, the same monster is selected. Thus, the bot continues to attack the same monster until it is alive. If the monster is alive after the first iteration of the loop, this process repeats on the next iteration. Moreover, the pickup command does not interrupt the attack. It means that the character does not stop attacking the monster after exceeding the five-second timeout for killing the monster.

There is still a problem with picking up only one dropped item. We can solve this issue by repeating a pickup action to the number of usually dropped items.

We can improve the script by moving each step of the algorithm to a separate function with a descriptive name. It makes the code more comprehensible. The `BlindBotFunc.au3` script in Listing 2-22 contains actions which are separated into functions:

Listing 2-22. The `BlindBotFunc.au3` Script

```
#RequireAdmin

Sleep(2000)

func SelectTarget()
    Send("{F9}")
    Sleep(200)
endfunc

func Attack()
    Send("{F1}")
    Sleep(5000)
endfunc

func Pickup()
    Send("{F8}")
    Sleep(1000)
endfunc

while True
    SelectTarget()
    Attack()
    Pickup()
wend
```

You can notice that this code is quite easy to read and understand. I recommend you always take a step back and check how easy it is to read your code. These efforts are always justified.

The Bot with Conditions

Let's improve our bot and make it more accurate. If the bot gets a possibility to check results of own actions, it will make much fewer mistakes. We will use a pixel analysis approach to check the state of the surrounding game objects.

Before we start to implement this feature, it is helpful to add a mechanism for printing log messages. This mechanism is known as **tracing**. It help us to trace bot decisions and detect possible bugs.

The code snippet in Listing 2-23 prints a log message into the file.

Listing 2-23. The LogWrite Function

```
global const $LogFile = "debug.log"

func LogWrite($data)
    FileWrite($LogFile, $data & chr(10))
endfunc

LogWrite("Hello world!")
```

After the execution of this script, you get a file named *debug.log*. It contains the "Hello world!" string. The *LogWrite* function is a wrapper for the *FileWrite* AutoIt function. You can change a name and a path of the output file by changing a value of the *LogFile* constant.

You should always consider a mechanism to debug your applications. The simplest solution is tracing the most important decisions of your algorithms.

The first condition which the bot should check is a result of choosing the monster for attacking. Please try to select several monsters on your own with a mouse. Do you notice the interface element which can signal about a successfully selected monster? The answer is the Target Window. It appears each time when you select the right unit. We can use the FastFind library to search this window. The *FFBestSpot* function provides the suitable algorithm for our case.

Now we should choose a color which is specific to the Target Window only. Our bot should distinguish this window and any other one. So, the color should be unique.

We can pick a color of a monster HP bar for example. The code snippet in Listing 2-24 checks a presence of the Target Window on the screen:

Listing 2-24. The IsTargetExist Function

```
func IsTargetExist()
    const $SizeSearch = 80
    const $MinNbPixel = 3
    const $OptNbPixel = 10
    const $PosX = 688
    const $PosY = 67

    $coords = FFBestSpot($SizeSearch, $MinNbPixel, $OptNbPixel, $PosX, $PosY, _
                        0x871D18, 10)

    const $MaxX = 800
    const $MinX = 575
    const $MaxY = 100

    if not @error then
        if $MinX < $coords[0] and $coords[0] < $MaxX and $coords[1] < $MaxY
        then
            LogWrite("IsTargetExist() - Success, coords = " & $coords[0] & _
                    ", " & $coords[1] & " pixels = " & $coords[2])
            return True
        else
            LogWrite("IsTargetExist() - Fail #1")
            return False
        endif
    else
        LogWrite("IsTargetExist() - Fail #2")
        return False
    endif
endfunc
```

Let us consider the *IsTargetExist* function in detail. We have *PosX* and *PosY* coordinates here. They define the approximate position of a monster HP bar. We pass the coordinates and the color of the full HP bar, which equals 0x871D18, to the *FFBestSpot* function.

It searches pixels of the specified color in any position on the screen. Therefore, the function can detect a player HP bar instead. This happens whether the Target Window is present or not. To avoid this mistake, we should check the coordinates of the detected area.

We compare the resulting x coordinate (*coords[0]*) with the maximum (*MaxX*) and minimum (*MinX*) allowed values. Also, there is the same comparison of the y coordinate (*coords[0]*) with the maximum (*MaxY*) value. The values of all coordinates depend on the screen resolution and position of the game window. You should adapt these coordinates to your screen configuration.

We do the *LogWrite* calls in the *IsTargetExist* function to trace each conclusion. It helps us to check the correctness of the allowed coordinates and the color value.

We can use the new *IsTargetExist* function in both the *SelectTarget* and *Attack* functions of the blind bot. It can check if the *SelectTarget* function is done successfully. So we ensure that a monster exists and the bot can perform the *Attack* function. Also, the *IsTargetExist* function can check if the monster is alive or not.

The *AnalysisBot.au3* script in Listing 2-25 concludes about the target monster presence and chooses an appropriate action.

Listing 2-25. The AnalysisBot.au3 Script

```
#include "FastFind.au3"

#RequireAdmin

Sleep(2000)

global const $LogFile = "debug.log"

func LogWrite($data)
    FileWrite($LogFile, $data & chr(10))
endfunc

func IsTargetExist()
    ; SEE ABOVE
endfunc
```

```
func SelectTarget()
    LogWrite("SelectTarget()")
    while not IsTargetExist()
        Send("{F9}")
        Sleep(200)
    wend
endfunc

func Attack()
    LogWrite("Attack()")
    while IsTargetExist()
        Send("{F1}")
        Sleep(1000)
    wend
endfunc

func Pickup()
    Send("{F8}")
    Sleep(1000)
endfunc

while True
    SelectTarget()
    Attack()
    Pickup()
wend
```

Pay attention to a new implementation of the *SelectTarget* and *Attack* functions. We try to select a target monster until the *IsTargetExist* function does not return the "true" value. Then we come to the loop of *Attack* function. Now the bot hits a monster (by pressing the F1 hotkey) while it is alive.

You can notice that we print log messages at the beginning of both the *SelectTarget* and *Attack* functions. This helps us to distinguish who calls the *IsTargetExist* function.

Further Improvements

Now our bot chooses its action according to the current game situation. However, there are several game situations when the bot makes a critical mistake and dies.

The first problem is aggressive monsters. Most of the monsters just stay in a game location and do not react to the player if it comes close to them. At the same time, some monsters attack the player in this case.

Our bot chooses the monster for attacking, but it ignores all other units. They are not visible for the bot because our algorithm does not consider them. Thus, aggressive monsters can attack our bot while it moves to its target. The bot supposes that it attacks one monster, but there are three or five instead. They can quickly kill the bot.

We can solve this issue if our bot prefers to choose the nearest units. The Lineage 2 interface has a command to select the nearest target. It is available via the F10 hotkey in our Shortcut Panel. Listing 2-26 demonstrates the new version of the *SelectTarget* function.

Listing 2-26. The SelectTarget Function

```
func SelectTarget()
    LogWrite("SelectTarget()")
    while not IsTargetExist()
        Send("{F10}")
        Sleep(200)

        if IsTargetExist() then
            exitloop
        endif

        Send("{F9}")
        Sleep(200)
    wend
endfunc
```

Now the bot tries to select the target via the F10 hotkey first. If it fails, the */target* command is used. This approach can solve the issue with the "invisible" aggressive monsters.

The second issue is obstacles in a hunting area. The bot can get stuck while moving to the target. The simplest solution is to make a timeout for the attack action. If the timeout expires and the target is still alive, we can conclude that the bot hits an obstacle. It can move randomly to avoid the obstacle.

The new versions of the *Attack* and *Move* functions (see Listing 2-27) provide the feature to avoid obstacles.

Listing 2-27. The Attack and Move Functions

```
func Move()
    SRandom(@MSEC)
    MouseClick("left", Random(300, 800), Random(170, 550), 1)
endfunc

func Attack()
    LogWrite("Attack()")

    const $TimeoutMax = 10
    $timeout = 0
    while IsTargetExist() and $timeout < $TimeoutMax
        Send("{F1}")
        Sleep(2000)

        Send("{F2}")
        Sleep(2000)

        $timeout += 1
    wend

    if $timeout == $TimeoutMax then
        Move()
    endif
endfunc
```

The *Attack* function contains the timeout counter. Each iteration of the while loop is incremented and compared with a threshold value of the *TimeoutMax* constant. When the timeout reaches the threshold, the bot concludes that it has gotten stuck. We call the *Move* function in this case.

The function performs a mouse click action via the *MouseClick* call at a random point. We use the *SRandom* and Random AutoIt functions to get the random point coordinates. The first function initializes a random number generator. When the generator is ready, it can produce the **pseudorandom numbers**; the *Random* function does it. We should pass the bounds of the interval via input parameters. A result is a random number in this interval.

Also, you should notice one new action in the new *Attack* function. This is the F2 hotkey press simulation. We can assign any attack skill to the hotkey, and the bot will use it in the fights. It allows killing monsters much faster.

Now our sample bot can work autonomously for an extended period. It can deal with obstacles and attack aggressive monsters. However, there is still one thing which can make the bot more durable. It is using health potions, which are bound to the F5 hotkey. To do so, we should analyze the level of the character's HP bar in the Status Window. You can do it as an exercise on your own. Just use the same pixel analysis approach that we have used in the *IsTargetExist* function.

Lineage 2 Summary

We have implemented a clicker bot for the Lineage 2 game. It uses the most common techniques to simulate game actions and analyze the game window events. Therefore, we can evaluate the effectiveness of our bot and approximately extrapolate the result for all clickers.

There is a list of our bot advantages:

1.   Easy to develop, extend functionality, and debug.

2.   Easy to integrate with any version of the game, even if there are significant differences in user interface between these versions.

3.   Protecting a game against this type of bot is difficult.

Here is a list of our bot's disadvantages:

1.   Each user needs to tune the pixel coordinates and colors for his case.

2.   The bot hangs in some unexpected cases (death, disconnect, NPC [nonplayer character] dialog, etc.).

3. Delays and timeouts lead to waste of time.

4. Pixel analysis can lead to unreliable results. Thus, the bot makes wrong actions in some cases.

A clicker bot is effective for solving strictly defined tasks which can be easily separated into steps and algorithmize. Also, a clicker bot works more reliably when the algorithm has a minimal count of conditions, and the cost of a mistake is cheap, so it can return to the regular work after making several wrong actions.

Protection Approaches

We already know how the clicker bots work. Let us now change sides and start to think like developers of the protection system. How we detect this kind of bot? This section answers the question.

We have considered the typical game application. As you remember, it has client-side and server-side parts. The protection system follows this architecture often and has the same two parts.

The client-side part controls points of interception and embedding data, which are related to devices, OS, and a game application itself. The server-side part of the protection system controls communication between a game application and a game server. Most techniques for clicker bot detection work on a client side.

The primary purpose of any protection system is to detect a game data violation. The bots manipulate this data, so reliable protection system should detect them.

When the detection step is done, there are several ways to react:

- Notify the system administrator of the game server about the suspicious player's actions. This can be done by writing a message to a server-side log file, for example.

- Break the connection between the suspicious player and the game server.

- Ban the account of the suspicious player or his IP address. It prevents his further connections to the game server.

We will focus on bot detection algorithms only. Also, ways to overcome these algorithms will be discussed.

Test Application

We will test our protection techniques with the Notepad application. Let us consider that the Notepad window is a game window. Also, we have a simple clicker bot that types a text there. Our goal is to detect the bot.

We will use AutoIt to make prototypes of protection scripts. It helps us to make source code shorter and clearer to understand. However, C++ language is preferred to develop real protection systems in most cases.

The *SimpleBot.*au3 script (see Listing 2-28) types "a", "b", and "c" letters consistently in the Notepad window.

Listing 2-28. The SimpleBot.au3 Script

```
$hWnd = WinGetHandle("[CLASS:Notepad]")
WinActivate($hWnd)
Sleep(200)

while true
    Send("a")
    Sleep(1000)
    Send("b")
    Sleep(2000)
    Send("c")
    Sleep(1500)
wend
```

You can launch Notepad first and then the *SimpleBot.au3* script. It switches to the Notepad window and types letters there in an infinite loop.

It is a starting point for our experiments. The purpose of each protection script is a detection of the launched *SimpleBot.au3* script: it should distinguish between user and bot actions.

Analysis of Actions

The *SimpleBot.au3* script performs regular actions. The regularity is the first thing that we can analyze. You can look at the bot script again and see the delays between each action. Humans cannot repeat their actions with such precise delays. Moreover, this precision does not have any sense for playing video games because a player should react to the game events. If somebody does things in this way, he is actually a computer program.

A protection algorithm can measure delays between the actions of one specific type. There is a very high probability that the actions are simulated by a bot when the delays between them are more precise than 100 milliseconds. Now we will implement a protection algorithm based on this time measurement.

An average computer user has an approximate reaction time of 300 milliseconds. This number is less for professional gamers (near 150 milliseconds).

Our protection script should solve two tasks: capture user actions and measure a delay between them. The code snippet in Listing 2-29 captures the pressed keys:

Listing 2-29. Capturing the Pressed Keys

```
global const $gKeyHandler = "_KeyHandler"

func _KeyHandler()
    $keyPressed = @HotKeyPressed

    LogWrite("_KeyHandler() - asc = " & asc($keyPressed) & " key = " &
    $keyPressed)
    AnalyzeKey($keyPressed)

    HotKeySet($keyPressed)
    Send($keyPressed)
    HotKeySet($keyPressed, $gKeyHandler)
endfunc

func InitKeyHooks($handler)
    for $i = 0 to 256
```

```
        HotKeySet(Chr($i), $handler)
    next
endfunc

InitKeyHooks($gKeyHandler)

while true
    Sleep(10)
wend
```

We use the *HotKeySet* AutoIt function here to assign a **handler** or **hook** for pressed keys. The *InitKeyHooks* function does this assignment. We call the *_KeyHandler* handler each time a user presses any key with ASCII codes from 0 to 255. The handler performs the following steps:

1. Pass the captured key to the *AnalyzeKey* function.
    The *@HotKeyPressed* macro provides the code of this key.

2. Disable the *_KeyHandler* by the *HotKeySet($keyPressed)* call.
    We need this step to allow the captured key reach the Notepad window.

3. Call the *Send* function to send the captured key to the Notepad window.

4. Enable the *_KeyHandler* again by the *HotKeySet($keyPressed, $gKeyHandler)* call.

Listing 2-30 shows a code of the *AnalyzeKey* function.

Listing 2-30. The AnalyzeKey Function

```
global $gTimeSpanA = -1
global $gPrevTimestampA = -1

func AnalyzeKey($key)
    local $timestamp = (@SEC * 1000 + @MSEC)
    LogWrite("AnalyzeKey() - key = " & $key & " msec = " & $timestamp)
    if $key <> 'a' then
        return
    endif
```

```
    if $gPrevTimestampA = -1 then
        $gPrevTimestampA = $timestamp
        return
    endif

    local $newTimeSpan = $timestamp - $gPrevTimestampA
    $gPrevTimestampA = $timestamp

    if $gTimeSpanA = -1 then
        $gTimeSpanA = $newTimeSpan
        return
    endif

    if Abs($gTimeSpanA - $newTimeSpan) < 100 then
        MsgBox(0, "Alert", "Clicker bot detected!")
    endif
endfunc
```

We measure the time spans between the "a" keys pressing here. Let us use a **trigger action** term to name this pressing. There are two global variables for storing a current state of the protection algorithm:

1. *gPrevTimestampA* – this is a **timestamp** of the last trigger action.

2. *gTimeSpanA* – this is a time span between the last two trigger actions.

Both these variables have a value of "-1" at the startup. It matches to the uninitialized state. Our algorithm requires a minimum of three trigger actions with the same delays to conclude that there is a bot. The first action initializes the *gPrevTimestampA* variable:

```
    if $gPrevTimestampA = -1 then
        $gPrevTimestampA = $timestamp
        return
    endif
```

Then we use the second action timestamp to calculate the *gTimeSpanA* variable. This variable equals to a subtraction between timestamps of the current and previous actions:

```
local $newTimeSpan = $timestamp - $gPrevTimestampA
$gPrevTimestampA = $timestamp

if $gTimeSpanA = -1 then
    $gTimeSpanA = $newTimeSpan
    return
endif
```

With the third action, we calculate the new time span and compare it with the previous one, which is stored in the *gTimeSpanA* variable:

```
if Abs($gTimeSpanA - $newTimeSpan) < 100 then
    MsgBox(0, "Alert", "Clicker bot detected!")
endif
```

As a result, we have measured two time spans here:

1. The time span between the first and the second trigger actions.

2. The time span between the second and the third trigger actions.

The subtraction of these two time spans matches the time precision of the user actions. Precision of less than 100 milliseconds is impossible for humans but it is typical for bots. Therefore, the protection script concludes that some program is simulating these actions. The script shows the "Clicker bot detected!" message in this case.

Listing 2-31 shows the code of the *TimeSpanProtection.au3* script with the skipped content of the *_KeyHandler* and *AnalyzeKey* functions because we considered them in the preceding.

Listing 2-31. The TimeSpanProtection.au3 Script

```
global const $gKeyHandler = "_KeyHandler"
global const $kLogFile = "debug.log"

global $gTimeSpanA = -1
global $gPrevTimestampA = -1
```

```
func LogWrite($data)
    FileWrite($kLogFile, $data & chr(10))
endfunc

func _KeyHandler()
    ; SEE ABOVE
endfunc

func InitKeyHooks($handler)
    for $i = 0 to 256
        HotKeySet(Chr($i), $handler)
    next
endfunc

func AnalyzeKey($key)
    ; SEE ABOVE
endfunc

InitKeyHooks($gKeyHandler)


while true
    Sleep(10)
wend
```

We can slightly improve our *SimpleBot.au3* script to avoid protection algorithms which analyze the time spans. The simplest way to do so is by adding random delays between simulated actions. The *RandomDelayBot.au3* script in Listing 2-32 is a fixed version of the bot.

Listing 2-32. The RandomDelayBot.au3 Script

```
SRandom(@MSEC)
$hWnd = WinGetHandle("[CLASS:Notepad]")
WinActivate($hWnd)
Sleep(200)

while true
    Send("a")
    Sleep(Random(800, 1200))
```

```
    Send("b")
    Sleep(Random(1700, 2300))
    Send("c")
    Sleep(Random(1300, 1700))
wend
```

We use the *Random* function each time we need a delay value. You can launch the *TimeSpanProtection.au3* script first and then *RandomDelayBot.au3*. The protection algorithm is not able to detect the bot in this case.

However, the bot has another regularity, which allows us to detect the *RandomDelayBot.au3* script. This regularity comes from repeated keypress sequences. It is evident that humans cannot repeat the same sequence hundreds of times. Even if a player wants to repeat his actions, he makes mistakes and presses wrong keys sometimes. The bot repeats pressing "a", "b", and "c" keys in a very regular manner which is impossible for humans.

The *ActionSequenceProtection.au3* script (see Listing 2-33) has a new version of the *AnalyzeKey* function. It checks the repeating sequence of the captured actions.

Listing 2-33. The ActionSequenceProtection.au3 Script

```
global const $gActionTemplate[3] = ['a', 'b', 'c']
global $gActionIndex = 0
global $gCounter = 0

func Reset()
    $gActionIndex = 0
    $gCounter = 0
endfunc

func AnalyzeKey($key)
    LogWrite("AnalyzeKey() - key = " & $key);

    $indexMax = UBound($gActionTemplate) - 1
    if $gActionIndex <= $indexMax and $key <>
$gActionTemplate[$gActionIndex] then
        Reset()
        return
    endif
```

```
    if $gActionIndex < $indexMax and $key = $gActionTemplate[$gActionIndex]
then
        $gActionIndex += 1
        return
    endif

    if $gActionIndex = $indexMax and $key = $gActionTemplate[$gActionIndex]
then
        $gCounter += 1
        $gActionIndex = 0

        if $gCounter = 3 then
            MsgBox(0, "Alert", "Clicker bot detected!")
            Reset()
        endif
    endif
endfunc
```

This is a list of global variables and constants which our algorithm uses:

1. *gActionTemplate* – this is a list of actions in the sequence which is specific for a particular bot script.

2. *gActionIndex* – this is an index of the last captured action which is present in the *gActionTemplate* list.

3. *gCounter* – this is a number of captured action repetitions.

The *AnalyzeKey* function processes the three cases of matching current captured action and elements of the *gActionTemplate* list. The first case happens when the captured action does not match any element of the *gActionTemplate* list:

```
    $indexMax = UBound($gActionTemplate) - 1
    if $gActionIndex <= $indexMax and $key <>
$gActionTemplate[$gActionIndex] then
        Reset()
        return
    endif
```

We call the *Reset* function in this case. It resets both *gActionIndex* and *gCounter* variables to zero.

The second case of the *AnalyzeKey* function happens when the captured action matches the element of the *gActionTemplate* list. Also, this element is not the last one in the list, and its index equals to the *gActionIndex* variable:

```
if $gActionIndex < $indexMax and $key = $gActionTemplate[$gActionIndex]
then
    $gActionIndex += 1
    return
endif
```

We increment the *gActionIndex* variable in this case.

The last case checks if the captured action equals to the last element of the *gActionTemplate* list:

```
if $gActionIndex = $indexMax and $key = $gActionTemplate[$gActionIndex]
then
    $gCounter += 1
    $gActionIndex = 0

    if $gCounter = 3 then
        MsgBox(0, "Alert", "Clicker bot detected!")
        Reset()
    endif
endif
```

We increment the *gCounter* and reset the *gActionIndex* variable to zero in this case. After these two steps, our algorithm can analyze the next sequence of the player actions.

When the key sequence, which is defined by the *gActionTemplate* list, repeats three times, the protection algorithm concludes that there is a bot. The *gCounter* variable calculates the number of repeating sequence. If it becomes equal to three, the protection script shows the "Clicker bot detected!" message. Then we call the *Reset* function and can detect the bot again.

You can launch the *ActionSequenceProtection.au3* and *RandomDelayBot.au3* scripts for testing. The new protection algorithm can detect the bot with random delays between simulated actions.

It is obvious that the considered approach is error-prone. It can make the wrong conclusion and detect a bot when a human player just repeats his actions several times. We can reduce a possibility of these false decisions by increasing a threshold value for *gCounter*:

```
if $gCounter = 3 then
    MsgBox(0, "Alert", "Clicker bot detected!")
    Reset()
endif
```

There is another serious issue of our *ActionSequenceProtection.au3* script. It detects only bots that press "a", "b", "c" sequence. If you make the bot which presses "a", "c", "b", the script cannot detect it. So, you should adapt your protection algorithm for each expected sequence of actions.

We can avoid this limitation if our algorithm accumulates all user actions in one huge array and searches for frequently repeated regularities there. These regularities warn us about possible usage of a bot.

Let us improve our bot script again to avoid protection algorithms that analyze actions' regularity. Listing 2-34 demonstrates a possible solution.

Listing 2-34. The RandomActionBot.au3 Script

```
SRandom(@MSEC)
$hWnd = WinGetHandle("[CLASS:Notepad]")
WinActivate($hWnd)
Sleep(200)

while true
    Send("a")
    Sleep(1000)
    if Random(0, 9, 1) < 5 then
        Send("b")
        Sleep(2000)
    endif
    Send("c")
    Sleep(1500)
wend
```

Now the bot simulates the actions irregularly. We do the action "b" with 50% probability. This breaks the conditions of the *AnalyzeKey* function of the protection algorithm. Each time then the bot skips "b", the algorithm resets the *gCounter* and starts to accumulate actions from the beginning. Thus, the *ActionSequenceProtection.au3* script is not able to detect our new bot.

Process Scanner

There is another approach for detecting clicker bots. It does not analyze the user actions but searches a bot process in the OS. If we know a name of the bot, we can get the list of all launched processes at the moment and search the bot there.

The *ProcessScanProtection.au3* script in Listing 2-35 checks the list of launched processes.

Listing 2-35. The ProcessScanProtection.au3 Script

```
global const $kLogFile = "debug.log"

func LogWrite($data)
    FileWrite($kLogFile, $data & chr(10))
endfunc

func ScanProcess($name)
    local $processList = ProcessList($name)

    if $processList[0][0] > 0 then
        LogWrite("Name: " & $processList[1][0] & " PID: " & $processList[1][1])
        MsgBox(0, "Alert", "Clicker bot detected!")
    endif
endfunc

while true
    ScanProcess("AutoHotKey.exe")
    Sleep(5000)
wend
```

We can get the process list from the *ProcessList* AutoIt function. It has an optional input parameter, which is a process name to search. We pass the *AutoHotKey.exe* name in our case. The *ProcessList* function returns a two-dimensional array. Table 2-8 describes elements of this array.

Table 2-8. *Resulting Array of the ProcessList Function*

Element	Description
processList[0][0]	The number of processes in the array
processList[1][0]	The name of the first process
processList[1][1]	The ID (PID) of the first process

If the *processList[0][0]* element is greater than zero, the *AutoHotKey.exe* process works now.

Why are we looking for the *AutoHotKey.exe* process instead of the *AutoIt.exe* one? There is a problem with testing the *ProcessScanProtection.au3* script. We write it on the AutoIt language. So, when we launch the script, the OS starts the *AutoIt.exe* process of the language **interpreter**. The interpreter executes our script but not the OS. It is the feature of all scripting languages. They typically work in the environment which is provided by the interpreter application. It means that the protection script can detect itself instead of the *SimpleBot.au3* script.

We can implement the bot with the AutoHotKey language. Listing 2-36 demonstrates the result.

Listing 2-36. The SimpleBot.ahk Script

```
WinActivate, Untitled - Notepad
Sleep, 200

while true
{
    Send, a
    Sleep, 1000
    Send, b
    Sleep, 2000
```

```
    Send, c
    Sleep, 1500
}
```

You can compare this script with the *SimpleBot.au3* one. They look very similar. There are some minor differences in the syntax of function calls. You should specify input parameters after a comma in AutoHotKey. The names of the used functions are the same as those in the AutoIt version.

Now we can test our protection algorithm. These are the steps to do it:

1. Launch the Notepad application.

2. Launch the *ProcessScanProtection.au3* script.

3. Launch the *SimpleBot.ahk* script. Do not forget to install the AutoHotKey interpreter first.

4. Wait until the protection script detects the *SimpleBot.ahk* script.

When the script detects the bot, you see the "Clicker bot detected!" message.

There are several simple ways to avoid this kind of protection algorithm. The most straightforward one is using the AutoHotKey compiler. The compiler allows converting the AutoHotKey script into the binary file, which can be executed by the OS directly without the interpreter. Thus, the bot gets its own name in the process list, and this name differs from the *AutoHotKey.exe* one.

These are the steps to create the *SimpleBot.exe* executable file from the *SimpleBot. ahk* script:

1. Launch the AutoHotKey compiler application. Its default path is *C:\Program Files (x86)\AutoHotkey\Compiler\Ahk2Exe.exe*. You will see the window as Figure 2-14 shows.

2. Select the *SimpleBot.ahk* script as a "Source (script file)" parameter in the "Required Parameters" panel.

3. Leave the "Destination (.exe file)" parameter empty in the "Required Parameters" panel. This means that we create the resulting file in the directory of the source script.

4. Press the "> Convert <" button.

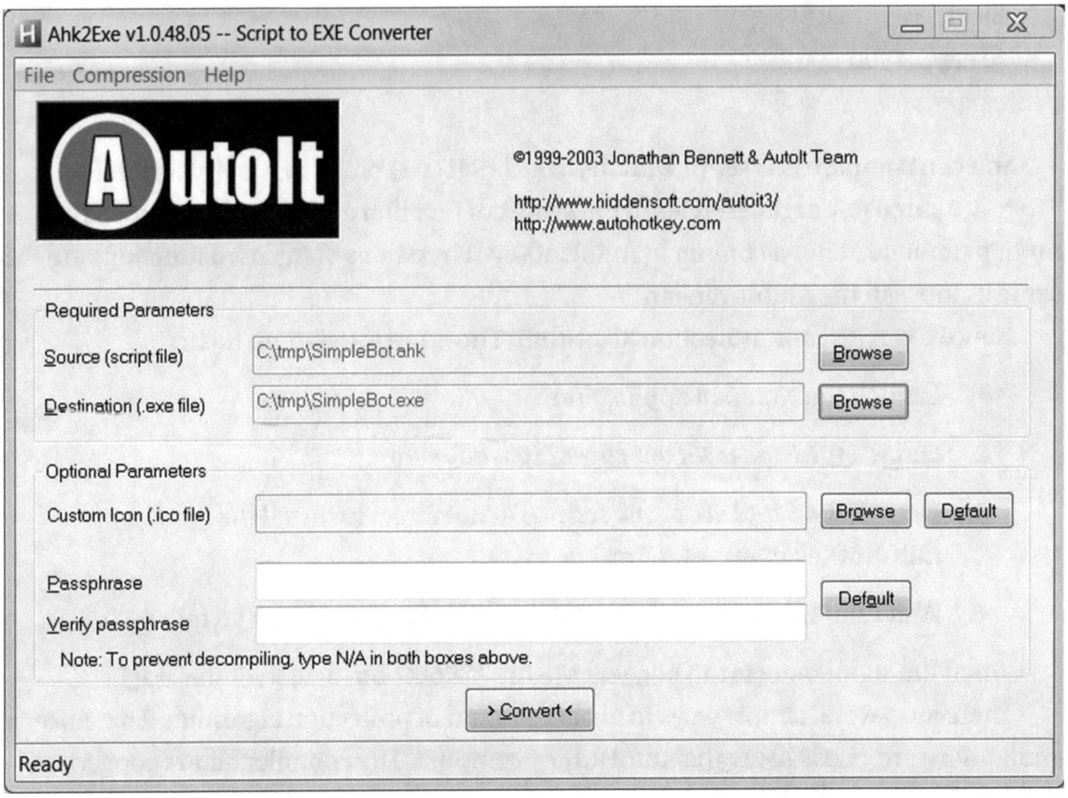

Figure 2-14. *The AutoHotKey compiler window*

You see the "Conversion complete" message when compilation finishes.

Now you can launch the generated *SimpleBot.exe* file instead of the *SimpleBot.ahk* script. It behaves the same as the script. The *ProcessScanProtection.au3* script cannot detect the bot this time. This is so because the compiled bot version has the *SimpleBot.exe* process name instead of the *AutoHotKey.exe*, which the protection script expects.

Can we somehow improve the *ProcessScanProtection.au3* script to detect the compiled versions of the bot? Changing a name of the binary file is easy. It is more difficult to change its content. There are many ways to distinguish files by their content. These are just several ideas to do it:

1. Calculate a **hash sum** for the content of the file and compare it with the predefined value.

2. Check a sequence of bytes in the specific place of the file.

3. Search a specific byte sequence or string in a whole file.

The *Md5ScanProtection.au3* script (see Listing 2-37) calculates an **MD5** hash sum for executable files of all launched processes and detects the bot if the hash sum matches to the predefined value.

Listing 2-37. The Md5ScanProtection.au3 Script

```
#include <Crypt.au3>

global const $kLogFile = "debug.log"
global const $kCheckMd5[2] = ["0x3E4539E7A04472610D68B32D31BF714B", _
 "0xD960F13A44D3BD8F262DF625F5705A63"]

func LogWrite($data)
    FileWrite($kLogFile, $data & chr(10))
endfunc

func _ProcessGetLocation($pid)
    local $proc = DllCall('kernel32.dll', 'hwnd', 'OpenProcess', 'int', _
                        BitOR(0x0400, 0x0010), 'int', 0, 'int', $pid)
    if $proc[0] = 0 then
        return ""
    endif
    local $struct = DllStructCreate('int[1024]')
    DllCall('psapi.dll', 'int', 'EnumProcessModules', 'hwnd', $proc[0], 'ptr', _
            DllStructGetPtr($struct), 'int', DllStructGetSize($struct),
            'int_ptr', 0)

    local $return = DllCall('psapi.dll', 'int', 'GetModuleFileNameEx', 'hwnd', _
                        $proc[0], 'int', DllStructGetData($struct, 1),
                        'str', _
                        ", 'int', 2048)
    if StringLen($return[3]) = 0 then
        return ""
    endif
    return $return[3]
endfunc
```

```
func ScanProcess()
    local $processList = ProcessList()
    for $i = 1 to $processList[0][0]
        local $path = _ProcessGetLocation($processList[$i][1])
        local $md5 = _Crypt_HashFile($path, $CALG_MD5)
        LogWrite("Name: " & $processList[$i][0] & " PID: " _
                    & $processList[$i][1] & " Path: " & $path & " md5: "
                    & $md5)

        for $j = 0 to Ubound($kCheckMd5) - 1
            if $md5 == $kCheckMd5[$j] then
                MsgBox(0, "Alert", "Clicker bot detected!")
            endif
        next
    next
endfunc

while true
    ScanProcess()
    Sleep(5000)
wend
```

The *ScanProcess* function contains the bot detection algorithm. We call the *ProcessList* function without a parameter this time. Therefore, the resulting *processList* array contains a list of all running processes at the moment. When we receive this list, we can retrieve a path of the executable files which start each process.

A process is a set of **modules**. Each module matches to one executable or DLL file, which is loaded into the process memory. A module contains full information about its file. The *_ProcessGetLocation* function retrieves the path of file modules.

When we have the executable file path, we can calculate its hash sum with the *_Crypt_HashFile* AutoIt function. Then we compare the hash sum with predefined values from the *kCheckMd5* array. The array contains hash sums of the *SimpleBot.exe* and AutoHotKey.exe files. If the sums match, the protection script detects the bot.

This is the _ProcessGetLocation function algorithm:

1. Call the OpenProcess WinAPI function to get a handle of the specified process.

2. Call the EnumProcessModules WinAPI function to get a list of process modules.

3. Call the GetModuleFileNameEx WinApi function to get a full path of the module file. The first module in the list, which is returned by the EnumProcessModules function, always matches to the executable file, and all others modules match to DLLs.

You can launch the Md5ScanProtection.au3 script and see how it detects both the SimpleBot.ahk and SimpleBot.exe variants of the bot.

It can happen that the SimpleBot.ahk script is not detected for your case. This means that you are using a version of AutoHotKey application that differs from mine. So, it has a hash sum, which is not specified in the kCheckMd5 array. To fix this, you should get the correct MD5 sum of the AutoHotKey.exe executable in the debug.log file and insert it into the kCheckMd5 array.

There are several ways to improve our bot and avoid the Md5ScanProtection.au3 script. All of them focus on changing a content of the executable file. We have two simple variants:

1. Perform a minor change of the SimpleBot.ahk script (for example in any delay value). Then compile a new version of the script.

2. Patch a header of the AutoHotKey.exe executable file with a binary files editor. You can use the **HT editor** (hte.sourceforge.net), for example.

When you change the executable file, you have a chance to damage it. The launched application crashes in this case. However, there is a place where the general information (like a creation time) about the file is stored. This place is the **COFF** header. It contains standard fields, that do not affect the behavior of the application.

Let us modify the file creation time. It is enough to change its MD5 checksum. So, the Md5ScanProtection.au3 script will not detect the bot anymore.

This is an algorithm to change the file creation time with HT editor:

1. Launch the HT editor with the administrator privileges. It is convenient to copy the editor into the directory with the *AutoHotKey.exe* file.

2. Press the F3 key to pop up the "open file" dialog.

3. Press Tab to switch to the "files" list. Then select the *AutoHotKey.exe* file. Press Enter to open this file.

4. Press the F6 key to open the "select mode" dialog with the list of available modes. Choose the "- pe/header" mode. Now you see a list of executable file headers.

5. Choose the "COFF header" and press Enter. Select the "time-data stamp" field of the header.

6. Press the F4 key to edit the timestamp value. Change the value. Figure 2-15 shows this step.

7. Press F4 and choose the "Yes" option in the "confirmation" dialog to save changes.

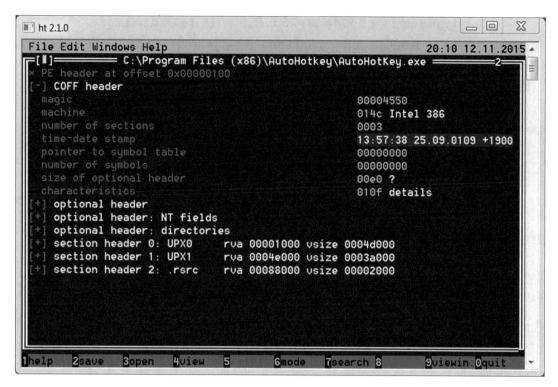

Figure 2-15. *Changing a timestamp in the HT editor*

You get a new *AutoHotKey.exe* executable file, which differs from the original one. You can launch the new interpreter first and then open the *SimpleBot.ahk* script. Test it together with the *Md5ScanProtection.au3* script. You see that now our protection mechanism does not detect the bot.

One way to improve the protection script is to skip the COFF header when calculating the MD5 sum. Another solution is calculating it only for a sequence of bytes in the specific place of the file.

Keyboard State Check

Windows OS provides a kernel-level mechanism to distinguish simulated keystrokes. Let us consider how we can use it.

First of all, we should capture all low-level keyboard input events. The *SetWindowsHookEx* WinAPI function allows setting a hook procedure, which is called each time when the specified event happens. The first function parameter defines a type of a hook procedure. Each type matches to the specific captured events. The *WH_KEYBOARD_LL* type matches to the keyboard input events.

We should implement the hook procedure. It receives the *KBDLLHOOKSTRUCT* structure. It contains detailed information about the captured event. All keyboard events, which are produced by the *SendInput* and *keybd_event* WinAPI functions, have the *LLKHF_INJECTED* flag in the *KBDLLHOOKSTRUCT* structure. On the other hand, keyboard events, which are produced by a keyboard driver, do not have this flag. This flag is set on the Windows kernel level, and it is impossible to disable the flag on the WinAPI level.

The *KeyboardCheckProtection.au3* script in Listing 2-38 checks the *LLKHF_INJECTED* flag and detects clicker bots.

Listing 2-38. The KeyboardCheckProtection.au3 Script

```
#include <WinAPI.au3>

global const $kLogFile = "debug.log"
global $gHook

func LogWrite($data)
    FileWrite($kLogFile, $data & chr(10))
endfunc

func _KeyHandler($nCode, $wParam, $lParam)
    if $nCode < 0 then
        return _WinAPI_CallNextHookEx($gHook, $nCode, $wParam, $lParam)
    endIf

    local $keyHooks = DllStructCreate($tagKBDLLHOOKSTRUCT, $lParam)

    LogWrite("_KeyHandler() - keyccode = " & DllStructGetData($keyHooks,
    "vkCode"));

    local $flags = DllStructGetData($keyHooks, "flags")
    if $flags = $LLKHF_INJECTED then
        MsgBox(0, "Alert", "Clicker bot detected!")
    endif

    return _WinAPI_CallNextHookEx($gHook, $nCode, $wParam, $lParam)
endfunc
```

```
func InitKeyHooks($handler)
    local $keyHandler = DllCallbackRegister($handler, "long", _
                                    "int;wparam;lparam")
    local $hMod = _WinAPI_GetModuleHandle(0)
    $gHook = _WinAPI_SetWindowsHookEx($WH_KEYBOARD_LL, _
                    DllCallbackGetPtr($keyHandler), $hMod)
endfunc

InitKeyHooks("_KeyHandler")

while true
    Sleep(10)
wend
```

We use the same technique to assign key press hooks as the *TimeSpanProtection.au3* and *ActionSequenceProtection.au3* scripts have. Now we use the WinAPI functions directly for this purpose. The *InitKeyHooks* function assigns the *_KeyHandler* hook procedure. The hook captures all low-level keyboard input events.

The *InitKeyHooks* function has the following algorithm:

1. Call the *DllCallbackRegister* AutoIt function to register a *_KeyHandler* procedure as a callback. This step allows passing this callback to other WinAPI functions.

2. Get a handle of the current module by the *GetModuleHandle* WinAPI function. Do not forget that we work in the interpreter process now.

3. Call the *SetWindowsHookEx* WinAPI function for adding the *_KeyHandler* procedure into a hook chain. We should pass to the function the handle of the module where the *_KeyHandler* is defined (we got it in step 2).

There is an algorithm to check the *LLKHF_INJECTED* flag in the *_KeyHandler* procedure:

1. Check the value of the *nCode* parameter. If the value is less than zero, we pass the captured keyboard event to the next hook in the chain without any processing. Both *wParam* and *lParam* parameters do not contain actual information about the keyboard event in this case.

2. If the *nCode* parameter is valid, we call the *DllStructCreate* function to create the *KBDLLHOOKSTRUCT* structure from the *lParam.*

3. Call the *DllStructGetData* function to extract the flags field from the *KBDLLHOOKSTRUCT* structure.

4. Check if the *LLKHF_INJECTED* flag is present. A clicker bot simulates keyboard events with this flag.

You can launch the *KeyboardCheckProtection.au3* script, the Notepad application, and the *SimpleBot.au3* script for testing our algorithm. When the bot simulates the first key, you see the "Clicker bot detected!" message immediately.

There are several ways to avoid this kind of protection algorithm. All of them focus on simulation keyboard events at the level below WinAPI. There are these ways:

1. VM usage.

2. Use a keyboard driver instead of WinAPI functions to simulate keyboard events. The InpOut32 (`www.highrez.co.uk/downloads/inpout32`) is an example of this kind of driver.

3. Emulate keyboard and mouse devices. We will consider this approach in Chapter 5.

The simplest way is to use VM. VM has **virtual device drivers**. These drivers solve two tasks: emulating hardware devices and providing access to real hardware. All events from emulated or real hardware are passed via virtual device drivers. It means that Windows OS inside the VM cannot distinguish the source of hardware events. If you do a keypress in the VM window, this action is legal from the point of view of the OS, which is launched inside the VM. If a bot simulates this keypress, its action is still legal too. It happens because the virtual device drivers process both these events in the same way.

There is an algorithm to use VM for avoiding our protection algorithm:

1. Install one of following VMs:

   - Virtual Box (www.virtualbox.org/wiki/Downloads)

   - VMWare (www.vmware.com/products/workstation-player/ workstation-player-evaluation.html)

   - Windows Virtual PC (www.microsoft.com/en-us/download/ details.aspx?id=3702)

2. Install Windows OS inside the VM.

3. Launch the Notepad application and the *KeyboardCheckProtection.au3* script inside the VM.

4. Launch the *VirtualMachineBot.au3* script outside the VM (i.e., on the host system).

The *VirtualMachineBot.au3* script (see Listing 2-39) is a modified version of our bot.

Listing 2-39. The VirtualMachineBot.au3 Script

```
Sleep(2000)

while true
    Send("a")
    Sleep(1000)
    Send("b")
    Sleep(2000)
    Send("c")
    Sleep(1500)
wend
```

There is only one difference between it and the SimpleBot.au3 script. We do not activate the Notepad window at startup. We have a two-second delay instead. You should activate the window of the VM application and the Notepad window inside it during the delay. Then the script starts to work, and the *KeyboardCheckProtection.au3* script cannot detect it.

Protection Summary

We have considered approaches to protect the game application against clicker bots. Each approach has its own drawbacks, and there are ways to overcome it. You can find an appropriate workaround if you know the protection algorithm well. There are few ideas how you can investigate the algorithm:

1. Hook WinAPI calls, which the protection system does. You can do it with the API Monitor or a similar application.

2. Apply reverse engineering methods to understand the executable and DLL files of the protection system.

3. Try several ways to avoid the protection system. If one of them works, you can assume how the protection algorithm works.

Most of the modern client-side protection systems combine several protection algorithms. Therefore, a reliable clicker bot should combine several methods to avoid them.

CHAPTER 3

In-game Bots

We will consider in-game bots in this chapter. First, we will get an overview of the tools that are often used for analyzing the process memory. Then we will consider a memory structure of a typical Windows process. We will learn how to search, read, and write specific variables in this memory. We will develop a sample bot for the game Diablo 2. Finally, we will consider the protection algorithms against in-game bots.

Tools

In-game bot development requires more advanced techniques than clicker bots. We should dive deeper into OS internals and consider them. Thus, our tools will became more complicated to use.

Programming Language

We will use C++ language only in this chapter. I recommend that you use freeware Microsoft Visual Studio IDE (`www.visualstudio.com/vs/express`) instead of the open source MinGW environment. MinGW has issues with importing some Windows libraries (for example, *dbghelp.dll*). You can try to compile examples of this chapter with MinGW, but you should be ready to switch to Visual Studio IDE in case there are issues.

Do not forget to update your **Internet Explorer** (windows.microsoft.com/en-us/internet-explorer/download-ie) for using the latest version of Visual Studio IDE.

Also, you should install **Windows SDK** (msdn.microsoft.com/en-us/library/ms717358%28v=vs.110%29.aspx), which allows accessing Windows Native API and linking with the *ntdll.dll* system library.

© Ilya Shpigor 2018
I. Shpigor, *Practical Video Game Bots*, https://doi.org/10.1007/978-1-4842-3736-6_3

Debugger

OllyDbg (`www.ollydbg.de`) is a freeware debugger. We will use it intensively in this chapter. The debugger has a user-friendly graphical interface, which simplifies work with it. OllyDbg provides extended functionality to analyze Windows applications without having the source code. However, it allows us to debug and **disassemble** 32-bit Windows applications only.

x64dbg (x64dbg.com) is an open source debugger for Windows. It has almost the same user-friendly interface as OllyDbg. The x64dbg supports both 32-bit and 64-bit applications. It has fewer features than OllyDbg debugger. Therefore, you should be prepared to do some memory addresses calculation manually if you decide to use it. I recommend using x64dbg for debugging 64-bit applications only and OllyDbg in other cases.

WinDbg (docs.microsoft.com/en-us/windows-hardware/drivers/download-the-wdk) is a freeware debugger with powerful features that allow you to debug user mode applications, device drivers, Windows libraries, and kernel. WinDbg supports both 32-bit and 64-bit applications. It has only one serious drawback—a poor user interface. However, we can easily solve this issue with the custom theme (github.com/Deniskore/ windbg-workspace). It improves the interface and makes it look like OllyDbg. Most of the WinDbg features are available through text commands (`www.windbg.info/doc/1-common-cmds.html`).

Here are the steps to install a custom WinDbg theme:

1. Unpack all files from the *windbg-workspace-master.zip* archive to the debugger directory with themes. It has a default path: *C:\Program Files (x86)\Windows Kits\8.1\Debuggers\x64\ themes.*

2. Launch the *windbg.reg file* and press the "Yes" button in both pop-up dialogs.

Now the main window of WinDbg should look like what is shown in Figure 3-1.

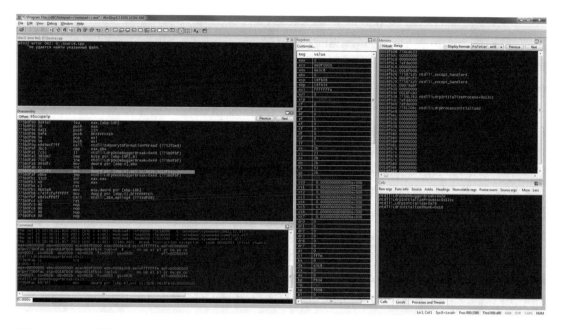

Figure 3-1. *The main window of WinDbg with the applied theme*

Memory Analyzing Tools

Cheat Engine (www.cheatengine.org) is an open source tool that combines features of memory scanner, debugger, and hex editor. It allows you to find an address of the specific variable in process memory and modify it.

HeapMemView (www.nirsoft.net/utils/heap_memory_view.html) is a freeware utility for analysis of the heap segments allocated by the process. It has special versions for 32-bit and 64-bit target applications.

Process Memory Analysis

Many books and articles describe process memory structure. We will consider only those aspects of this topic that are essential for process memory analysis.

Process Memory Overview

First of all, we should understand well the difference between an executable binary file and a launched process. The file is some record on the storage device. The executable file contains instructions (**machine code**) that the CPU can understand and perform.

When you ask OS to launch an executable file, OS copies its content from the storage device to the **random-access memory** (RAM). This operation allows the CPU to access file instructions much faster because the RAM-to-CPU interface has a bandwidth of several orders of magnitude more than the storage device.

Also, OS loads to the RAM all libraries that are required for the loaded file. Then OS provides some CPU time to perform the executable file instructions. At this point, we get the process. So, a process is the executed application.

What does the process do? To answer this question, let us look into the executable file. In general, it contains algorithms to process some data and description of ways to interpret them. Rules of the **type system** encode this description. So, we can conclude that typical process work is manipulation with data.

The next question is where process data is stored. We know that OS keeps CPU instructions into the RAM. However, this is a process responsibility to choose a place to store its data. It can be a storage device, RAM, or remote host (such as a game server). Most of the data that is used for current execution is copied into the RAM because of a quick access benefit. Therefore, we can read a game state from the RAM when the game process works. This period of the process execution is also known as **runtime**.

Figure 3-2 shows components of a typical process. It consists of several modules. The EXE module, which matches the executable file, presents always. All other modules (DLL_1 and DLL_2) are the libraries that are used by the EXE module.

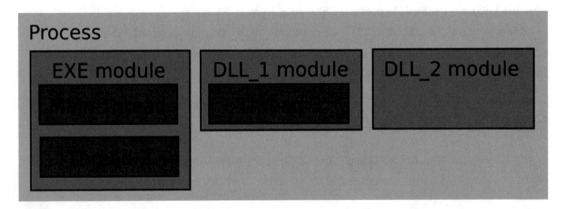

Figure 3-2. *Components of a typical Windows process*

All Windows applications use at least one library that provides access to WinAPI functions. The compiler links some system libraries implicitly even if your application does not call any WinAPI functions. However, the compiler inserts some WinAPI functions (for example, `ExitProcess` or `VirtualQuery`) automatically during the compilation process. They are responsible for process termination and memory management.

There are two types of the libraries: **dynamic-link libraries** (DLL) and static libraries. The primary difference between them is the time to resolve dependencies.

If an executable file depends on a static library, the library must be available at compile time. A linker produces one resulting file, which contains machine code of both the static library and the executable file. So, the EXE module in Figure 3-2 contains a code of the static library and the executable file.

If an executable file depends on a DLL, the DLL should be available at the compile time too. However, the resulting file does not contain machine code of the library. OS searches and loads this code into the process memory at runtime. The launched process crashes if OS does not find the required DLL. You can see two DLL modules in Figure 3-2.

Now let us look how the CPU executes the process. The process can have many algorithms, and sometimes they can be executed in parallel. The **thread** is the smallest portion of machine code that can be executed separately from others in a parallel manner. Threads interact with each other via shared resources (for example RAM). OS chooses which thread is executed at the moment. The number of CPU cores defines the number of simultaneously executed threads.

You can see in Figure 3-2 that each module contains one or more threads. Some modules do not contain threads at all. The EXE module always contains the main thread, which is launched by OS on application start.

Figure 3-2 focuses on the details of process execution. Now we consider the memory layout of a typical process.

Figure 3-3 shows an **address space** of some process with two modules: EXE and one DLL. The address space is divided into memory blocks or **segments**. Each segment has a **base address**, length, and a set of permissions (for example write, read, execute). Segments simplify memory management for OS. This happens because OS can operate by memory blocks instead of the memory cells.

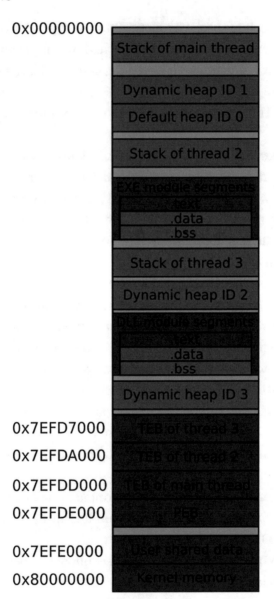

Figure 3-3. *Memory layout of a typical process*

The process on Figure 3-3 has three threads (including the main). Each thread has own **stack segment**. Also, there are several **heap segments**, which are shared between all threads.

Each of process modules has mandatory segments like .*text*, .*data*, and .*bss*. Also, there are some segments (like .*rsrc*) that are not mentioned in our scheme.

Table 3-1 describes each segment briefly.

Table 3-1. *Description of the Segments*

Segment	Description
Stack of main thread	It contains call stack, parameters of the called functions, and **automatic variables**. The segment is used only by the main thread.
Dynamic heap ID 1	The heap, which is created by default on the process start. Dynamic heaps are created and destroyed on the fly during the process execution.
Default heap ID 0	OS creates this heap on the process start. Global and local memory management functions use it by default. However, you can specify another heap for them.
Stack of thread 2	Thread 2 stores here call stack, function parameters, and automatic variables.
EXE module `.text`	It contains machine code of the EXE module.
EXE module `.data`	It contains non-constant **globals** and **static variables** of the EXE module, which have predefined values.
EXE module `.bss`	It contains non-constant globals and static variables without predefined values.
Stack of thread 3	Thread 3 stores here call stack, function parameters, and automatic variables.
Dynamic heap ID 2	**Heap manager** creates this heap automatically when the default heap reaches the maximum available size. This heap extends the default heap.
DLL module `.text`	It contains machine code of the DLL module.
DLL module `.data`	It contains DLL module-specific non-constant globals and static variables with predefined values.
DLL module `.bss`	It contains non-constant globals and static variables without predefined values.
Dynamic heap ID 3	Automatically created heap, which extends the dynamic heap with ID 2 when it reaches the maximum available size.
TEB of thread 3	It contains **Thread Environment Block** (TEB) or **Thread Information Block** (TIB) data structure. This structure stores information about thread 3.

(continued)

Table 3-1. (*continued*)

Segment	Description
TEB of thread 2	It contains TEB with information about thread 2.
TEB of main thread	It contains TEB with information about the main thread.
PEB	It contains **Process Environment Block** (PEB) data structure with information about a whole process.
User shared data	It contains memory that is shared by the current process with other processes.
Kernel memory	It contains memory that is reserved for OS purposes like device drivers and system cache.

Let us assume that Figure 3-3 shows a memory layout of the game process. Some segments contain data related to the game objects. They have been marked with a red color.

OS assigns base addresses of these segments when the game process starts. It means that these addresses can differ each time when you launch the application. Moreover, an order of the red segments in the process memory can vary. However, some segments have permanent base addresses that stay unchanged on each process launch. Examples of these segments are PEB, user shared data, and kernel memory.

OllyDbg debugger allows you to get a memory map of a launched process.

Figure 3-4 shows the beginning of the process address space.

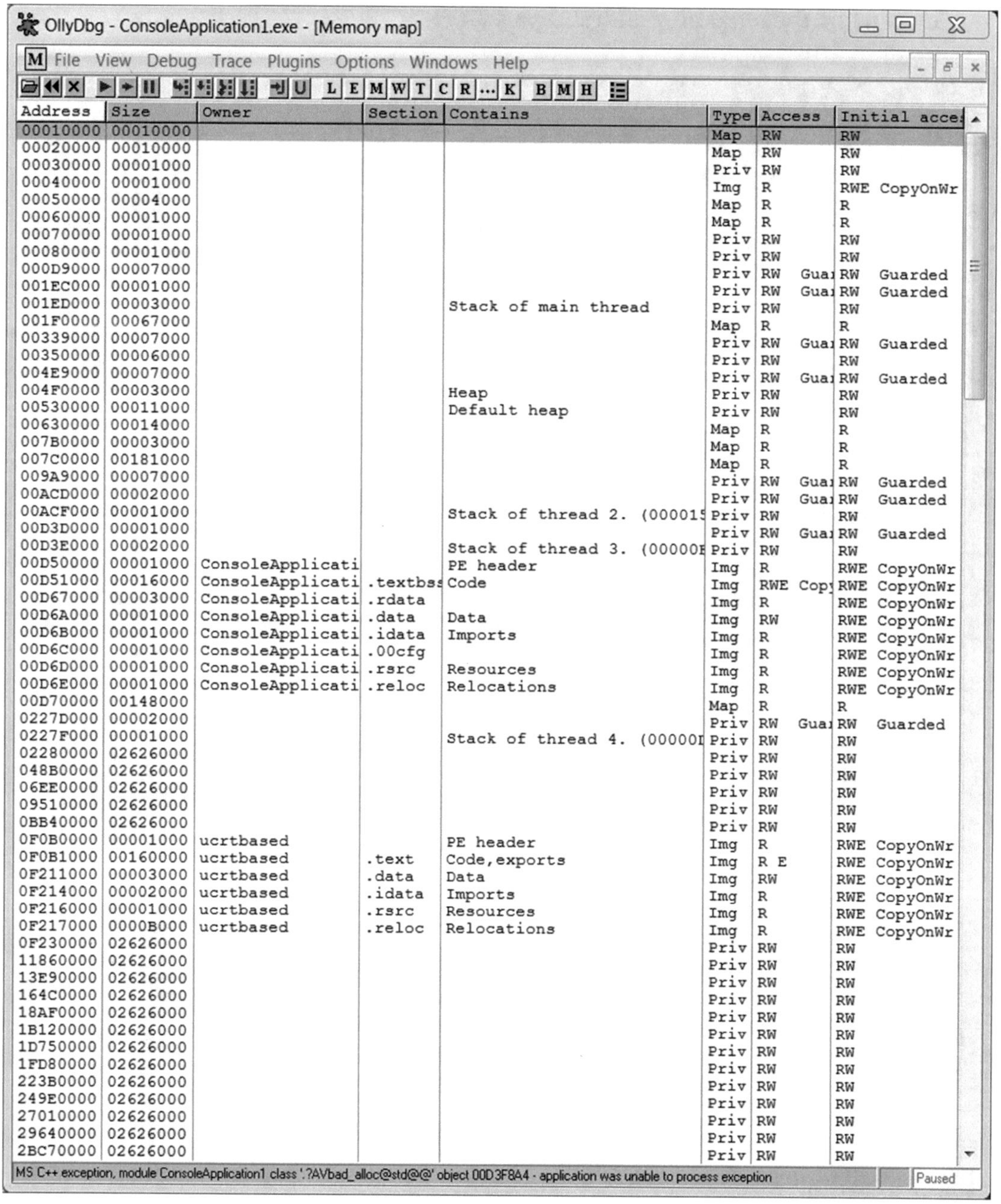

Address	Size	Owner	Section	Contains	Type	Access	Initial acce:
00010000	00010000				Map	RW	RW
00020000	00010000				Map	RW	RW
00030000	00001000				Priv	RW	RW
00040000	00001000				Img	R	RWE CopyOnWr
00050000	00004000				Map	R	R
00060000	00001000				Map	R	R
00070000	00001000				Priv	RW	RW
00080000	00001000				Priv	RW	RW
000D9000	00007000				Priv	RW Gua	RW Guarded
001EC000	00001000				Priv	RW Gua	RW Guarded
001ED000	00003000			Stack of main thread	Priv	RW	RW
001F0000	00067000				Map	R	R
00339000	00007000				Priv	RW Gua	RW Guarded
00350000	00006000				Priv	RW	RW
004E9000	00007000				Priv	RW Gua	RW Guarded
004F0000	00003000			Heap	Priv	RW	RW
00530000	00011000			Default heap	Priv	RW	RW
00630000	00014000				Map	R	R
007B0000	00003000				Map	R	R
007C0000	00181000				Map	R	R
009A9000	00007000				Priv	RW Gua	RW Guarded
00ACD000	00002000				Priv	RW Gua	RW Guarded
00ACF000	00001000			Stack of thread 2. (00001	Priv	RW	RW
00D3D000	00001000				Priv	RW Gua	RW Guarded
00D3E000	00002000			Stack of thread 3. (00000	Priv	RW	RW
00D50000	00001000	ConsoleApplicati		PE header	Img	R	RWE CopyOnWr
00D51000	00016000	ConsoleApplicati	.textbss	Code	Img	RWE Cop	RWE CopyOnWr
00D67000	00003000	ConsoleApplicati	.rdata		Img	R	RWE CopyOnWr
00D6A000	00001000	ConsoleApplicati	.data	Data	Img	RW	RWE CopyOnWr
00D6B000	00001000	ConsoleApplicati	.idata	Imports	Img	R	RWE CopyOnWr
00D6C000	00001000	ConsoleApplicati	.00cfg		Img	R	RWE CopyOnWr
00D6D000	00001000	ConsoleApplicati	.rsrc	Resources	Img	R	RWE CopyOnWr
00D6E000	00001000	ConsoleApplicati	.reloc	Relocations	Img	R	RWE CopyOnWr
00D70000	00148000				Map	R	R
0227D000	00002000				Priv	RW Gua	RW Guarded
0227F000	00001000			Stack of thread 4. (00000	Priv	RW	RW
02280000	02626000				Priv	RW	RW
048B0000	02626000				Priv	RW	RW
06EE0000	02626000				Priv	RW	RW
09510000	02626000				Priv	RW	RW
0BB40000	02626000				Priv	RW	RW
0F0B0000	00001000	ucrtbased		PE header	Img	R	RWE CopyOnWr
0F0B1000	00160000	ucrtbased	.text	Code,exports	Img	R E	RWE CopyOnWr
0F211000	00003000	ucrtbased	.data	Data	Img	RW	RWE CopyOnWr
0F214000	00002000	ucrtbased	.idata	Imports	Img	R	RWE CopyOnWr
0F216000	00001000	ucrtbased	.rsrc	Resources	Img	R	RWE CopyOnWr
0F217000	0000B000	ucrtbased	.reloc	Relocations	Img	R	RWE CopyOnWr
0F230000	02626000				Priv	RW	RW
11860000	02626000				Priv	RW	RW
13E90000	02626000				Priv	RW	RW
164C0000	02626000				Priv	RW	RW
18AF0000	02626000				Priv	RW	RW
1B120000	02626000				Priv	RW	RW
1D750000	02626000				Priv	RW	RW
1FD80000	02626000				Priv	RW	RW
223B0000	02626000				Priv	RW	RW
249E0000	02626000				Priv	RW	RW
27010000	02626000				Priv	RW	RW
29640000	02626000				Priv	RW	RW
2BC70000	02626000				Priv	RW	RW

***Figure 3-4.** The memory map of a launched process (beginning)*

You can find the remaining address space in Figure 3-5.

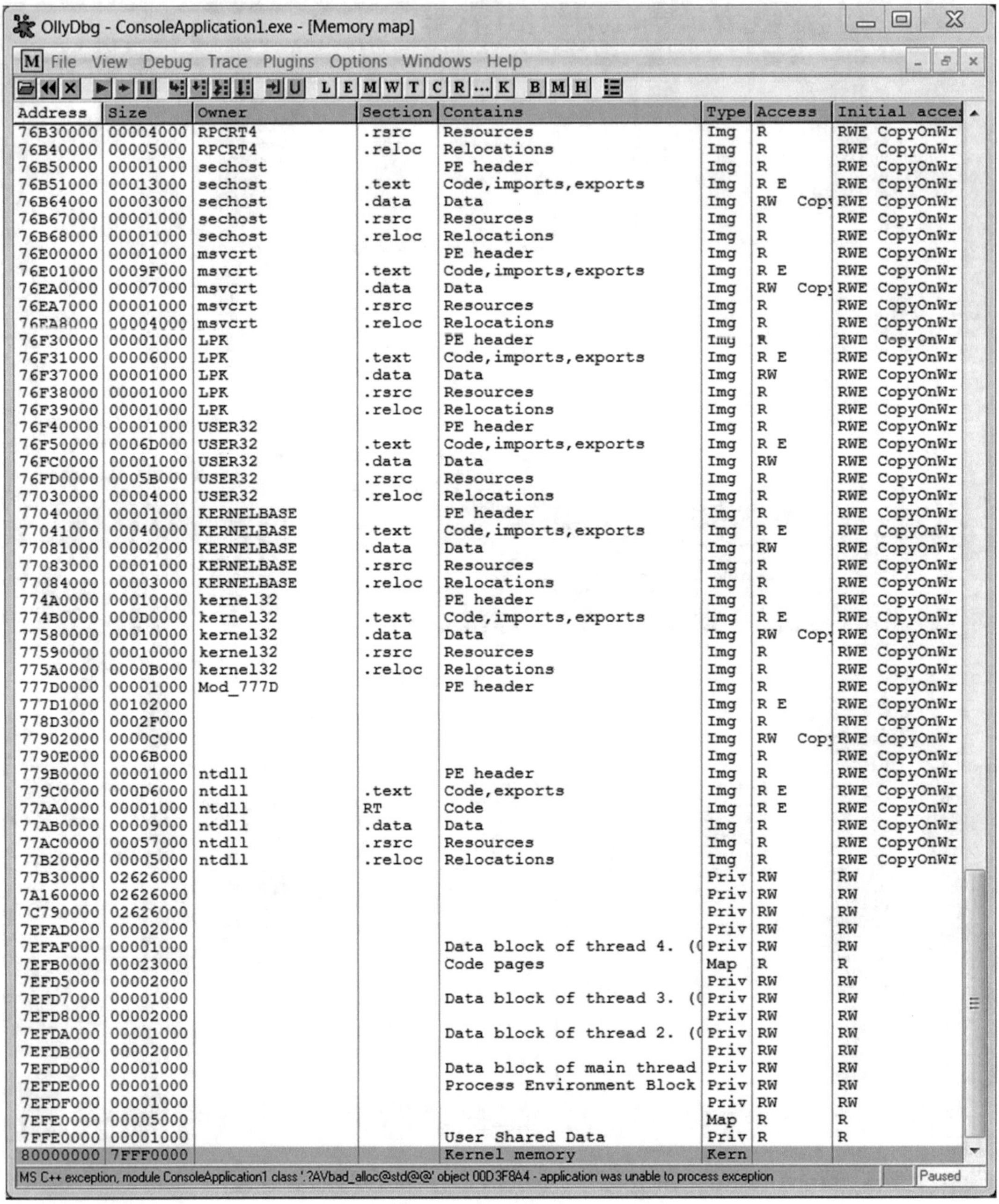

Address	Size	Owner	Section	Contains	Type	Access	Initial acces
76B30000	00004000	RPCRT4	.rsrc	Resources	Img	R	RWE CopyOnWr
76B40000	00005000	RPCRT4	.reloc	Relocations	Img	R	RWE CopyOnWr
76B50000	00001000	sechost		PE header	Img	R	RWE CopyOnWr
76B51000	00013000	sechost	.text	Code,imports,exports	Img	R E	RWE CopyOnWr
76B64000	00003000	sechost	.data	Data	Img	RW Copy	RWE CopyOnWr
76B67000	00001000	sechost	.rsrc	Resources	Img	R	RWE CopyOnWr
76B68000	00001000	sechost	.reloc	Relocations	Img	R	RWE CopyOnWr
76E00000	00001000	msvcrt		PE header	Img	R	RWE CopyOnWr
76E01000	0009F000	msvcrt	.text	Code,imports,exports	Img	R E	RWE CopyOnWr
76EA0000	00007000	msvcrt	.data	Data	Img	RW Copy	RWE CopyOnWr
76EA7000	00001000	msvcrt	.rsrc	Resources	Img	R	RWE CopyOnWr
76EA8000	00004000	msvcrt	.reloc	Relocations	Img	R	RWE CopyOnWr
76F30000	00001000	LPK		PE header	Img	R	RWE CopyOnWr
76F31000	00006000	LPK	.text	Code,imports,exports	Img	R E	RWE CopyOnWr
76F37000	00001000	LPK	.data	Data	Img	RW	RWE CopyOnWr
76F38000	00001000	LPK	.rsrc	Resources	Img	R	RWE CopyOnWr
76F39000	00001000	LPK	.reloc	Relocations	Img	R	RWE CopyOnWr
76F40000	00001000	USER32		PE header	Img	R	RWE CopyOnWr
76F50000	0006D000	USER32	.text	Code,imports,exports	Img	R E	RWE CopyOnWr
76FC0000	00001000	USER32	.data	Data	Img	RW	RWE CopyOnWr
76FD0000	0005B000	USER32	.rsrc	Resources	Img	R	RWE CopyOnWr
77030000	00004000	USER32	.reloc	Relocations	Img	R	RWE CopyOnWr
77040000	00001000	KERNELBASE		PE header	Img	R	RWE CopyOnWr
77041000	00040000	KERNELBASE	.text	Code,imports,exports	Img	R E	RWE CopyOnWr
77081000	00002000	KERNELBASE	.data	Data	Img	RW	RWE CopyOnWr
77083000	00001000	KERNELBASE	.rsrc	Resources	Img	R	RWE CopyOnWr
77084000	00003000	KERNELBASE	.reloc	Relocations	Img	R	RWE CopyOnWr
774A0000	00010000	kernel32		PE header	Img	R	RWE CopyOnWr
774B0000	000D0000	kernel32	.text	Code,imports,exports	Img	R E	RWE CopyOnWr
77580000	00010000	kernel32	.data	Data	Img	RW Copy	RWE CopyOnWr
77590000	00010000	kernel32	.rsrc	Resources	Img	R	RWE CopyOnWr
775A0000	0000B000	kernel32	.reloc	Relocations	Img	R	RWE CopyOnWr
777D0000	00001000	Mod_777D		PE header	Img	R	RWE CopyOnWr
777D1000	00102000				Img	R E	RWE CopyOnWr
778D3000	0002F000				Img	R	RWE CopyOnWr
77902000	0000C000				Img	RW Copy	RWE CopyOnWr
7790E000	0006B000				Img	R	RWE CopyOnWr
779B0000	00001000	ntdll		PE header	Img	R	RWE CopyOnWr
779C0000	000D6000	ntdll	.text	Code,exports	Img	R E	RWE CopyOnWr
77AA0000	00001000	ntdll	RT	Code	Img	R E	RWE CopyOnWr
77AB0000	00009000	ntdll	.data	Data	Img	R	RWE CopyOnWr
77AC0000	00057000	ntdll	.rsrc	Resources	Img	R	RWE CopyOnWr
77B20000	00005000	ntdll	.reloc	Relocations	Img	R	RWE CopyOnWr
77B30000	02626000				Priv	RW	RW
7A160000	02626000				Priv	RW	RW
7C790000	02626000				Priv	RW	RW
7EFAD000	00002000				Priv	RW	RW
7EFAF000	00001000			Data block of thread 4. ((	Priv	RW	RW
7EFB0000	00023000			Code pages	Map	R	R
7EFD5000	00002000				Priv	RW	RW
7EFD7000	00001000			Data block of thread 3. ((	Priv	RW	RW
7EFD8000	00002000				Priv	RW	RW
7EFDA000	00001000			Data block of thread 2. ((	Priv	RW	RW
7EFDB000	00002000				Priv	RW	RW
7EFDD000	00001000			Data block of main thread	Priv	RW	RW
7EFDE000	00001000			Process Environment Block	Priv	RW	RW
7EFDF000	00001000				Priv	RW	RW
7EFE0000	00005000				Map	R	R
7FFE0000	00001000			User Shared Data	Priv	R	R
80000000	7FFF0000			Kernel memory	Kern		

MS C++ exception, module ConsoleApplication1 class '.?AVbad_alloc@std@@' object 00D3F8A4 - application was unable to process exception Paused

Figure 3-5. *The memory map of a launched process (ending)*

Let us make a match between the Figure 3-3 memory layout and segments of the real process. Table 3-2 summarizes this.

Table 3-2. *Segments of the Real Process*

Address	Segment
001ED000	Stack of main thread.
004F0000	Dynamic heap with ID 1.
00530000	Default heap with ID 0.
00ACF000	Stacks of additional threads.
00D3E000	
0227F000	
00D50000-00D6E000	Segments of the EXE module named "ConsoleApplication1".
02280000-0BB40000	Extra dynamic heaps.
0F230000-2BC70000	
0F0B0000-0F217000	Segments of the DLL module named "ucrtbased".
7EFAF000	TEB of additional threads.
7EFD7000	
7EFDA000	
7EFDD000	TEB of main thread.
7EFDE000	PEB of main thread.
7FFE0000	User shared data.
80000000	Kernel memory.

You have probably noticed that OllyDbg does not detect all dynamic heaps automatically. You can use WinDbg debugger or HeapMemView utility to find all heap segments and get their base addresses.

Variable Searching

In-game bots read states of game objects from the game process memory. Variables from several segments can keep this state. The base addresses of these segments and offsets of the variables inside them can change each time we restart a game. This means that the absolute address of each variable is not a constant. Therefore, the bot should have an algorithm to search variables in process memory. The algorithm should calculate an absolute address of the specified variable.

We use the term "absolute address" here, but it is not a precise name in terms of the **x86 memory segmentation model**. If we follow the naming of this model, the absolute address is named **linear address**. This is a formula to calculate a linear address:

```
linear address = base address + offset
```

We will continue to use the term "absolute address" for simplicity's sake, as it is more intuitively understandable. The term "linear address" will appear when it becomes important to emphasize aspects of the memory segmentation model.

We can divide the search of a specific variable in process memory into three steps to make a **variable searching algorithm**:

1. Find a segment that contains the variable.

2. Define a base address of the segment.

3. Define an offset of the variable inside the segment.

It is very likely that the variable will fit in the same segment after application restart. However, the heap segments break this rule. This happens because of a mechanism that creates dynamic heaps. If the target variable is not in the heap segment, we can perform the first step of our algorithm manually and hard-code the result in our bot. Otherwise, we should apply more sophisticated techniques.

The in-game bot should solve the second algorithm step by his own because segment address changes after application restart.

It is not guaranteed that a variable offset inside the segment stays unchanged on each process launch. However, it may remain the same in some cases. It depends on the segment type. Table 3-3 shows the dependency between segment types and offsets of its variables.

Table 3-3. *Variable Offsets in Different Types of Segments*

Segment Type	Offset Constancy
.bss	Always constant.
.data	Always constant.
stack	The offset is constant in most cases. It can vary when **control flow** of application execution differs between new application launches.
heap	The offset varies in most cases.

Thus, we can solve the third step of the algorithm manually in some cases and hard-ode the result.

32-Bit Application Analysis

We will analyze the memory of the ColorPix 32-bit application. This allows us to apply our variable searching algorithm in practice. After we have completed this exercise, we will understand each step of the algorithm better.

We have already used the ColorPix application in Chapter 2. Figure 3-6 shows the application window.

Let us find a variable that matches the x coordinate of the selected pixel on a screen. A red line underlines this value in Figure 3-6.

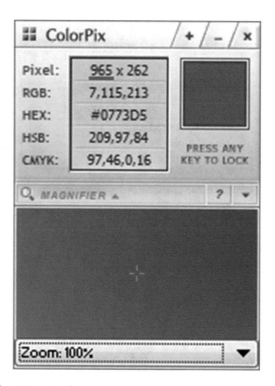

Figure 3-6. *The ColorPix window*

You should not close the ColorPix application during our analysis. If you do, you should repeat the search steps from the beginning.

The first step of the variable searching algorithm is to find a memory segment that contains the x coordinate. We can split this task into two stages:

1. Find the absolute address of the variable with the Cheat Engine scanner.

2. Compare the discovered absolute address with the base addresses and lengths of all memory segments. This allows us to deduce a segment that contains the variable.

This is an algorithm to find the absolute address of the variable with the Cheat Engine scanner:

1. Launch the 32-bit version of the Cheat Engine scanner with administrator privileges.

2. Select the "File"➤"Open Process" menu item. You will see the dialog with a list of launched applications at the moment (Figure 3-7).

Figure 3-7. *The process list dialog*

3. Select a process with the "ColorPix.exe" name in the list and press the "Open" button. Now the process name is displayed above the progress bar at the top of the Cheat Engine window.

4. Type the current value of the x coordinate into the "Value" control of the Cheat Engine window. You can read this value in the ColorPix window.

5. Press the "First Scan" button to find the typed x value in a memory of the ColorPix process.

The number in the "Value" control should match the x coordinate, which is displayed in the ColorPix window at the moment when you are pressing the "First Scan" button. You can use the Tab and Shift+Tab keys to switch between the "Value" control and the "First Scan" button. This allows you to keep the pixel coordinate unchanged during switching.

The list control in the Cheat Engine window shows the search results (Figure 3-8).

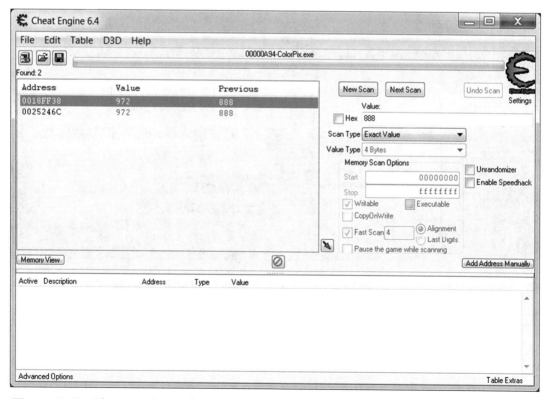

Figure 3-8.   *The search results in the Cheat Engine window*

If there are more than two absolute addresses in the list, you should filter inappropriate results. To do so, just move the mouse to change the x coordinate of the current pixel. Then type a new value of the x coordinate in the "Value" control and press the "Next Scan" button. Be sure that the new value differs from the previous one.

After filtering inappropriate results, you will get two variables as Figure 3-8 shows. Their absolute addresses equal to "0018FF38" and "0025246C" in my case. You can get other addresses. It is not an issue for our exercise.

Now we know absolute addresses of two variables that match to the x coordinate of the selected pixel. The next step is to find segments that contain these variables. We can usc OllyDbg debugger to get it.

This is an algorithm to search the segment:

1. Launch OllyDbg debugger with administrator privileges. The default path of the executable file is *C:\Program Files (x86)\ odbg201\ollydbg.exe.*

2. Select the "File"➤"Attach" menu item. You will see the dialog with a list of launched 32-bit applications at the moment (Figure 3-9).

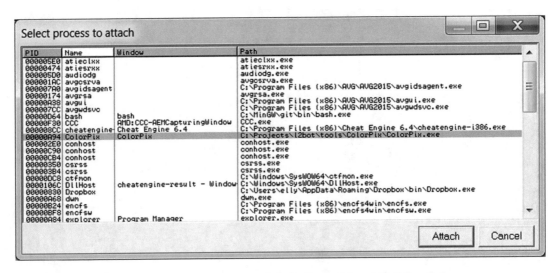

Figure 3-9. *The "Select process to attach" dialog of the OllyDbg debugger*

3. Select the "ColorPix.exe" process in the list and press the "Attach" button. When the debugger attaches, you see the "Paused" text in the bottom right corner of the OllyDbg window.

4. Press Alt+M to open a memory map of the ColorPix process. Now the OllyDbg window looks like what Figure 3-10 shows.

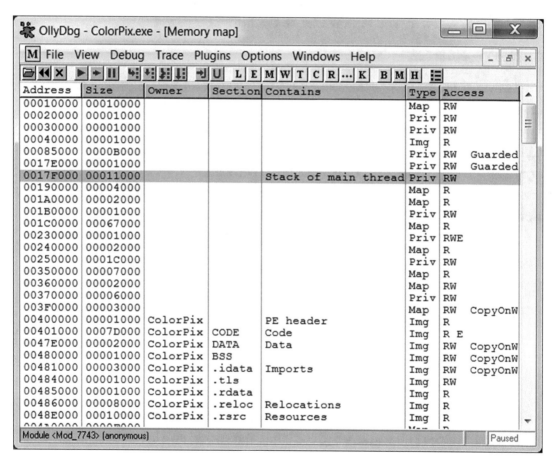

Figure 3-10. *The memory map of the ColorPix process*

You can see that the variable with the absolute address 0018FF38 matches the "Stack of main thread" segment. This segment starts at the "0017F000" address. It ends at the "00190000" address because the next segment starts at the "00190000". The second variable with absolute address 0025246C matches an unknown segment with a "00250000" base address. It will be more reliable to choose the "Stack of main thread" segment to read a value of the x coordinate. It is much easier to find a stack segment than some unknown segment.

The last step of our variable searching algorithm is to calculate a variable offset inside the owning segment. The stack segment grows down for x86 architecture. This means that the stack grows from higher addresses to lower addresses. Therefore, the base address of the stack segment equals its upper bound (i.e., 00190000 in our case). The lower segment bound will change when the stack grows.

An offset of the variable equals the subtraction of its absolute address from a base address of the segment. This is a calculation example for our case:

```
00190000 - 0018FF38 = C8
```

The variable offset inside the owning segment equals C8. This formula differs for heap, *.bss*, and *.data* segments. Heap grows up, and its base address equals the lower segment bound. The *.bss* and *.data* segments do not grow at all. Their base addresses equal to lower segment bounds too. You can follow the rule to subtract a smaller address from a larger one to calculate the variable offset correctly.

Now we have enough information to find and read a value of the x coordinate for any launched ColorPix process. This is the algorithm to do it:

1. Get the base address of the main thread stack segment. You can get this address from the TEB segment.

2. Calculate the absolute address of the x coordinate variable by subtraction the offset C8 from the base address of the stack segment.

3. Read four bytes from the ColorPix application memory at the calculated absolute address.

As you see, it is quite simple to write a bot that follows this algorithm.

You can read the TEB segment with OllyDbg. You should do a left-button double-click on the "Data block of main thread" segment in the "Memory Map" window. Then you will see the window shown in Figure 3-11.

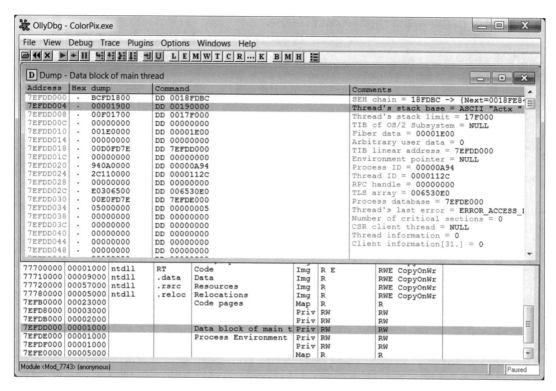

Figure 3-11. *The TEB dump of the ColorPix application*

The base address of the stack segment equals "00190000" according to Figure 3-11. This address can vary, and you should reread it again each time when you restart the ColorPix application.

64-Bit Application Analysis

Let us apply our variable searching algorithm to a 64-bit application.

We cannot use the OllyDbg debugger for this exercise because it does not support 64-bit applications. We will use the WinDbg debugger instead.

We will analyze the Resource Monitor Windows 7 utility. The bitness of this application matches the bitness of the Windows OS. If you have the 64-bit Windows version, you have the 64-bit Resource Monitor. To launch it, you should open the "Start" Windows menu and type the following command in a search box:

```
perfmon.exe /res
```

Figure 3-12 shows the application window.

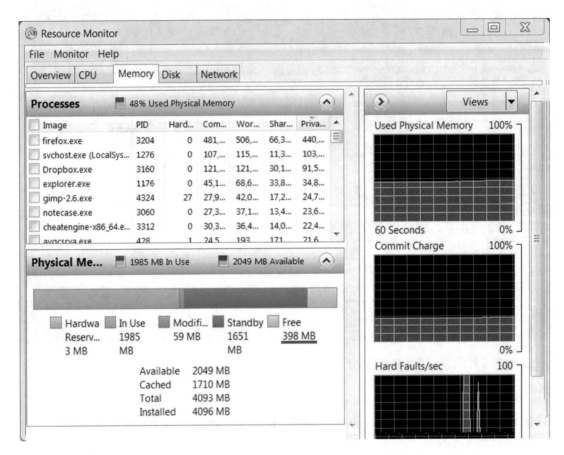

Figure 3-12. *The Resource Monitor window*

A red line underlines the "Free" memory amount. We will find this variable in the process memory.

The first step of our algorithm is finding the segment that contains the target variable. We can use the 64-bit version of the Cheat Engine scanner to get an absolute address of the variable. The 64-bit version of the Cheat Engine has the same user interface as the 32-bit version.

I get two addresses for the "Free" memory amount variable: "00432FEC" and "00433010".

The second step is comparing the process memory map and variable addresses. This step differs from the 32-bit application analysis because we will use another debugger.

This is an algorithm to get a process memory map with WinDbg:

1. Launch the 64-bit version of the WinDbg debugger with administrator privileges. The default path of the executable file is *C:\Program Files (x86)\Windows Kits\8.1\Debuggers\x64\windbg.exe.*

2. Select the "File"➤"Attach to a Process..." menu item. You will see a dialog with a list of launched 64-bit applications at the moment (see Figure 3-13).

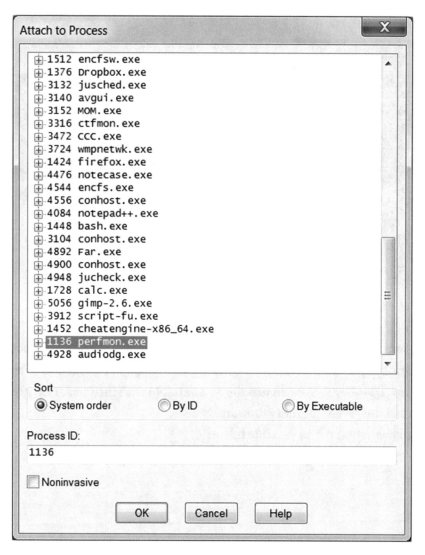

Figure 3-13. *The "Attach to Process" dialog*

3. Select the "perfmon.exe" process in the list and press the "OK" button.

4. Type the *!address* command in a control at the bottom of the "Command" window, and press Enter. You will see a memory map of the Resource Monitor application in the "Command" window as Figure 3-14 shows.

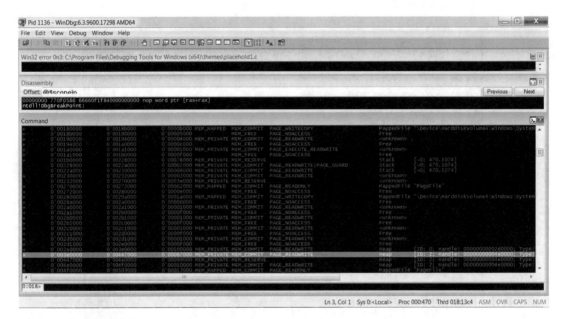

Figure 3-14. *Memory map in the WinDbg debugger*

You can see that both variables with absolute addresses 00432FEC and 00433010 match the first heap segment with ID 2. This segment occupies addresses from "003E0000" to "00447000". We can use the first variable with the 00432FEC absolute address to read the "Free" memory amount.

This is a calculation of the variable offset:

```
00432FEC - 003E0000 = 52FEC
```

This is an algorithm to find and read a "Free" memory amount from the Resource Monitor process:

1. Get a base address of the heap segment with ID 2. You can use this set of WinAPI functions to traverse heap segments of the process:

    *   `CreateToolhelp32Snapshot`

    *   `Heap32ListFirst`

    *   `Heap32ListNext`

2. Calculate an absolute address of the variable by adding the offset 52FEC to the base address of the heap segment.

3. Read four bytes from the Resource Monitor process memory at the calculated absolute address.

Process Memory Analysis Summary

We have considered the memory layout of a typical Windows application. We made the variable searching algorithm and applied it to analysis of both 32-bit and 64-bit applications. We got the practical skills to use both OllyDbg and WinDbg debuggers.

Process Memory Access

We already know how to find a variable in the process memory manually. Let us implement a code that automates this algorithm. In-game bots cannot use a debugger (like OllyDbg). Instead, they should have some debugger mechanism to repeat their features.

Open Process

As you remember, the first step of accessing a process memory is attaching to this process. Now we consider the WinAPI functions to do it.

Almost all Windows objects and resources can be accessed via **handles**. The *OpenProcess* WinAPI function provides a handle of the specified process. Each process in the system has a unique number, which is named the **process identifier** (PID). We should pass the PID to the *OpenProcess* function and get the handle back. Once we get a process handle, we can access its memory via WinAPI functions.

Windows has high-level abstractions for its resources. Windows objects (for example, processes) use these abstractions. Some objects wrap system resources and provide a unified interface for other objects. So, Windows objects interact with other objects in most cases. This approach simplifies interfaces and application development very much.

How can our application interact with the Windows object? Each object has a unified structure, which consists of a **header** and **body**. The header contains metainformation about the object, and **Object Manager** uses this information. This manager responds by providing access to system resources. The body contains the object-specific data.

The Windows **security model** restricts processes that can access the system objects and perform various system administration tasks. The security model requires a process to have special privileges to access another process with the *OpenProcess* function. An **access token** is a system object that allows manipulating the security attributes of the process. We can use the access token features to grant privileges for our application. So, it can use the *OpenProcess* function without limitations.

This is the **opening the target process algorithm** from the current process with the *OpenProcess* function:

1. Get a handle of a current process.

2. Get an access token of the current process.

3. Grant *SE_DEBUG_NAME* privilege for the access token of the current process. This privilege allows the process to debug others.

4. Get a handle of the target process with the *OpenProcess* call.

We should launch our application with administrator privileges to perform this algorithm. Otherwise, we cannot grant the *SE_DEBUG_NAME* privilege with the *AdjustTokenPrivileges* function.

You might ask why it is not enough to launch the application with administrator privileges and let it access other processes. It is a good question. If you are a system administrator, you should have access to the system configuration features. However, this does not mean that all applications that you run can easily violate the common system rules (for example accessing the resources of other processes). If the system behaves in the same way, it becomes very unstable and fragile.

Listing 3-1 demonstrates an application that opens the target process with the specified PID.

Listing 3-1. The OpenProcess.cpp Application

```c
#include <windows.h>
#include <stdio.h>

BOOL SetPrivilege(HANDLE hToken, LPCTSTR lpszPrivilege, BOOL bEnablePrivilege)
{
    TOKEN_PRIVILEGES tp;
    LUID luid;

    if (!LookupPrivilegeValue(NULL, lpszPrivilege, &luid))
    {
        printf("LookupPrivilegeValue error: %u\n", GetLastError());
        return FALSE;
    }

    tp.PrivilegeCount = 1;
    tp.Privileges[0].Luid = luid;
    if (bEnablePrivilege)
        tp.Privileges[0].Attributes = SE_PRIVILEGE_ENABLED;
    else
        tp.Privileges[0].Attributes = 0;

    if (!AdjustTokenPrivileges(hToken, FALSE, &tp, sizeof(TOKEN_PRIVILEGES),
                            (PTOKEN_PRIVILEGES)NULL, (PDWORD)NULL))
    {
        printf("AdjustTokenPrivileges error: %u\n", GetLastError());
        return FALSE;
    }

    if (GetLastError() == ERROR_NOT_ALL_ASSIGNED)
    {
        printf("The token does not have the specified privilege. \n");
        return FALSE;
    }
    return TRUE;
}
```

```
int main()
{
    HANDLE hProc = GetCurrentProcess();

    HANDLE hToken = NULL;
    if (!OpenProcessToken(hProc, TOKEN_ADJUST_PRIVILEGES, &hToken))
        printf("Failed to open access token\n");

    if (!SetPrivilege(hToken, SE_DEBUG_NAME, TRUE))
        printf("Failed to set debug privilege\n");

    DWORD pid = 1804;
    HANDLE hTargetProc = OpenProcess(PROCESS_ALL_ACCESS, FALSE, pid);
    if (hTargetProc)
        printf("Target process handle = %p\n", hTargetProc);
    else
        printf("Failed to open process: %u\n", GetLastError());

    CloseHandle(hTargetProc);
    return 0;
}
```

The application opens a process with a PID that equals 1804. To test it, you should specify the PID of any existing process in your system. Windows Task Manager allows you to get PIDs of all launched processes.

You should specify the PID in this code line:

```
DWORD pid = 1804;
```

We implement each step of the opening a process algorithm in the separate functions. Then, we call all these functions from the *main* function of the *OpenProcess.cpp* application. Let us consider these steps.

The first step is getting a handle of the current process with the *GetCurrentProcess* call. We save it in the *hProc* variable.

The second step is getting an access token of the current process with the *OpenProcessToken* call. We pass the *hProc* variable and *TOKEN_ADJUST_PRIVILEGES* access mask to this function. The function returns a handle to the access token. We save it in the *hToken* variable.

The third step is to grant the *SE_DEBUG_NAME* privilege for the current process. We encapsulate this action in the *SetPrivilege* function. There are two steps to grant the privilege:

1. Get the **locally unique identifier** (LUID) of the *SE_DEBUG_NAME* privilege constant with the *LookupPrivilegeValue* WinAPI function.

2. Grant the privilege with the specified LUID with the *AdjustTokenPrivileges* WinAPI function. This function operates with LUID values instead of privilege constants.

An example of the *SetPrivilege* function with a detailed explanation is available in the MSDN article (msdn.microsoft.com/en-us/library/aa446619%28VS.85%29.aspx).

The last step is the *OpenProcess* WinAPI function call. We pass the *PROCESS_ALL_ACCESS* access rights and a PID of the target process to this function. It returns a handle, which we can use to access memory of this process.

Read and Write Operations

We have a handle of the target process. Let us consider ways to access its memory. WinAPI provides appropriate functions for this task.

The *ReadProcessMemory* function reads data from a memory area of the target process to the memory of the current process. The *WriteProcessMemory* function writes specified data to a memory area of the target process.

We will consider the usage of these functions with a sample application (see Listing 3-2). Our application writes the hexadecimal value 0xDEADBEEF at the specified absolute address of the target process memory. Then it reads a value at the same absolute address. If the write operation succeeds, the read operation returns the 0xDEADBEEF value.

Listing 3-2. The ReadWriteProcessMemory.cpp Application

```
#include <stdio.h>
#include <windows.h>
```

```
BOOL SetPrivilege(HANDLE hToken, LPCTSTR lpszPrivilege, BOOL
bEnablePrivilege)
{
    // See function's implementation in the OpenProcess.cpp application
}

DWORD ReadDword(HANDLE hProc, DWORD_PTR address)
{
    DWORD result = 0;

    if (ReadProcessMemory(hProc, (void*)address, &result, sizeof(result),
    NULL) == 0)
    {
        printf("Failed to read memory: %u\n", GetLastError());
    }
    return result;
}

void WriteDword(HANDLE hProc, DWORD_PTR address, DWORD value)
{
    if (WriteProcessMemory(hProc, (void*)address, &value, sizeof(value),
    NULL) == 0)
    {
        printf("Failed to write memory: %u\n", GetLastError());
    }
}

int main()
{
    HANDLE hProc = GetCurrentProcess();

    HANDLE hToken = NULL;
    if (!OpenProcessToken(hProc, TOKEN_ADJUST_PRIVILEGES, &hToken))
        printf("Failed to open access token\n");

    if (!SetPrivilege(hToken, SE_DEBUG_NAME, TRUE))
        printf("Failed to set debug privilege\n");

    DWORD pid = 5356;
```

```
HANDLE hTargetProc = OpenProcess(PROCESS_ALL_ACCESS, FALSE, pid);
if (!hTargetProc)
    printf("Failed to open process: %u\n", GetLastError());

DWORD_PTR address = 0x001E0000;
WriteDword(hTargetProc, address, 0xDEADBEEF);
printf("Result of reading dword at 0x%llx address = 0x%x\n", address,
        ReadDword(hTargetProc, address));

CloseHandle(hTargetProc);
return 0;
}
```

The write operation to the 0x001E0000 absolute address can crash the target process. Therefore, I recommend to not use any Windows system services as a target process to test the *ReadWriteProcessMemory.cpp* application. It is better to launch Notepad and use it as the target process.

This is an algorithm to launch our application:

1. Launch a Notepad.

2. Get a PID of the Notepad process with the Windows Task Manager.

3. Assign the Notepad PID to the *pid* variable in this line of the *main* function:

   ```
   DWORD pid = 5356;
   ```

4. Get a base address of any heap segment of the Notepad process with WinDbg debugger. You can use the *!address* command to get a full memory map of the Notepad process.

5. Detach the WinDbg debugger from the Notepad process with the *.detach* command.

6. Assign the base address of the heap segment to the *address* variable in this line of the *main* function:

   ```
   DWORD_PTR address = 0x001E0000;
   ```

7. Rebuild the *ReadWriteProcessMemory.cpp* application. The application binary should have the same target architecture (x86 or x64) as Notepad.

8. Launch the sample application with administrator privileges.

This is a console output after successful execution of the application:

```
Result of reading dword at 0x1e0000 address = 0xdeadbeef
```

The output contains a memory address where our application reads and writes data. We use *WriteDword* and *ReadDword* wrapper functions for WinAPI. These wrappers encapsulate type casts and error processing. However, you should know input parameters of both *WriteProcessMemory* and *ReadProcessMemory* WinAPI functions. Table 3-4 explains these parameters.

Table 3-4. *Parameters of the WriteProcessMemory and ReadProcessMemory WinAPI Functions*

Parameter	Description
hProc	A handle of the target process. We access the memory of this process.
address	An absolute address of a memory area to access.
&result or *&value*	A pointer to store the result of the read operation in case of *ReadProcessMemory* function. The buffer contains data for writing in case of the *WriteProcessMemory* function.
sizeof(...)	A number of bytes to read from memory or to write there.
NULL	A pointer to a variable that stores an actual number of transferred bytes.

TEB and PEB Access

We know how to access data of the target process memory. However, we should know an absolute address to read or write the specific variable. There is only one reliable way for calculating the variable address. We should consider the segment where our variable is stored.

You probably remember that each process has places where we can find information about its segments. These places are special TEB and PEB segments. Now we consider ways to find and access them.

If a process has several threads, each of them has its own TEB segment. It contains a base address of the stack segment that belongs to the thread. We can get the first half of the thread variables from its stack.

The default heap segment contains the remaining half (with some exceptions) of the variables. How can we find this segment? This task is quite easy because the PEB segment contains a base address of the default heap. Also, if we find a TEB segment, we automatically find a PEB segment too because all TEB segments contain a base address of the PEB.

A process has only one PEB segment (unlike few TEB segments).

Current Process

Let us consider methods to access a TEB segment. We start with the most simple variant of this task. This variant answers the question of how we can access the TEB of the main thread of our sample application.

There are several ways to access a TEB segment. The first is to use segment registers in the same way as Windows does. There is an **FS segment register** for the x86 architecture and a **GS segment register** for the x64 architecture. Both of these registers point to the TEB segment of the thread that is executed at the moment.

The *GetTeb* function retrieves a pointer to the *TEB* structure for x86 architecture application:

```
#include <winternl.h>

PTEB GetTeb()
{
    PTEB pTeb;

    __asm {
        mov EAX, FS:[0x18]
        mov pTeb, EAX
    }
    return pTeb;
}
```

You can see that we read a 32-bit value with the 0x18 offset from the TEB segment. This value matches to the base address of the TEB segment.

You might ask why we cannot just use the value of the FS register. Does it make sense for the TEB segment to store its own base address?

This question requires us to take one step back and consider the way that OS accesses the process segments.

Most of the modern OS (like Windows) use the **protected processor mode** (en.wikipedia.org/wiki/Protected_mode). This means that **segment addressing** (en.wikipedia.org/wiki/X86_memory_segmentation#Protected_mode) works via a **descriptor table** (en.wikipedia.org/wiki/Global_Descriptor_Table) mechanism. The FS and GS registers contain a selector that defines the index of entry inside the descriptor table. The descriptor table contains an actual base address of the TEB segment that matches to the specified index. A segmentation unit of the CPU performs this kind of request to the descriptor table. The resulting address of a calculation that is performed by the segmentation unit is kept inside the CPU and is accessible neither by the user application nor by the OS. There is a way to access entries in the descriptor tables via the *GetThreadSelectorEntry* and *Wow64GetThreadSelectorEntry* WinAPI functions. However, Windows cannot use these functions because of the overhead. The probable reason that the TEB segment contains its own base address is to overcome the overhead of the direct access the descriptor tables.

An example of the use of the *GetThreadSelectorEntry* function may be found at reverseengineering.stackexchange.com/questions/3139/how-can-i-find-the-thread-local-storage-tls-of-a-windows-process-thread.

The *TEB* structure varies between different Windows versions. The *winternal.h* header file defines the structure. Windows SDK provides this file. You should clarify the structure fields for your environment before starting to work with it. In over words, versions of the Windows SDK and your Windows system should match.

This is an example of the *TEB* structure for Windows 8.1 version:

```
typedef struct _TEB {
    PVOID Reserved1[12];
    PPEB ProcessEnvironmentBlock;
    PVOID Reserved2[399];
    BYTE Reserved3[1952];
    PVOID TlsSlots[64];
    BYTE Reserved4[8];
```

```
    PVOID Reserved5[26];
    PVOID ReservedForOle;   // Windows 2000 only
    PVOID Reserved6[4];
    PVOID TlsExpansionSlots;
} TEB, *PTEB;
```

You can see that the structure has the *ProcessEnvironmentBlock* field, which points to the PEB structure. We can use this pointer to access the PEB segment.

This approach to accessing a TEB segment register via inline assembler code does not work for x64 architecture. Visual Studio C++ compiler does not support the inline assembler for the x64 target architecture. The **compiler intrinsics** should be used instead of the inline assembler in this case.

Listing 3-3 shows a source code of the *GetTeb* function, which uses compiler intrinsics.

Listing 3-3. The GetTeb Function

```
#include <windows.h>
#include <winternl.h>

PTEB GetTeb()
{
#if defined(_M_X64) // x64
    PTEB pTeb = reinterpret_cast<PTEB>(__readgsqword(0x30));
#else // x86
    PTEB pTeb = reinterpret_cast<PTEB>(__readfsdword(0x18));
#endif
    return pTeb;
}
```

This version of the *GetTeb* function works for both x86 and x64 target architectures. We use the *_M_X64* macro to define an architecture of the application.

The *__readgsqword* compiler intrinsic reads a qword of 64-bit size with the 0x30 offset from the GS segment register in the case of x64 architecture.

The *__readfsdword* intrinsic reads a double word of 32-bit size with the 0x18 offset from the FS segment register in the case of x86 architecture.

There is another question about the TEB segment. Why does the structure field with a TEB segment base address have these different offsets inside the TEB segment for the x86 and x64 architectures? Let us look at the definition of the *NT_TIB* structure, which is used for interpreting the **NT subsystem**-independent part of the TEB segment:

```
typedef struct _NT_TIB {
    struct _EXCEPTION_REGISTRATION_RECORD *ExceptionList;
    PVOID StackBase;
    PVOID StackLimit;
    PVOID SubSystemTib;
     union
     {
         PVOID FiberData;
         ULONG Version;
     };
    PVOID ArbitraryUserPointer;
    struct _NT_TIB *Self;
} NT_TIB;
```

There are six pointers before the *Self* field of the *NT_TIB* structure. The pointer size equals 32 bits (or four bytes) for the x86 architecture. It equals 64 bits (or eight bytes) for the x64 architecture. This is a calculation of the *Self* field offset for the x86 architecture:

```
6 * 4 = 24
```

The 24 in the decimal numeral system equals 0x18 in hexadecimal. The same offset calculation for x64 architecture gives the 0x30 result in the hexadecimal numeral system.

Listing 3-4 demonstrates a portable version of the *GetTeb* function with an explicit usage of the *NT_TIB* structure.

Listing 3-4. The Portable Version of the GetTeb Function

```
#include <windows.h>
#include <winternl.h>
```

```
PTEB GetTeb()
{
#if defined(_M_X64) // x64
    PTEB pTeb = reinterpret_cast<PTEB>(__readgsqword(reinterpret_cast<QWORD>(
                                &static_cast<PNT_TIB>(nullptr)->Self)));
#else // x86
    PTEB pTeb = reinterpret_cast<PTEB>(__readfsdword(reinterpret_cast<DWORD>(
                                &static_cast<PNT_TIB>(nullptr)->Self)));
#endif
    return pTeb;
}
```

This implementation of the *GetTeb* function is taken from the article www. autoitscript.com/forum/topic/164693-implementation-of-a-standalone-teb-and-peb-read-method-for-the-simulation-of-getmodulehandle-and-getprocaddress-functions-for-loaded-pe-module. You can see that the same *__readgsqword* and *__readfsdword* compiler intrinsics are used there.

Now we use the *NT_TIB* structure to calculate the offset of the base TEB address. It allows us to avoid magical numbers and to adapt our application to future Windows versions where the *NT_TIB* structure may change.

The second way to access the TEB segment is to use WinAPI functions. The *NtCurrentTeb* function implements the same algorithm as the preceding *GetTeb*. It allows us to get the *TEB* structure of the current thread. This code snippet shows how to use the *NtCurrentTeb* function:

```
#include <windows.h>
#include <winternl.h>

PTEB pTeb = NtCurrentTeb();
```

Now we delegate the responsibility to choose an appropriate register calculation to WinAPI. Therefore, the function provides a correct result for all architectures that are supported by Windows (x86, x64, and ARM).

The *NtQueryInformationThread* WinAPI function provides information about any thread. Listing 3-5 shows a version of the *GetTeb* function that calls the *NtQueryInformationThread* internally.

Listing 3-5. The GetTeb Function, Which Calls `NtQueryInformationThread`

```
#include <windows.h>
#include <winternl.h>

#pragma comment(lib,"ntdll.lib")

typedef struct _CLIENT_ID {
    DWORD UniqueProcess;
    DWORD UniqueThread;
} CLIENT_ID, *PCLIENT_ID;

typedef struct _THREAD_BASIC_INFORMATION {
    typedef PVOID KPRIORITY;
    NTSTATUS ExitStatus;
    PVOID TebBaseAddress;
    CLIENT_ID ClientId;
    KAFFINITY AffinityMask;
    KPRIORITY Priority;
    KPRIORITY BasePriority;
} THREAD_BASIC_INFORMATION, *PTHREAD_BASIC_INFORMATION;

typedef enum _THREADINFOCLASS2 {
    ThreadBasicInformation,
    ThreadTimes,
    ThreadPriority,
    ThreadBasePriority,
    ThreadAffinityMask,
    ThreadImpersonationToken,
    ThreadDescriptorTableEntry,
    ThreadEnableAlignmentFaultFixup,
    ThreadEventPair_Reusable,
    ThreadQuerySetWin32StartAddress,
    ThreadZeroTlsCell,
    ThreadPerformanceCount,
    ThreadAmILastThread,
    ThreadIdealProcessor,
    ThreadPriorityBoost,
```

```
    ThreadSetTlsArrayAddress,
    _ThreadIsIoPending,
    ThreadHideFromDebugger,
    ThreadBreakOnTermination,
    MaxThreadInfoClass
} THREADINFOCLASS2;

PTEB GetTeb()
{
    THREAD_BASIC_INFORMATION threadInfo;
    if (NtQueryInformationThread(GetCurrentThread(),
                                (THREADINFOCLASS)ThreadBasicInformation,
                                &threadInfo, sizeof(threadInfo), NULL))
    {
        printf("NtQueryInformationThread return error\n");
        return NULL;
    }
    return reinterpret_cast<PTEB>(threadInfo.TebBaseAddress);
}
```

Table 3-5 describes the input parameters of the *NtQueryInformationThread* function.

Table 3-5. *Parameters of the NtQueryInformationThread WinAPI Function*

Parameter	Description
GetCurrentThread()	A handle of the target thread. There is a handle of the current thread in our case.
ThreadBasicInformation	A constant of the *THREADINFOCLASS* enumeration type. The constant defines a type of the resulting structure.
&threadInfo	A pointer to the structure where the function writes its result value.
sizeof(...)	Size of the structure with the function result.
NULL	A pointer to a variable with an actual number of bytes that were written to the resulting structure.

The *NtQueryInformationThread* function receives a constant of the *THREADINFOCLASS* enumeration type. We should use the *ThreadBasicInformation* constant in our case. However, this constant is not documented. Moreover, it is absent from the *winternl.h* header file. The header defines only one constant with the *ThreadIsIoPending* name.

If you want to use the undocumented constants of the *THREADINFOCLASS* enumeration, you should define a custom enumeration. It should contain the undocumented constants you want to use. You can get a list of these constants in the unofficial documentation (undocumented.ntinternals.net/index.html?page=UserM ode%2FUndocumented%20Functions%2FNT%20Objects%2FThread%2FTHREAD_ INFORMATION_CLASS.html).

We add a custom enumeration named *THREADINFOCLASS2* in our sample. Also, we rename the *ThreadIsIoPending* constant to *_ThreadIsIoPending*. Otherwise, we get a compilation error because of conflicts with the constant from the *winternl.h* header.

The *NtQueryInformationThread* function returns a structure. When we pass the undocumented *ThreadBasicInformation* constant to the function, it returns a structure of the undocumented type. Thus, we should define a type of the structure. It has the *THREAD_BASIC_INFORMATION* type. You can get it in the unofficial documentation that we mentioned previously.

Please have a look at the *THREAD_BASIC_INFORMATION* structure. You will find the *TebBaseAddress* field there. It contains a base address of the TEB segment.

Windows Native API provides the *NtQueryInformationThread* function. The *ntdll. dll* dynamic library contains an implementation of this API. The library is a part of the Windows distribution. However, you need the *ntdll.lib* **import library** and the *winternl.h* header to access Native API. Windows SDK provides both of these files.

You can use the import library via the **pragma directive**:

```
#pragma comment(lib, "ntdll.lib")
```

This is a line that adds the *ntdll.lib* file to the linker list of import libraries.

You can find the *TebPebSelf.cpp* application in the source code examples that are provided with this book. It demonstrates all of the ways that we have considered to access the TEB and PEB of the current process.

Target Process

You already know how to access the TEB segment of your application process. This task does not make sense in most cases because you can get all variables of your application directly by their names. However, our investigation helps you to understand the TEB segment better.

Now we will consider methods to access the TEB and PEB segments of the target process. You can test the code examples given in this section with any Windows application. This application is our target process.

This is an algorithm to launch the target process and an example application:

1. Launch a 32-bit or 64-bit Windows application.

2. Get a PID of the target process with the Windows Task Manager.

3. Assign a PID of the target process to the *pid* variable in this line of the *main* function:

   ```
   DWORD pid = 5356;
   ```

4. Launch an example application with the administrator privileges.

The first approach to access the TEB segment relies on the assumption that base addresses of TEB segments are the same for all processes in a system. We should get base addresses of the TEB segments for the current process, and then read memory at the same addresses from another process. Listing 3-6 shows the code that does it.

Listing 3-6. The TebPebMirror.cpp Application

```
#include <windows.h>
#include <winternl.h>

BOOL SetPrivilege(HANDLE hToken, LPCTSTR lpszPrivilege, BOOL
bEnablePrivilege)
{
    // See function's implementation in the OpenProcess.cpp application
}

BOOL GetMainThreadTeb(DWORD dwPid, PTEB pTeb)
{
    LPVOID tebAddress = NtCurrentTeb();
```

```
    printf("TEB = %p\n", tebAddress);

    HANDLE hProcess = OpenProcess(PROCESS_VM_READ, FALSE, dwPid);
    if (hProcess == NULL)
        return false;

    if (ReadProcessMemory(hProcess, tebAddress, pTeb, sizeof(TEB), NULL) ==
    FALSE)
    {
        CloseHandle(hProcess);
        return false;
    }

    CloseHandle(hProcess);
    return true;
}

int main()
{
    HANDLE hProc = GetCurrentProcess();

    HANDLE hToken = NULL;
    if (!OpenProcessToken(hProc, TOKEN_ADJUST_PRIVILEGES, &hToken))
        printf("Failed to open access token\n");

    if (!SetPrivilege(hToken, SE_DEBUG_NAME, TRUE))
        printf("Failed to set debug privilege\n");

    DWORD pid = 7368;

    TEB teb;
    if (!GetMainThreadTeb(pid, &teb))
        printf("Failed to get TEB\n");

    printf("PEB = %p StackBase = %p\n", teb.ProcessEnvironmentBlock,
            teb.Reserved1[1]);

    return 0;
}
```

When you launch the *TebPebMirror.cpp* application, you get three base addresses of the target process memory in the console output:

- TEB segment.

- PEB segment.

- Stack segment of the main thread.

Here we use an already considered approach to grant the *SE_DEBUG_NAME* privilege to the current process with the *OpenProcessToken* and *SetPrivilege* functions. Then we call the *GetMainThreadTeb* function. This receives a PID of the target process and returns a pointer to the *TEB* structure.

This is an algorithm that the function does:

1. Call the *NtCurrentTeb* WinAPI function to get the TEB segment base address of the current thread.

2. Call the *OpenProcess* WinAPI function to get a handler of the target process with the *PROCESS_VM_READ* access.

3. Call the *ReadProcessMemory* WinAPI function to read a *TEB* structure from the target process.

In general, when a new process starts, Windows assigns an address for the TEB segment without any pattern. However, I have experimentally discovered that Windows assigns the same address for 32-bit applications in most cases. We can assume that the address of the TEB segment in one 32-bit process matches to this address in another process.

This approach provides stable results for 32-bit target processes. It does not work for 64-bit processes. A base address of the TEB segment varies each time when you restart 64-bit applications. Nevertheless, this approach has a significant advantage. It is easy to implement.

It is important to emphasize that the bitness of the *TebPebMirror.cpp* application should be the same as the bitness of a target process. This rule works for all examples in this chapter. To build the proper version of the example application, you should select the target architecture in the "Solution Platforms" control of the Visual Studio window.

The second approach to access a TEB segment is to use WinAPI functions to traverse all threads that are launched in the system at the moment. When you get a thread handle, you can get its TEB segment via the *NtQueryInformationThread* function.

This is a list of necessary functions:

- *CreateToolhelp32Snapshot* provides a system snapshot with processes and their threads, modules and heaps. You can pass the PID parameter to get modules and heaps of the specific process. The snapshot always contains all threads that are launched in the system at the moment.

- *Thread32First* starts to traverse threads of the specified snapshot. The output parameter of the function is a pointer to the *THREADENTRY32* structure. The structure contains information about the first thread in the snapshot.

- *Thread32Next* continues to traverse threads of the snapshot. It has the same output parameter as the *Thread32First* function.

The *TebPebTraverse.cpp* application (see Listing 3-7) implements the traversing algorithm.

Listing 3-7. The TebPebTraverse.cpp Application

```
#include <windows.h>
#include <tlhelp32.h>
#include <winternl.h>

#pragma comment(lib,"ntdll.lib")

typedef struct _CLIENT_ID {
    // See struct definition in the TebPebSelf.cpp application
} CLIENT_ID, *PCLIENT_ID;

typedef struct _THREAD_BASIC_INFORMATION {
    // See struct definition in the TebPebSelf.cpp application
} THREAD_BASIC_INFORMATION, *PTHREAD_BASIC_INFORMATION;

typedef enum _THREADINFOCLASS2
{
    // See enumeration definition in the TebPebSelf.cpp application
}   THREADINFOCLASS2;
```

```cpp
PTEB GetTeb(HANDLE hThread)
{
    THREAD_BASIC_INFORMATION threadInfo;
    NTSTATUS result = NtQueryInformationThread(hThread,
                            (THREADINFOCLASS)ThreadBasicInformation,
                            &threadInfo, sizeof(threadInfo), NULL);
    if (result)
    {
        printf("NtQueryInformationThread return error: %d\n", result);
        return NULL;
    }
    return reinterpret_cast<PTEB>(threadInfo.TebBaseAddress);
}

void ListProcessThreads(DWORD dwOwnerPID)
{
    HANDLE hThreadSnap = INVALID_HANDLE_VALUE;
    THREADENTRY32 te32;

    hThreadSnap = CreateToolhelp32Snapshot(TH32CS_SNAPTHREAD, 0);

    if (hThreadSnap == INVALID_HANDLE_VALUE)
        return;

    te32.dwSize = sizeof(THREADENTRY32);

    if (!Thread32First(hThreadSnap, &te32))
    {
        CloseHandle(hThreadSnap);
        return;
    }

    DWORD result = 0;
    do
    {
        if (te32.th32OwnerProcessID == dwOwnerPID)
        {
```

```
            printf("\n      THREAD ID = 0x%08X", te32.th32ThreadID);

            HANDLE hThread = OpenThread(THREAD_ALL_ACCESS, FALSE,
                                            te32.th32ThreadID);
            PTEB pTeb = GetTeb(hThread);
            printf("\n      TEB = %p\n", pTeb);

            CloseHandle(hThread);
        }
    } while (Thread32Next(hThreadSnap, &te32));

    printf("\n");
    CloseHandle(hThreadSnap);
}

int main()
{
    DWORD pid = 4792;

    ListProcessThreads(pid);

    return 0;
}
```

The application prints a list of threads that belong to the target process. Also, a thread ID in terms of OS and a TEB segment base address is printed for each thread in this list.

The *main* function does the *ListProcessThreads* call with the PID of the target process. The *SE_DEBUG_NAME* privilege is not needed to traverse threads. It happens because the *TebPebTraverse.cpp* application does not debug any process. Instead, it makes a system snapshot. This action requires administrator privileges only.

These are the steps that the *ListProcessThreads* function does:

1. Call the *CreateToolhelp32Snapshot* function to make a system snapshot.

2. Call *Thread32First* to start the traversing of the threads in the snapshot.

3. Compare a PID of the owner process with the PID of target process for each thread.

4. If the PIDs match, call the *GetTeb* function to get the *TEB* structure.

5. Print a thread handle and a resulting base address of its TEB segment.

6. Call *Thread32Next* to continue thread traversing. Repeat steps 3, 4, and 5 for each thread.

This approach of TEB segment access is more reliable than the previous one.

It provides access to TEB segments of all threads of the target process. However, you can access the TEBs of all threads with the *TebPebMirror.cpp* application too. To do this, you should create the same number of threads in the current process as the target process has. Then you can get base addresses of all TEB segments of the current process and use them to access the TEBs of the target process. As we mentioned in the preceding, this approach is error-prone.

You might ask how to distinguish threads that we traverse with the *Thread32Next* WinAPI function. For example, you are looking for a base address of the stack for the main thread. The *THREADENTRY32* structure does not contain information about thread ID in terms of the process. Instead, there are thread IDs in terms of Windows Object Manager.

The answer is that you can rely on the assumption that TEB segments are sorted in the reverse order. This means that the TEB segment with the maximum base address matches to the main thread. The TEB segment with the next lower base address matches to the thread with the first ID in terms of the target process. Then the TEB segment with the second ID has the next lower base address, and so on.

You can check this assumption with the memory map feature of the WinDbg debugger.

Heap Access

We have considered how you can get a base address of the default heap from the PEB segment. However, the process can have several heap segments. Thus, we should have a mechanism to access them.

WinAPI provides the necessary functions. They allow traversing all heap segments (and their blocks) of the target process. The algorithm of traversing heaps is reminiscent of that for traversing all threads in the system, which we considered previously.

This is a list of WinAPI functions to access heap:

- *CreateToolhelp32Snapshot* makes a system snapshot.

- *Heap32ListFirst* starts to traverse heap segments of the specified snapshot. The function result is a pointer to the *HEAPLIST32* structure. This structure contains information about the first heap segment in the snapshot.

- *Heap32ListNext* continues to traverse heap segments in the snapshot. It provides the same result value as the *Heap32ListFirst* function.

Also, there are two extra WinAPI functions: *Heap32First* and *Heap32Next*. These functions allow us to traverse memory blocks inside each heap segment. We will not use these functions in our example.

Traversing of memory blocks takes considerable time if the target process is a complex application.

Listing 3-8 demonstrates traversing of the heap segments.

Listing 3-8. The HeapTraverse.cpp Application

```
#include <windows.h>
#include <tlhelp32.h>

void ListProcessHeaps(DWORD pid)
{
    HEAPLIST32 hl;

    HANDLE hHeapSnap = CreateToolhelp32Snapshot(TH32CS_SNAPHEAPLIST, pid);

    hl.dwSize = sizeof(HEAPLIST32);

    if (hHeapSnap == INVALID_HANDLE_VALUE)
```

```
    {
        printf("CreateToolhelp32Snapshot failed (%d)\n", GetLastError());
        return;
    }

    if (Heap32ListFirst(hHeapSnap, &hl))
    {
        do
        {
            printf("\nHeap ID: 0x%lx\n", hl.th32HeapID);
            printf("\Flags: 0x%lx\n", hl.dwFlags);
        } while (Heap32ListNext(hHeapSnap, &hl));
    }
    else
        printf("Cannot list first heap (%d)\n", GetLastError());

    CloseHandle(hHeapSnap);
}

int main()
{
    DWORD pid = 6712;

    ListProcessHeaps(pid);

    return 0;
}
```

The *HeapTraverse.cpp* application prints base addresses and flags of the heap segments of the target process. An ID of a heap segment matches to its base address. The segment flags are important because they allow us to distinguish the default heap segment. The non-zeroed flags match to the default heap.

The *ListProcessHeaps* function works similarly to the *ListProcessThreads* one from the *TebPebTraverse.cpp* application.

These are the steps that the *ListProcessHeaps* function does:

1. Call *CreateToolhelp32Snapshot* to make a system snapshot.

2. Call *Heap32ListFirst* to start traversing of the heap segments in the snapshot.

3.   Print ID and flags for each heap segment.

4.   Repeat step 3 until all heap segments in the system snapshot are not enumerated by the *Heap32ListNext* function.

Heap segments are traversed in order of their IDs. This means that the segment with a smaller ID will be traversed before the segment with a greater ID. This ordering can help us to distinguish them.

Process Memory Access Summary

We have considered ways to get base addresses of the stack and heap segments, which can contain information about game objects. Any in-game bot application should use these approaches to capture (or embed) data from the game process memory.

Example with Diablo 2

Now we know enough to write a simple in-game bot. The bot will partially control a player character in the famous game Diablo 2. Its gameplay is quite typical for the RPG genre. A player should do quests, kill monsters, and improve his character.

Our bot will analyze the state of the player character. When one of the character parameters reaches the threshold value, the bot does some action. First of all, we should consider the game interface to understand its control elements. Then we will examine character parameters and find one that the bot can control.

Figure 3-15 shows a screenshot of the game window. You can see the player character in the center of the screen. The monsters stand to his left and right. The mouse cursor selects one of the monsters. There is a control panel on the bottom side of the screen. The most important element of this panel for our case is the four hotkey slots where you can see red potions. Our bot can use items from these slots to affect the character parameters.

Figure 3-15. *Screenshot of the game window*

Figure 3-16 shows two windows with all character parameters. The left window contains common information about the character. For example: his name is Kain, the class is "Paladin," he has a level of 70, and 285,160,782 experience points. This information is available at the top of the window. In the following you can see the attributes that define a behavior of the character during a game. For example, the "Strength" attribute defines damage to the monsters.

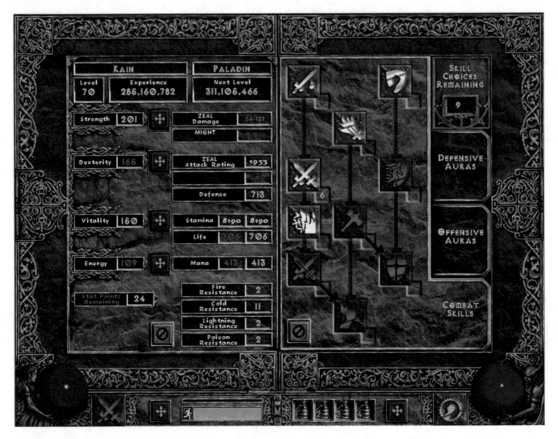

Figure 3-16. *Screenshot of the player parameter window*

The right window contains a tree of character skills. There are special abilities and combos that allow him to do more damage or to improve his attributes significantly. Each skill has a level that defines its effectiveness.

You can get detailed information about character parameters on the wiki page (diablo.gamepedia.com/Classes_(Diablo_II)).

Diablo 2 has single-player and multiplayer game modes. We will consider the single-player mode only. It allows us to stop the execution of the game process at any moment and to explore its memory without any time limitations. If we try to do the same in the multiplayer mode, we get an issue. The game client that does not respond to requests of a game server is disconnected by a timeout. This limitation does not allow us to use a debugger and to break the game process in this mode.

You can buy Diablo 2 at the Blizzard Entertainment website (eu.shop.battle.net/en-b/product/diablo-ii) and try our in-game bot.

If you do not want to buy Diablo 2, you can use an open source game that has very similar mechanics and interface. This game is Flare, and it is free to download on the official website (flarerpg.org). You can apply all methods from this section to the Flare game too.

The main difference between these two games is complexity. Diablo 2 has many more libraries and game objects in the memory than Flare does. Thus, analysis of Diablo 2 is a more difficult task.

Bot Overview

First of all, we should strictly define what we are going to do. We do not want to **hack** a game. In other words, we will not change the normal behavior of Diablo 2 and break its rules. You can find examples of such hacks in two Jan Miller articles: extreme-gamerz.org/diablo2/viewdiablo2/hackingdiablo2 and `www.battleforums.com/threads/howtohackd2-edition-2.111214`. Our bot should work differently.

It reacts when a game object's state changes. A possible reaction is to simulate player action or legally change a game state. Meanwhile, the game process is still working within its original algorithms, and the state of all objects is valid according to the game rules.

We have considered character parameters. The parameter that we can control in the simplest way is health level. When the character receives damage from monsters, the level decreases. When a player uses a healing potion, the level increases.

I suggest implementing the in-game bot with the following algorithm:

1. Read a current health level of the player character.

2. Compare the level with the threshold value.

3. If the level is below the threshold, use a healing potion.

This algorithm allows us to keep the player character alive while the healing potions are available. Nevertheless, the implementation of such a simple algorithm requires in-depth research into Diablo 2's process memory.

Diablo 2 Memory Analysis

Now we are ready to start our analysis of Diablo 2's process memory. Our goal is to find a variable that keeps the character health level. Let us consider the steps to configure the game before we start.

First of all, you should launch the game. It starts in the fullscreen mode by default. However, it is more convenient for us to use the windowed mode. It allows quick switching to the memory scanner window and back.

Here are the instructions for launching the game in the windowed mode:

1. Right-click the "Diablo II" icon to open the popup menu and click the "Properties" menu item.

2. Click the "Shortcut" tab in the "Properties" dialog.

3. Add the "-w" key at the end of the "Target" field. This is an example:

    ```
    "C:\DiabloII\Diablo II.exe" -w
    ```

Now launch the game via the changed icon. When it starts, you should select the "Single player" option in the main menu, create a new character, and start the game.

Search the Parameters

We are looking for a character health level in Diablo 2's process memory. The first idea to solve this task is to use Cheat Engine memory scanner. This is a special tool that is designed exactly for this purpose.

You can follow the Cheat Engine tutorial (cheatengine.org/tutorials.php) and try to search a current value of the character health without any configuration of the search options. This approach does not work for me. Most probably, you will get a long list of resulting addresses. If you continue searching by pressing the "Next Scan" button after updating the health value, the resulting list becomes empty.

The straightforward approach does not work. The primary reason for our issue is the complexity of the Diablo 2 game model. There are a lot of game objects in the memory. Some of them have parameters with similar values at one moment. Now, we do not know how the object parameters are stored into the memory. Therefore, it will be better to find an approach to detect a specific object in the memory first; then we can analyze its parameters.

Let us look at the game window with the player character attributes again. There are several parameters that should be unique for the character object. We can name this kind of parameter as **artifacts** for the sake of brevity. What are the artifacts for the character object? I suggest the following list:

1. **Character name.**

   It is unlikely that another game object has the same name as the player character. If it happens, you can create a new character with another unique name.

2. **Experience points.**

   This is a long positive integer number. The same number of such a length can appear in other objects rarely. However, if you get several results, you can change experience points easily by killing several monsters. Then update its value and press the "Next Scan" button. You will find an address of the right variable.

3. **Stamina value.**

   This is a long positive number. It changes if the player character runs outside the city.

I suggest choosing the experience points for searching. In case its value equals zero, you should kill several monsters to increase it. Figure 3-17 shows a possible memory scan result. The scanner found several addresses that have equal experience point values. However, some of them are parameters of other game objects.

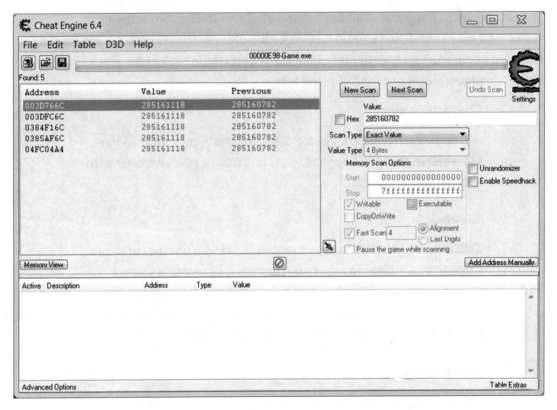

Figure 3-17. *Memory scan results for the experience points of a character*

The next step is to distinguish the value that matches the character object. First of all, we should clarify a type of the owning segment for each of these variables.

You can launch the WinDbg debugger and perform the *!address* command. This is the shortened output the command for my case:

```
+ 0`003c0000  0`003e0000  0`00020000  MEM_PRIVATE MEM_COMMIT PAGE_READWRITE
<unknown>
+ 0`03840000  0`03850000  0`00010000  MEM_PRIVATE MEM_COMMIT PAGE_READWRITE
<unknown>
+ 0`03850000  0`03860000  0`00010000  MEM_PRIVATE MEM_COMMIT PAGE_READWRITE
<unknown>
+ 0`04f50000  0`04fd0000  0`00080000  MEM_PRIVATE MEM_COMMIT PAGE_READWRITE
<unknown>
```

CHAPTER 3   IN-GAME BOTS

The output told us that all found variables are stored in the segments of the "unknown" type. What is the "unknown" type? We already know the stack and heap segments. WinDbg debugger can distinguish them well. Therefore, we conclude that these "unknown" segments are neither stack nor heap type.

The *VirtualAllocEx* WinAPI function can allocate these segments. We can verify this assumption by writing a simple test application (it has the *VirtualAllocEx.cpp* name and is provided with this book) that uses the function. In case you launch it with the WinDbg debugger, you see a segment of "unknown" type in the process memory map. The `VirtualAllocEx` function returns a base address of this segment.

We get types of owning segments, but this does not help us to distinguish the experience point variable that belongs to the character object. All of these "unknown" segments have the same type and flags.

We can try another approach to find the character object. It is evident that object parameters change when a player does some game actions. For example, when the character moves, its coordinates change. Also, a health value decreases when monsters hit the character.

We can analyze how memory data that is located near the experience point variable changes. The Cheat Engine can display changes of a memory region in real time. You should open the Memory Viewer window for accessing this feature. These are the actions to open the window:

1. Select one address in the resulting list.

2. Left-click the address.

3. Select the "Browse this memory region" item in the pop-up menu.

You will see the Memory Viewer window as Figure 3-18 shows. The window has two parts. The upper part contains the disassembled code of the memory region near the selected address. The bottom part shows a dump in the hexadecimal format. It is the same memory region, but we see it in two different formats.

We will focus on the memory dump (a bottom part) in our case. A red line marks the experience point variable. You may ask why the "9E 36 FF 10" hexadecimal number equals the "285161118" experience points in decimal.

We launch the Diablo 2 application in the x86 architecture. This architecture has the **little-endian byte order**. It means that you should reverse order the four-byte integer to get its value. The hexadecimal value becomes equal to "10 FF 36 9E" in our case. You can use the standard Windows Calculator and check that this hexadecimal value equals "285161118" in decimal.

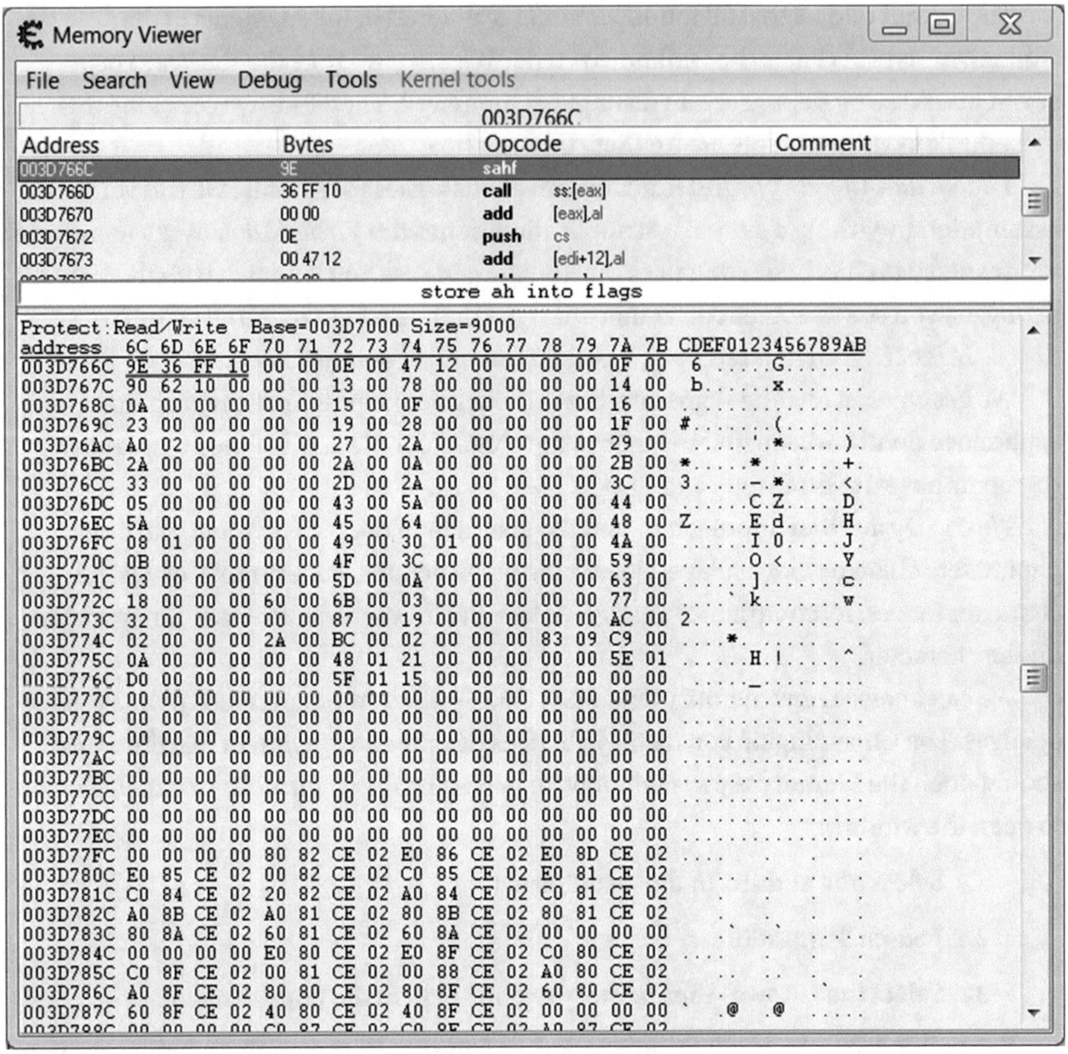

```
   Memory Viewer                                                    _  □  ☒

 File   Search   View   Debug   Tools   Kernel tools

                              003D766C
 Address                Bytes              Opcode             Comment        ▲
 003D766C               9E                 sahf                              
 003D766D               36 FF 10           call    ss:[eax]                  ≡
 003D7670               00 00              add     [eax],al
 003D7672               0E                 push    cs
 003D7673               00 47 12           add     [edi+12],al               ▼
                        store ah into flags

 Protect:Read/Write  Base=003D7000 Size=9000                                 ▲
 address   6C 6D 6E 6F 70 71 72 73 74 75 76 77 78 79 7A 7B CDEF0123456789AB
 003D766C  9E 36 FF 10 00 00 0E 00 47 12 00 00 00 00 0F 00  6.....G.......
 003D767C  90 62 10 00 00 00 13 00 78 00 00 00 00 00 14 00  b......x.......
 003D768C  0A 00 00 00 00 00 15 00 0F 00 00 00 00 00 16 00  ..............
 003D769C  23 00 00 00 00 00 19 00 28 00 00 00 00 00 1F 00  #.......(.....
 003D76AC  A0 02 00 00 00 00 27 00 2A 00 00 00 00 00 29 00  ......'.*.....).
 003D76BC  2A 00 00 00 00 00 2A 00 0A 00 00 00 00 00 2B 00  *.....*.......+.
 003D76CC  33 00 00 00 00 00 2D 00 2A 00 00 00 00 00 3C 00  3.....-.*.....<.
 003D76DC  05 00 00 00 00 00 43 00 5A 00 00 00 00 00 44 00  ......C.Z.....D.
 003D76EC  5A 00 00 00 00 00 45 00 64 00 00 00 00 00 48 00  Z.....E.d.....H.
 003D76FC  08 01 00 00 00 00 49 00 30 01 00 00 00 00 4A 00  ......I.0.....J.
 003D770C  0B 00 00 00 00 00 4F 00 3C 00 00 00 00 00 59 00  ......O.<.....Y.
 003D771C  03 00 00 00 00 00 5D 00 0A 00 00 00 00 00 63 00  ......].......c.
 003D772C  18 00 00 00 60 00 6B 00 03 00 00 00 00 00 77 00  ....`.k.......w.
 003D773C  32 00 00 00 00 00 87 00 19 00 00 00 00 00 AC 00  2.............
 003D774C  02 00 00 00 2A 00 BC 00 02 00 00 00 83 09 C9 00  ....*.........
 003D775C  0A 00 00 00 00 00 48 01 21 00 00 00 00 00 5E 01  ......H.!.....^.
 003D776C  D0 00 00 00 00 00 5F 01 15 00 00 00 00 00 00 00  ......_.......
 003D777C  00 00 00 00 00 00 00 00 00 00 00 00 00 00 00 00  ..............
 003D778C  00 00 00 00 00 00 00 00 00 00 00 00 00 00 00 00  ..............
 003D779C  00 00 00 00 00 00 00 00 00 00 00 00 00 00 00 00  ..............
 003D77AC  00 00 00 00 00 00 00 00 00 00 00 00 00 00 00 00  ..............
 003D77BC  00 00 00 00 00 00 00 00 00 00 00 00 00 00 00 00  ..............
 003D77CC  00 00 00 00 00 00 00 00 00 00 00 00 00 00 00 00  ..............
 003D77DC  00 00 00 00 00 00 00 00 00 00 00 00 00 00 00 00  ..............
 003D77EC  00 00 00 00 00 00 00 00 00 00 00 00 00 00 00 00  ..............
 003D77FC  00 00 00 00 80 82 CE 02 E0 86 CE 02 E0 8D CE 02  ....            .
 003D780C  E0 85 CE 02 00 82 CE 02 C0 85 CE 02 E0 81 CE 02
 003D781C  C0 84 CE 02 20 82 CE 02 A0 84 CE 02 C0 81 CE 02
 003D782C  A0 8B CE 02 A0 81 CE 02 80 8B CE 02 80 81 CE 02
 003D783C  80 8A CE 02 60 81 CE 02 60 8A CE 02 00 00 00 00
 003D784C  00 00 00 00 E0 80 CE 02 E0 8F CE 02 C0 80 CE 02
 003D785C  C0 8F CE 02 00 81 CE 02 00 88 CE 02 A0 80 CE 02
 003D786C  A0 8F CE 02 80 80 CE 02 80 8F CE 02 60 80 CE 02
 003D787C  60 8F CE 02 40 80 CE 02 40 8F CE 02 00 00 00 00  `  .@  .@  .....
                                                                             ▼
```

Figure 3-18. Memory Viewer window of Cheat Engine

You can automate a reverse byte operation if you change the format of integers in the memory dump. To do so, do a left mouse click on the dump part of the window and choose the "Display Type" item of the pop-up menu. However, I recommend that you keep the "Byte hex" format. The custom display type can confuse you in some cases, because you may not know an actual size of a variable that you are looking for.

Now we are ready to analyze memory data changes. You should place both windows — Memory Viewer and the Diablo 2 application — near each other. This allows you to do actions in the game window and to inspect the memory region in the Memory Viewer simultaneously. Figure 3-19 shows both windows and results of the memory inspection.

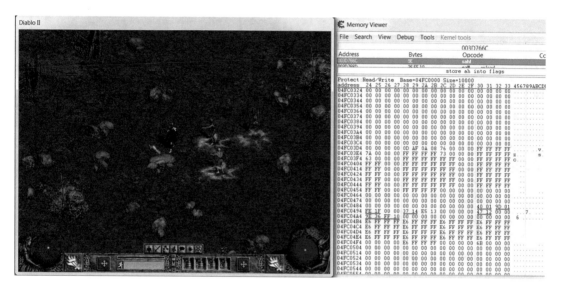

Figure 3-19. *Results of the memory inspection process*

You can see the memory region near the "04FC04A4" address in the Memory Viewer window. It is the address of the experience point variable, which we got by a process memory scanning. Let us do this analysis for each variable address in the scanning resulting list.

How do we understand that the variable belongs to the character object? I suggest a simple rule. If the region around the variable contains more character parameters then others, this region contains the character object. Therefore, the variable belongs to this character object.

In our case, the last address in the scanning resulting list belongs to the character object. We come to this conclusion through trial and error by changing the values via in-game actions. My resulting address, "04FC04A4", may differ in your case.

Table 3-6 shows parameters that we detected in the character object.

Table 3-6. *Found Parameters in the Memory Region*

Parameter	Address	Offset	Size	Hex Value	Dec Value
Life (Health)	04FC0490	490	2	40 01	320
Mana	04FC0492	492	2	9D 01	413
Stamina	04FC0494	494	2	FE 1F	8190
Coordinate X	04FC0498	498	2	37 14	5175
Coordinate Y	04FC04A0	4A0	2	47 12	4679
Experience	04FC04A4	4A4	4	9E 36 FF 10	285161118

The red lines mark these parameters in Figure 3-19. I performed the following actions to deduce the parameters:

1. Stay in one place and get the damage from any monster. Only the health parameter changes in this case. When a character gets a hit, the variable with the "04FC0490" address changes. So, it is the health variable.

2. Stay in one place and cast any spell. Then the mana parameter changes. It has the "04FC0492" address.

3. Run outside the city. Movement of the character leads to a change of three parameters at the same time: stamina, x coordinate, and y coordinate. However, if you move the character a long time, the stamina parameter becomes equal to 0. It allows us to distinguish this parameter from coordinates. When I move the character in horizontal and vertical directions, I find that the x variable has "04FC0498" address and the y one has "04FC04A0" address.

4. Kill any random monster. When the player kills the monster, the experience increases. You can easily distinguish this parameter from the health and mana because they decrease during the fight. This way I found that the experience variable has the "04FC04A4" address.

Did we learn something new about the character parameters? First of all, the size of the health parameter equals two bytes. It means that you should specify the "2 Byte" item of the "Value Type" option in the Cheat Engine window if you want to search the health parameter.

Also, you can see that some parameters have **alignment** that is not equal to four bytes. For example, let us consider the mana parameter at the 04FC0492 address. You can check with a calculator that the 04FC0492 value is not divided by 4 without a remainder. This means that you should deselect the "Fast Scan" check box in the Cheat Engine window to find unaligned parameters.

Figure 3-20 shows the Cheat Engine window with the correct configuration.

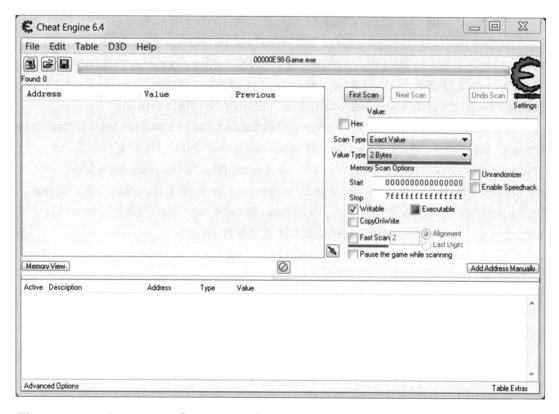

Figure 3-20. *Correct configuration of the Cheat Engine to find a health parameter*

The red color marks the changed search options. Now we can find any parameter of the character when scanning the game process.

Probably you have noticed the "Offset" column in Table 3-6. It defines the offset of each parameter from the beginning of the character object in memory.

Search the Object

Let us consider a question: how will a bot find the health parameter in the process memory? The most straightforward way is to find the character object first. Then, the bot should add the constant offset to the object address and get the required variable.

We know how to find the character object with the memory dump analysis in real time. However, a bot cannot use the Cheat Engine or a similar scanner. It should rely on its own algorithms. Therefore, we should find a reliable way to detect the object when only one memory snapshot is available.

Please scroll up the Memory Viewer window, which contains a memory region near the experience point variable (the 04FC04A4 address). You will find the character name as it appeared in my case. Figure 3-21 shows the result that you should get.

The four underscored bytes equal the "Kain" string. **String** values do not have the reversed byte order on the little-endian architecture, unlike the integers. It happens because a string has the same internal structure as the simple byte array. In Figure 3-21, you can see that the memory block above the character name is zeroed.

Now we start making assumptions and check them. Let us assume that the character name is stored close to the upper bound of the character object. How can we check this assumption? We can use OllyDbg to make the breakpoint on the memory address of the character name. When the game process reads or writes this memory, it is stopped by the breakpoint. Then we can analyze the application code that tries to access this memory. So, we can find some footprints of the object bounds.

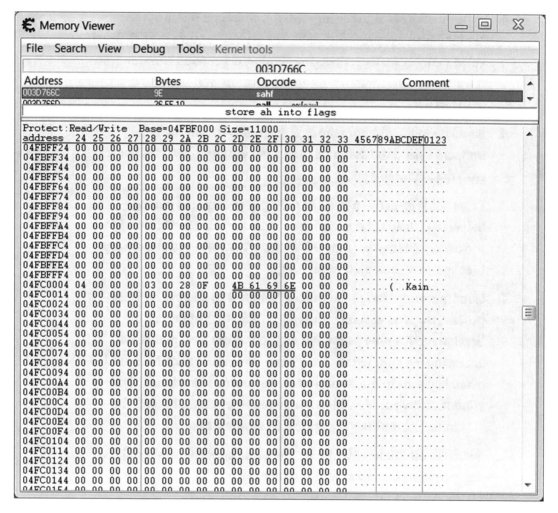

Figure 3-21. *The character name in the memory dump*

This is an algorithm to search the object bounds with OllyDbg:

1. Launch the debugger with administrator privileges. Attach to the launched Diablo 2 process.

2. Select by the left mouse click the bottom left subwindow of the debugger with a memory dump in the hex format.

3. Press Ctrl+G to open the "Enter expression to follow" dialog.

4. Type an address of the string with the character name in the "Enter address expression" field. The address equals the 04FC00D value in my case. Then press the "Follow expression" button. Now the cursor in the memory dump subwindow points to the first byte of the string.

5. Scroll up in the memory dump subwindow to find the first nonzero byte at the assumed object beginning. Select this byte with the left mouse click.

6. Press Shift+F3 to open the "Set memory breakpoint" dialog. Select the "Read access" and the "Write access" check boxes in the dialog. Then press the "OK" button. Now we set the memory breakpoint at the object beginning.

7. Continue execution of the Diablo 2 process by F9 keypress. The process stops on several events. One of them is our memory breakpoint. Another event that happens often is a break when accessing the guarded memory page. You can check which kind of event happens in the status bar at the bottom side of the OllyDbg window. Now you should continue process execution until the "Running" status does not appear in the status bar.

8. Switch to the Diablo 2 window. The game application should be stopped immediately after this switching.

9. Switch back to the OllyDbg window. Figure 3-22 shows how the window should look.

You can see the highlighted gray line of the disassembled code in the upper left side of the debugger window. This code line at the "03668D9F" address tries to access the memory, which has our breakpoint:

```
CMP DWORD PTR DS:[ESI+4], 4
```

This code line compares an integer of the DWORD type, which has the "ESI + 4" address, and the "4" constants.

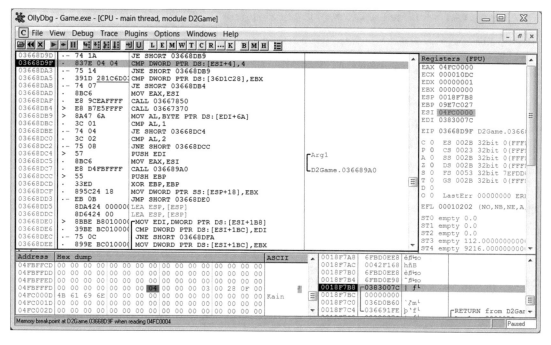

Figure 3-22. *A breakpoint on the object beginning*

ESI is the source index **CPU register**. ESI and **DS** registers are always used in pairs. The DS register holds a base address of the data segment. The ESI register equals the "04FC0000" address in our case. You can find it on the upper right side of the debugger window, which contains current values of all CPU registers. It is a common practice to hold an object address in the ESI register.

Let us inspect the disassembled code below the breakpoint line. You can see these lines, which are started at the "03668DE0" address:

```
MOV EDI,DWORD PTR DS:[ESI+1B8]
CMP DWORD PTR DS:[ESI+1BC],EDI
JNE SHORT 03668DFA
MOV DWORD PTR DS:[ESI+1BC],EBX
```

These operations look like processing of the object fields. The "1B8" and "1BC" values define offsets of the fields from the object beginning. If you scroll down this disassembling listing, you will find similar operations with object fields. Thus, we can conclude that the beginning address of the character object equals the "04FC0000" value of the ESI register.

Now we can calculate the offset of the health parameter. This is a formula for the calculation:

```
04FC0490 - 04FC0000 = 0x490
```

The offset equals 490 in hexadecimal.

The next question is how the bot finds the beginning address of the object. We know that the segment that contains the object has the "unknown" type. Also, the segment has a size of 80000 bytes (in hexadecimal). It has the MEM_PRIVATE, MEM_COMMIT, and PAGE_READWRITE flags. There are a minimum of ten other segments that have the same size and flags. It means that we cannot find the required segment by traversing them and checking their sizes and flags.

Let us look at the first bytes of the character object:

```
00 00 00 00 04 00 00 00 03 00 28 0F 00 4B 61 69 6E 00 00 00
```

If you restart the Diablo 2 process and find the character object again, you see the same byte sequence at the object beginning. We can assume that this byte sequence matches to the unchanged character parameters. These parameters are defined when a player creates his character. Once they are set, they have never changed again.

This is the list of unchanged parameters:

- The character name.

- The expansion character flag (diablo.wikia.com/wiki/Expansion_ Character).

- The hardcore mode flag (diablo.wikia.com/wiki/Hardcore).

- The encoded class of the character.

This unchanged byte sequence can be used as the **magic numbers** to search the object in memory. Be aware that these "magic numbers" differ in your case. The lack of flexibility is the main disadvantage of this approach.

You can check the correctness of the magic numbers with the Cheat Engine. Select the "Array of byte" item of the "Value Type" option. Then select the "Hex" check box and copy the magic numbers into the "Array of byte" field.

Figure 3-23 shows the possible search results.

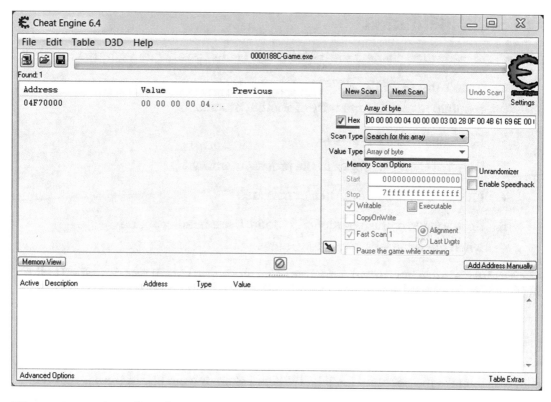

Figure 3-23. *Search a character object in memory via magic numbers*

You will notice that the address of the character object changes each time when you restart the Diablo 2 process. Now it equals "04F70000". However, offsets of all character parameters inside the object are still the same. It means that the new address of the health parameter equals "04F70490".

You can apply an alternative way to find health level of a player character. The Cheat Engine scanner provides the pointer scanning feature. It allows you to find a base address and offset of the specified variable after several memory scans. This feature does not work in some cases. You can learn more about it in the article sethioz.com/mediawiki/index.php/Pointer_Scanning_/_Finding_Pointer.

Bot Implementation

Now we are ready to implement the in-game bot. Let us consider its algorithm in detail:

1. Enable the *SE_DEBUG_NAME* privilege for the current process. This is required to read the memory of another process.

2. Open the Diablo 2 process.

3. Search a character object in the process memory.

4. Calculate an offset of the health parameter.

5. Read a value of the parameter in a loop. Use a healing potion when the value falls below 100 points.

We already know how to implement the first algorithm step. It was described in the "Process Memory Access" section of this chapter.

We can implement the second step in two ways. We can either hard-code a PID value (as we did before) or get a PID of the process that owns a currently active window. We assume that the Diablo 2 window is active when we launch the bot. Thus, getting a PID allows us to make the bot more flexible. We avoid changing the PID in the source code and the recompilation each time before launching.

The code snippet in Listing 3-9 gets a PID and opens the game process.

Listing 3-9. The Code to Open a Game Process

```
int main()
{
    Sleep(4000);

    HWND wnd = GetForegroundWindow();
    DWORD pid = 0;
    if (!GetWindowThreadProcessId(wnd, &pid))
    {
        printf("Error of the pid detection\n");
        return 1;
    }

    HANDLE hTargetProc = OpenProcess(PROCESS_ALL_ACCESS, FALSE, pid);
    if (!hTargetProc)
```

```
        printf("Failed to open process: %u\n", GetLastError());

    return 0;
}
```

We use two WinAPI functions here. The *GetForegroundWindow* call gets a handle of the window that has the foreground (or active) mode at the moment. The *GetWindowThreadProcessId* function retrieves a PID of the process that owns the specified window. We store the PID value in the *pid* variable when the code snippet finishes.

Also, we do a four-second delay at the first line of the *main* function. It provides us enough time to switch the Diablo 2 window after launching the bot.

The third step of the bot algorithm is to find the player object. I suggest using an approach that is described in the series of video tutorials you can view at www.youtube.com/watch?v=YRPMdb1YMS8. The tutorials explain the implementation of the simple memory scanner. Its algorithm is very similar to what Cheat Engine has. The idea is to traverse all memory segments of a target process by the *VirtualQueryEx* WinAPI function. We will use this function to access the memory segments of the Diablo 2 process.

Listing 3-10 demonstrates a code that searches the character object in the Diablo 2 process memory.

Listing 3-10. The Code to Find a Character Object in the Game Memory

```
SIZE_T IsArrayMatch(HANDLE proc, SIZE_T address, SIZE_T segmentSize, BYTE
array[], SIZE_T arraySize)
{
        BYTE* procArray = new BYTE[segmentSize];

        if (ReadProcessMemory(proc, (void*)address, procArray, segmentSize,
        NULL) != 0)
        {
                printf("Failed to read memory: %u\n", GetLastError());
                delete[] procArray;
                return 0;
        }

        for (SIZE_T i = 0; i < segmentSize; ++i)
```

```
        {
                if ((array[0] == procArray[i]) && ((i + arraySize)
                < segmentSize))
                {
                        if (!memcmp(array, procArray + i, arraySize))
                        {
                                delete[] procArray;
                                return address + i;
                        }
                }
        }

        delete[] procArray;
        return 0;
}

SIZE_T ScanSegments(HANDLE proc, BYTE array[], SIZE_T size)
{
        MEMORY_BASIC_INFORMATION meminfo;
        LPCVOID addr = 0;
        SIZE_T result = 0;

        if (!proc)
                return 0;

        while (1)
        {
                if (VirtualQueryEx(proc, addr, &meminfo, sizeof(meminfo))
                == 0)
                        break;

                if ((meminfo.State & MEM_COMMIT) && (meminfo.Type &
                MEM_PRIVATE) && (meminfo.Protect & PAGE_READWRITE) &&
                !(meminfo.Protect & PAGE_GUARD))
                {
                        result = IsArrayMatch(proc, (SIZE_T)meminfo.
                        BaseAddress,
                                meminfo.RegionSize, array, size);
```

```
                    if (result != 0)
                            return result;
                }
                addr = (unsigned char*)meminfo.BaseAddress + meminfo.
                RegionSize;
        }
        return 0;
}

int main()
{
        // Enable `SE_DEBUG_NAME` privilege for current process here.

        // Open the Diablo 2 process here.

        BYTE array[] = { 0, 0, 0, 0, 0x04, 0, 0, 0, 0x03, 0, 0x28, 0x0F, 0,
        0x4B, 0x61, 0x69, 0x6E, 0, 0, 0 };

        SIZE_T objectAddress = ScanSegments(hTargetProc, array,
        sizeof(array));

        return 0;
}
```

The *ScanSegments* function implements an algorithm for traversing the memory segments. There are four steps in the loop of this function:

1. Make a *VirtualQueryEx* call to read the memory segment with a base address that equals the *addr* variable.

2. Compare flags of the current segment with the flags of a typical "unknown" segment. Skip the segment if the comparison does not pass.

3. Search the "magic numbers" of the character object in the current segment.

4. Return a resulting address of the object.

The *IsArrayMatch* function implements an algorithm that finds the "magic numbers" in the current segment. The *ScanSegments* function calls the *IsArrayMatch* one.

We do two steps in the *IsArrayMatch* function:

1. Read all data of the specified segment by the *ReadProcessMemory* WinAPI function.

2. Search the "magic numbers" in this data.

Also, the code snippet contains the *main* function. It demonstrates how you can call the *ScanSegments* function from your code. You see that the function has three input parameters:

1. A handle of the Diablo 2 process.

2. A pointer to the "magic numbers" array.

3. The size of this array.

Do not forget that the "magic numbers" differ in your case.

The fourth step of the bot algorithm is a calculation of the health parameter address. We use the *objectAddress* variable, which stores a result of the *ScanSegments* function, for this calculation:

```
SIZE_T hpAddress = objectAddress + 0x490;
```

The *hpAddress* variable stores the address of the health parameter when this code line finishes.

The last step of the bot algorithm is checking the health parameter in the loop. The bot should use a healing potion in case the value becomes less than the threshold. Listing 3-11 shows a corresponding code.

Listing 3-11. The Code to Check the Health Parameter

```
WORD ReadWord(HANDLE hProc, DWORD_PTR address)
{
        WORD result = 0;

        if (ReadProcessMemory(hProc, (void*)address, &result,
        sizeof(result), NULL) == 0)
```

```
            printf("Failed to read memory: %u\n", GetLastError());

        return result;
}

int main()
{
        // Enable `SE_DEBUG_NAME` privilege for current process here.

        // Open the Diablo 2 process here.

        // Search a player character object here.

        // Calculate an offset of character's life parameter here.

        ULONG hp = 0;

        while (1)
        {
                hp = ReadWord(hTargetProc, hpAddress);
                printf("HP = %lu\n", hp);

                if (hp < 100)
                        PostMessage(wnd, WM_KEYDOWN, 0x31, 0x1);

                Sleep(2000);
        }
        return 0;
}
```

We read the parameter in the infinite loop with the *ReadWord* function. It is just a wrapper around the *ReadProcessMemory* WinAPI function. When the *ReadWord* call is done, we print the parameter to a console. You can compare it with the actual health points that are displayed in the Diablo 2 window.

If the value falls below the 100 points, the bot presses the "1" hotkey. This is the command for a character to consume a healing potion. We use the *PostMessage* WinAPI function for simulating a keypress.

I agree that the *PostMessage* call is not a "pure" way to embed data in the process memory. We do not modify the memory explicitly. Instead, we inject the *WM_KEYDOWN* message that matches the keypress action into the event queue of the Diablo 2 process. It is the simplest way to simulate the player action. We will consider more complex approaches further.

The *PostMessage* function has four input parameters:

1. A handle of the target window that receives the message.

2. The message code. It equals the *WM_KEYDOWN* code in our case.

3. The **virtual code** of the pressed key (msdn.microsoft.com/en-us/library/windows/desktop/dd375731(v=vs.85).aspx).

4. The mask with several parameters. The most important parameter in the mask is a number to repeat a sent message. The bits from 0 to 15 store it. The number equals "1" in our case.

The keypress simulation does not work if you specify zero as the fourth parameter of the *PostMessage* function.

The complete implementation of our in-game bot is available in the *AutohpBot.cpp* source file that is provided with this book.

This is an algorithm to launch the bot:

1. Change the "magic numbers" according to your character. This is the code line to change:

    ```
    BYTE array[] = { 0, 0, 0, 0, 0x04, 0, 0, 0, 0x03, 0, 0x28,
    0x0F, 0, 0x4B, 0x61, 0x69, 0x6E, 0, 0, 0 };
    ```

2. Compile the bot with the changed "magic numbers".

3. Launch Diablo 2 in the windowed mode.

4. Launch the bot with the administrator privileges.

5. Switch the Diablo 2 window during the four-second delay. After the delay, the bot captures an active window and starts to analyze its process.

6. Get damage from any monsters in the game to decrease the health parameter of your character. It should fall below 100 points.

The bot presses the "1" hotkey when the health points become low. Do not forget to assign a healing potion to the "1" hotkey.

You can press the H key to view quick tips about the user interface. The "Belt" hotkey panel is in the bottom right corner of the game window. You can drag and drop the healing potions to the panel by left-clicking them.

Further Improvements

Our in-game bot has several issues. Let us consider ways to improve it.

The first issue is that the bot uses only a first slot of the hotkey panel. It can be more efficient when using all slots.

The code snippet in Listing 3-12 shows a new version of the loop that checks the health parameter.

Listing 3-12. Using All Slots of the Hotkey Panel

```
ULONG hp = 0;
BYTE keys[] = { 0x31, 0x32, 0x33, 0x34 };
BYTE keyIndex = 0;

while (1)
{
        hp = ReadWord(hTargetProc, hpAddress);
        printf("HP = %lu\n", hp);

        if (hp < 100)
        {
                PostMessage(wnd, WM_KEYDOWN, keys[keyIndex], 0x1);
                ++keyIndex;
                if (keyIndex == sizeof(keys))
                        keyIndex = 0;
        }
        Sleep(2000);
}
```

Now we store a list of the virtual key codes in the *keys* array. We use the *keyIndex* variable for indexing elements of the array. We increment the index each time the bot uses a healing potion. If the *keyIndex* value reaches the end of the key code array, we reset it back to zero. This approach allows us to use all slots of the hotkey panel one after each other. When the first row of the slots becomes empty, the bot uses the second one, and so on.

The second possible improvement of our bot is a feature to check a mana parameter of the character. The algorithm to control the mana level is the same as we have for health. If the parameter becomes low, the bot consumes a mana potion.

It is simple to calculate an offset of the mana parameter and read its value in the same checking loop where we process the health parameter. The bot can choose either the healing or the mana potion to use when the corresponding parameter becomes low.

Simulating the keypress action with the *PostMessage* function is one of several possible ways to embed data in the process memory. Another way is to write the new value of the parameter directly to the process memory.

Listing 3-13 demonstrates this approach.

Listing 3-13. Writing a New Value into the Process Memory

```
void WriteWord(HANDLE hProc, DWORD_PTR address, WORD value)
{
        if (WriteProcessMemory(hProc, (void*)address, &value,
        sizeof(value), NULL) == 0)
                printf("Failed to write memory: %u\n", GetLastError());
}

int main()
{
        // Enable `SE_DEBUG_NAME` privilege for current process here.

        // Open a game process here.

        // Search a player character object here.

        // Calculate an offset of character's life parameter here.

        ULONG hp = 0;

        while (1)
```

```
    {
            hp = ReadWord(hTargetProc, hpAddress);
            printf("HP = %lu\n", hp);

            if (hp < 100)
                    WriteWord(hTargetProc, hpAddress, 100);

            Sleep(2000);
    }
        return 0;
}
```

You can see that we added a new *WriteWord* function. It is a wrapper around the *WriteProcessMemory* WinAPI function. Now the bot writes the health value directly to the process memory when the parameter becomes low. This approach has one issue. It breaks the game rules because our write operation is a workaround. We change the parameter bypassing game algorithms. Therefore, the state of the game objects can become inconsistent with it.

You can test a new version of the bot. The health parameter is still unchanged after the write operation. It happens because the game stores this parameter in several places (not only in the character object that we found). I assume that some control algorithm compares these parameter values regularly. It can fix the wrong values according to other ones. The game server does the same fixing of the inconsistent values in online games. So, we can use this approach just for games that do not protect data by controlling algorithms.

There is a third way to embed data in the process memory. There are the code injection techniques. The following two articles describe them:

- www.codeproject.com/Articles/4610/Three-Ways-to-Inject-Your-Code-into-Another-Proces.

- www.codeproject.com/Articles/9229/RemoteLib-DLL-Injection-for-Win-x-NT-Platforms.

The idea of these techniques to force a game process to execute your code. When you reach it, you can call any function (or algorithm) of the game process. You do not need to simulate any keypress actions anymore. Instead, you can call the "UsePotion" function directly. However, this powerful approach requires in-depth analysis and reverse engineering of the game application.

Our in-game bot implements a very simple algorithm. It automates the consumption of health potions, so a player can pay attention to other aspects of the game.

You may ask whether it is possible to implement a more complex bot that hunts the monsters. Yes, we can do it. The primary task of this bot is searching for the monster objects in the game memory. Now, we know both x and y coordinates of the character (they are available in its object). Table 3-6 mentions both coordinates. They are two bytes in size. Also, the y coordinate follows the x one without any gap.

Now we assume that monsters that stand near the player have almost the same coordinates. The bot can scan the game memory to a four-byte number that matches a couple of two-byte coordinates. Then we add each appropriate search result to the list of "possible" monsters. The next action is to filter the wrong results. The hint for a filtering algorithm is an assumption that monster coordinates belong the same memory segment (or their addresses are close).

The bot can remember the memory segment that stores the monster coordinates. We can use this segment for all further memory scan operations. Finally, the bot can do a *PostMessage* call to simulate attacking actions.

Example Summary

We implemented a typical in-game bot for the Diablo 2 game. Let us consider its advantages and disadvantages. We can generalize our evaluation for a whole class of the bots.

These are the advantages:

- The bot receives precise information about the game objects. There is a very low probability that the bot makes mistakes during his work.

- The bot has a lot of ways to modify a state of the game objects. Possible options are as follows: to simulate the player actions, to write new the values directly to the game process memory, and to call the internal game functions.

This is a list of the in-game bot's disadvantages:

- The analysis and reverse engineering of the game require a lot of effort and time.

- The bot is compatible with one specific version of the game (in most cases). We should adapt the bot for each new game version.

- There are a lot of effective approaches to protect applications against the reverse engineering and debugging techniques.

You can see that in-game bots require much more effort to develop and to support them than clicker bots. At the same time, they are quite reliable because they can gather detailed information about a state of the game objects.

Protection Approaches

We have considered an implementation of the in-game bot for Diablo 2. We know the algorithms and techniques that it uses. Let us consider the ways to protect a game application from this kind of bot.

There are two groups of protection methods that can prevent the usage of in-game bots:

- Methods to protect an application against reverse engineering.

- Methods for blocking bot algorithms.

The first group has a long history. Many applications that process sensitive user data and software license managers use these methods. They are well known, and you can find many articles about this topic on the Internet. The primary goal of these methods is to force the bot developer to spend more time on investigating the game application internals. At some point, he can decide that a game analysis costs too much time, and there is no sense in doing it.

The second group of methods focuses on breaking the normal work of a bot by protecting data from being read and written, so that the bot cannot reliably receive the game state.

Some of the protection methods refer to both groups.

Test Application

Let us remember a typical online game architecture. It has a client-side application and a game server. Most of the protection techniques against in-game bots should be applied on the client side.

How will we consider the protection methods? We can take a game application and develop a protection system for it. However, this way requires a lot of effort and time.

Another possibility is to make a simple application that implements some game model. Also, we can develop a primitive in-game bot that controls our test application. Then we will try several protection techniques and estimate their effectiveness against the bot.

The test game application has the following algorithm:

1. Set a maximum value of the health parameter.

2. Check a state of the "1" key every second in a loop.

3. Decrement the health if the key is not pressed. Otherwise, increment the value.

4. Finish the loop and stop the application when the health value becomes equal to zero.

Listing 3-14 demonstrates a source code of the *TestApplication.cpp*.

Listing 3-14. The TestApplication.cpp Code

```cpp
#include <stdio.h>
#include <stdint.h>
#include <windows.h>

static const uint16_t MAX_LIFE = 20;
static uint16_t gLife = MAX_LIFE;

int main()
{
        SHORT result = 0;

        while (gLife > 0)
        {
                result = GetAsyncKeyState(0x31);
                if (result != 0xFFFF8001)
                        --gLife;
                else
                        ++gLife;

                printf("life = %u\n", gLife);
                Sleep(1000);
```

```
    }
    printf("stop\n");
    return 0;
}
```

We store the health value in the *gLife* global variable. When the application starts, we assign the *MAX_LIFE* constant to this variable.

The *main* function has a *while* loop where we check the state of a keyboard key with the *GetAsyncKeyState* WinAPI function. The function has only one input parameter, which specifies a key for checking. The parameter equals the 0x31 virtual-key code in our case. It is the code of the "1" key. If it is not pressed, we decrement the health value. Otherwise, we increment it. Then we do a one-second delay with the *Sleep* WinAPI function. This provides the player enough time to press or release the keyboard key.

You can compile *TestApplication.cpp* with the "Debug" configuration of Visual Studio compiler, and launch it for testing.

Analysis of Test Application

Now we will develop a bot for our test application. We will apply the same bot algorithm as we have implemented in the "Example with Diablo 2" section. The algorithm is simply that if the health value falls below 10, the bot presses the "1" key.

The bot should control the health value. So, let us find it in the application process memory. The application is quite simple and small. Therefore, we can use OllyDbg only to consider its internals.

These are the steps to find a segment that contains the health variable:

1. Launch the OllyDbg debugger. Open the "TestApplication.exe" binary in the "Select 32-bit executable" dialog (you can open the dialog with the F3 key). Now, launch the application from the debugger instead of attaching it; the debugger stops the target process at its start point.

2. Press Ctrl+G to open the "Enter expression to follow" dialog.

3. Type the full name of the *main* function into the "Enter address expression" field. The full name is "TestApplication.main". Then press the "Follow expression" button. Now a cursor in the disassembler subwindow points to the first instruction of the *main* function.

4. Set a breakpoint on the instruction by pressing the F2 key.

5. Start the execution of the target process by pressing the F9 key. Our breakpoint will stop it.

6. Click the left button on the following line of disassembled code (the cursor position should look like Figure 3-24):

```
MOV AX,WORD PTR DS:[gLife]
```

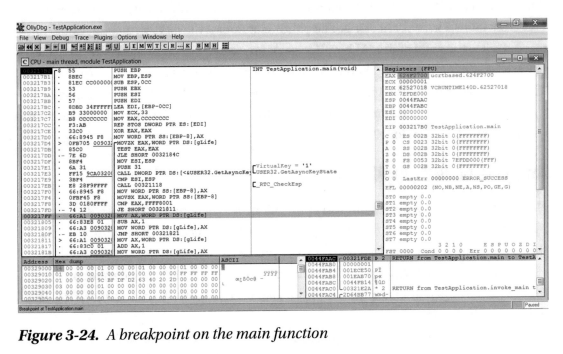

Figure 3-24. *A breakpoint on the main function*

7. Select the "Follow in Dump" ➤ "Memory address" item in the pop-up menu. Now the cursor of the memory dump subwindow should be on the *gLife* variable. It equals "14" in hexadecimal and has the "329000" address in my case.

8. Open the "Memory map" window with an Alt+M keypress.

9. Find a memory segment that contains the address of the *gLife* variable. It should be a ".data" segment of the "TestApplication" module (see Figure 3-25).

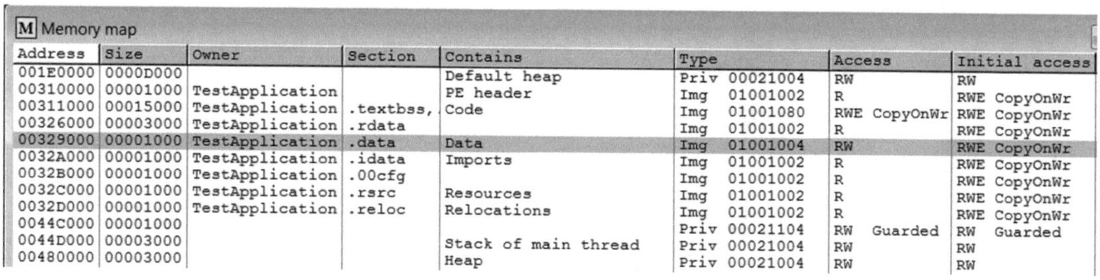

Address	Size	Owner	Section	Contains	Type	Access	Initial access
001E0000	0000D000			Default heap	Priv 00021004	RW	RW
00310000	00001000	TestApplication		PE header	Img 01001002	R	RWE CopyOnWr
00311000	00015000	TestApplication	.textbss,	Code	Img 01001080	RWE CopyOnWr	RWE CopyOnWr
00326000	00003000	TestApplication	.rdata		Img 01001002	R	RWE CopyOnWr
00329000	00001000	TestApplication	.data	Data	Img 01001004	RW	RWE CopyOnWr
0032A000	00001000	TestApplication	.idata	Imports	Img 01001002	R	RWE CopyOnWr
0032B000	00001000	TestApplication	.00cfg		Img 01001002	R	RWE CopyOnWr
0032C000	00001000	TestApplication	.rsrc	Resources	Img 01001002	R	RWE CopyOnWr
0032D000	00001000	TestApplication	.reloc	Relocations	Img 01001002	R	RWE CopyOnWr
0044C000	00001000				Priv 00021104	RW Guarded	RW Guarded
0044D000	00003000			Stack of main thread	Priv 00021004	RW	RW
00480000	00003000			Heap	Priv 00021004	RW	RW

Figure 3-25. *A memory map of the TestApplication*

We learned that the *gLife* variable occupies the beginning of the ".data" segment. So, its address equals the segment base address. It will be enough for our bot to find the ".data" segment. Then, the bot just reads a health variable.

The Bot for Test Application

We have considered the general algorithm of our bot. Now let us view the bot actions step by step:

1. Enable the *SE_DEBUG_NAME* privilege for the current process.
2. Open the test application process.
3. Search the memory segment that contains the `gLife` variable.
4. Read the variable in a loop. Write the 20 value to the `gLife` variable when it falls below 10.

Listing 3-15 shows a source code of the `SimpleBot.cpp` application.

Listing 3-15. The `SimpleBot.cpp` Application

```
#include <windows.h>

BOOL SetPrivilege(HANDLE hToken, LPCTSTR lpszPrivilege, BOOL bEnablePrivilege)
{
        // Implementation of the function is still the same
        // and it is available in the SimpleBot.cpp source file
}

SIZE_T ScanSegments(HANDLE proc)
```

```
{
        MEMORY_BASIC_INFORMATION meminfo;
        LPCVOID addr = 0;

        if (!proc)
                return 0;

        while (1)
        {
                if (VirtualQueryEx(proc, addr, &meminfo,
                sizeof(meminfo)) == 0)
                        break;

                if ((meminfo.State == MEM_COMMIT) && (meminfo.Type &
                MEM_IMAGE) && (meminfo.Protect == PAGE_READWRITE) &&
                (meminfo.RegionSize == 0x1000))
                {
                        return (SIZE_T)meminfo.BaseAddress;
                }
                addr = (unsigned char*)meminfo.BaseAddress + meminfo.
                RegionSize;
        }
        return 0;
}

WORD ReadWord(HANDLE hProc, DWORD_PTR address)
{
        // Implementation of the function is still the same
        // and it is available in the SimpleBot.cpp source file
}

void WriteWord(HANDLE hProc, DWORD_PTR address, WORD value)
{
        if (WriteProcessMemory(hProc, (void*)address, &value,
        sizeof(value), NULL) == 0)
                printf("Failed to write memory: %u\n", GetLastError());
}
```

```
int main()
{
        // Enable `SE_DEBUG_NAME` privilege for current process here.

        // Open the test application process here.

        SIZE_T lifeAddress = ScanSegments(hTargetProc);

        ULONG hp = 0;
        while (1)
        {
                hp = ReadWord(hTargetProc, lifeAddress);
                printf("life = %lu\n", hp);

                if (hp < 10)
                        WriteWord(hTargetProc, lifeAddress, 20);

                Sleep(1000);
        }
        return 0;
}
```

The primary difference of this bot from our Diablo 2 in-game bot is the *ScanSegments* function. Now we can distinguish the segment that contains the *gLife* variable. It has the unique set of flags and the specific size. We can get these data from the "Memory map" window of OllyDbg. Table 3-7 explains the meaning of the segment flags.

Table 3-7. *Meaning of the Segment Flags*

Meminfo field	OllyDbg value	WinAPI value	Description
Type	Img	MEM_IMAGE	Indicates that the memory pages within the region are mapped into the view of an executable image.
Access	RW	PAGE_READWRITE	Enables read-only or read/write access to the committed region of pages.

All segments that are related to an executable image have the *MEM_COMMIT* state flag. It means that address space of the segment was allocated on some physical storage (RAM or the paging file on disk).

These are the steps to launch our bot:

1. Launch the TestAplication.

2. Launch the bot with administrator privileges.

3. Switch to a window of the TestAplication (it should be a console).

4. Wait until the health value falls below 10.

You will see that the bot overwrites the health value when it becomes low.

Approaches Against Analysis

Now we will consider ways to make an investigation of game internals more difficult. Our example with Diablo 2 shows that it is necessary to know these internals to develop a bot. If we apply protection techniques, bot developers will need to spend more time for their work, and they will probably give up.

WinAPI for Debugger Detection

Here we will consider WinAPI functions that check if some process is debugged. Some of them prevent debugging of the protected process.

IsDebuggerPresent

The most straightforward way to protect an application against debugging is the *IsDebuggerPresent* WinAPI function. When we detect the debugger, we can abort the game process.

The following code snippet shows naive usage of the *IsDebuggerPresent* function:

```
int main()
{
        if (IsDebuggerPresent())
        {
                printf("debugger detected!\n");
                exit(EXIT_FAILURE);
        }
```

```
        // Rest function is the same as in TestApplication.cpp
}
```

We check the debugger presence at the beginning of the *main* function.
If the check succeeds, we abort the process by the *exit* function. This usage of the
IsDebuggerPresent function is ineffective. Yes, it detects the debugger when the
application starts. It means that you cannot launch TestApplication from the OllyDbg as
we did it before. However, you can attach the debugger to the working TestApplication
process. The *IsDebuggerPresent* check has already happened and it does not detect the
debugger in this case.

The *IsDebuggerPresent.cpp* application in Listing 3-16 demonstrates the proper
usage of the WinAPI function.

Listing 3-16. The IsDebuggerPresent.cpp Application

```cpp
int main()
{
        SHORT result = 0;

        while (gLife > 0)
        {
                if (IsDebuggerPresent())
                {
                        printf("debugger detected!\n");
                        exit(EXIT_FAILURE);
                }
                result = GetAsyncKeyState(0x31);
                if (result != 0xFFFF8001)
                        --gLife;
                else
                        ++gLife;

                printf("life = %u\n", gLife);
                Sleep(1000);
        }
        printf("stop\n");
        return 0;
}
```

Now, the *IsDebuggerPresent* check happens regularly in the *while* loop, so it detects the debugger even when it attaches to the working process.

How can we bypass this protection? The first way is to modify the CPU register at the moment when the check happens. Thus, we change the check result and avoid execution of the positive case branch of the *if* condition.

The following algorithm explains the steps to modify a CPU register:

1. Launch OllyDbg and open the "TestApplication.exe" binary.

2. Press Ctrl+N to open the "Names in TestApplication" window. Here you can see the **symbol table** of TestApplication.

3. Type the "IsDebuggerPresent" text in the "Names in TestApplication" window.

4. Select the "&KERNEL32.IsDebuggerPresent" symbol name by left-clicking.

5. Press Ctrl+R to search references to the *IsDebuggerPresent* function. You will see the "Search - References to..." dialog. It shows a list of places in the code that do the *IsDebuggerPresent* call.

6. By left-clicking, select the first item in the "Search - References to..." dialog. You should see the *IsDebuggerPresent* call from the *main* function in the disassembler subwindow.

7. By left-clicking, select the *TEST EAX,EAX* instruction, which follows the *IsDebuggerPresent* call. Press the F2 key to set a breakpoint on this instruction.

8. Continue the execution of the TestApplication by the F9 key. Our breakpoint should trigger.

9. Set the value of the EAX register to zero. To do so, double-click the value of EAX register in the "Registers (FPU)" subwindow. It opens the "Modify EAX" dialog, as Figure 3-26 shows. Then type value "0" in the "Signed" row of the "EAX" column. Press the "OK" button.

10. Continue the execution of the TestApplication by the F9 key.

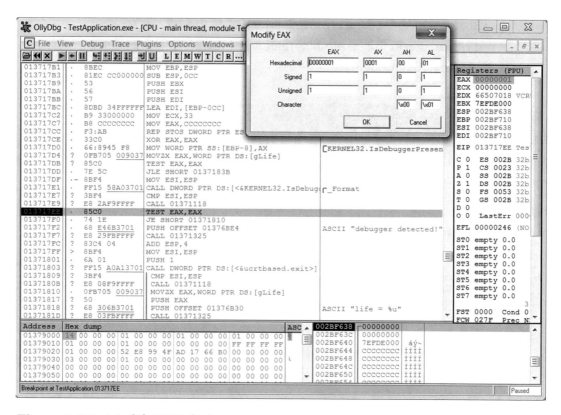

Figure 3-26. *Modify EAX dialog*

The application does not detect the debugger after our modification of the CPU register. However, the *IsDebuggerPresent* check happens on the next iteration of the `while` loop. It means that you should modify the register on each iteration.

Another way to avoid the debugger detection is to make a permanent patch for the TestApplication code. The code is already loaded into the process memory, and OllyDbg has a feature to change it.

These are the steps to make a code patch:

1. Launch the OllyDbg debugger and open the "TestApplication.exe" binary.

2. Find a place of the *IsDebuggerPresent* call.

3. By left-clicking, select the `JE SHORT 01371810` instruction, which follows the `IsDebuggerPresent` call and the `TEST EAX,EAX` line. Press the Space key to edit the selected instruction.

4. Change the *JE SHORT 01371810* instruction to the *JNE SHORT 01371810* one in the "Assemble" dialog, as Figure 3-27 shows. Then press the "Assemble" button.

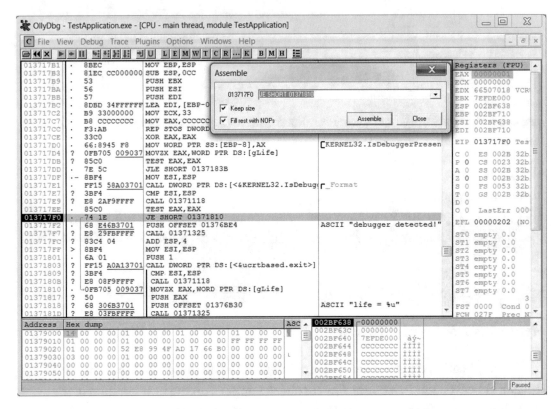

Figure 3-27. *The assemble dialog*

5. Continue the execution of the TestApplication by the F9 key.

The application cannot detect OllyDbg after this patch.

What is the meaning of changing the instruction from *JE* to *JNE*? Let us consider the C++ code that matches to each instruction.

This is a variant for the original *JE* instruction:

```
if (IsDebuggerPresent())
{
        printf("debugger detected!\n");
        exit(EXIT_FAILURE);
}
```

This is a variant for the new *JNE* instruction:

```
if ( ! IsDebuggerPresent())
{
        printf("debugger detected!\n");
        exit(EXIT_FAILURE);
}
```

As you see, we inverse the *if* condition. So, if there is no debugger, the process terminates with the "debugger detected!" message. Otherwise, it continues. We hacked this check, and it becomes broken in a suitable way for us.

If you restart the TestApplication, you should do the same code patch again. You can solve this issue by using the **OllyDumpEx** plug-in (low-priority.appspot.com/ollydumpex) for OllyDbg. It provides a feature to save a modified code back to the binary file.

These are the steps to install OllyDbg plug-ins:

1. Download an archive with a plug-in from the developer website.

2. Unpack the archive to the OllyDbg directory. The default path to the directory is "C:\Program Files (x86)\odbg200".

3. Check that OllyDbg uses the right directory with plug-ins. To do so, select the "Options"➤"Options..." item of the main menu. It opens the "Options" dialog. Then, choose the "Directories" item of a tree control on the left side of the dialog. The "Plug-in directory" field should match your installation path of OllyDbg (for example "C:\Program Files (x86)\odbg200").

4. Restart the debugger.

You will see a new main menu item, which has the "Plug-ins" label. Now, we consider the steps to save patched code to the binary file:

1. Select the "Plug-ins"➤"OllyDumpEx"➤"Dump process" item. You will see the "OllyDumpEx" dialog.

2. Press the "Dump" button. You will see the "Save Dump to File" dialog.

3. Select the path to the saved binary in this dialog.

After these actions, you will find the modified binary file on the hard drive. You can launch this file. It should work correctly for simple applications like our TestApplication. However, if the patched binary is a complex application, it can crash when you launch it.

WinAPI has another function named *CheckRemoteDebuggerPresent*, which detects a debugger. We have considered the *IsDebuggerPresent* function. It returns the *TRUE* value if the process that calls the function is debugged. The *CheckRemoteDebuggerPresent* function does the same check but for another process. This feature is useful when you implement an external protection system that works separately from a game process.

The *CheckRemoteDebuggerPresent* function does the *NtQueryInformationProcess* call. It provides detailed information about the specified process. The information contains the debugging state.

CloseHandle

The considered *IsDebuggerPresent* function does a straightforward check for debugger presence. It has one significant disadvantage. We can easily find this check in the application code and disable it.

The *CloseHandle* WinAPI function has a side effect feature, which we can use for indirect checking for debugger presence. If you use this approach, it will be much more difficult to find and disable the protection. Let us consider how it works.

We should use the *CloseHandle* function to notify OS that we finish our work with some object. It means that somebody else can use the object or OS can remove it. The function receives one input parameter, which is an object handle. So, it is evident that complex applications use the CloseHandle function intensively.

The function generates the *EXCEPTION_INVALID_HANDLE* exception if we call it with an invalid handle or we call it twice for the same handle. Now there comes an important point. The exception is generated only when the process that does the *CloseHandle* call is debugged at the moment. If it is not debugged, the function behaves differently. It returns the error value instead of raising an exception. So, we can check how the function behaves and conclude the debugger presence.

When somebody analyzes the protected application, he should consider all *CloseHandle* calls and check if they are used for object release or for debugger detection.

The following code snippet demonstrates this check:

```
BOOL IsDebug()
{
        __try
        {
                CloseHandle((HANDLE)0x12345);
        }
        __except (GetExceptionCode() == EXCEPTION_INVALID_HANDLE ?
                EXCEPTION_EXECUTE_HANDLER : EXCEPTION_CONTINUE_SEARCH)
        {
                return TRUE;
        }
        return FALSE;
}
```

We use the **try-except statement** here. It is not a C++ standard **try-catch statement**. It is a Microsoft extension for both C and C++ languages, which is part of **Structured Exception Handling** (SEH) mechanism. You can read more about the SEH in MSDN (msdn.microsoft.com/en-us/library/windows/desktop/ms680657(v=vs.85).aspx).

Let us modify our TestApplication and substitute replace the *IsDebuggerPresent* call with the new *IsDebug* function. The *CloseHandle.cpp* file demonstrates the modified version. You can launch it and test with the OllyDbg and WinDbg debuggers. You will see that the application cannot detect the OllyDbg, but it detects WinDbg well. This happens because OllyDbg uses a special technique to bypass this kind of protection.

We can do the same debugger check with the *DebugBreak* WinAPI function. The following code snippet shows its usage:

```
BOOL IsDebug()
{
        __try
        {
                DebugBreak();
        }
        __except (GetExceptionCode() == EXCEPTION_BREAKPOINT ?
                EXCEPTION_EXECUTE_HANDLER : EXCEPTION_CONTINUE_SEARCH)
        {
```

```
                return FALSE;
        }
        return TRUE;
}
```

The full code of this example is available in the *DebugBreak.cpp* file.

Unlike the *CloseHandle* call, the *DebugBreak* function always generates an exception. It is the *EXCEPTION_BREAKPOINT*. If the application is debugged, the debugger handles the exception. It means that we do not reach the code inside the *__except* block. If there is no debugger, our application catches the exception and concludes that there is no debugger.

This approach detects both OllyDbg and WinDbg debuggers.

The *DebugBreak* function has an alternative variant named *DebugBreakProcess*, which allows you to check another process.

CreateProcess

There is a technique that prevents debugging of the process at all. Windows has a limitation that only one debugger can attach to a process at any one time. Thus, if the application debugs itself, nobody else can do it. This technique is known as self-debugging.

The principal idea of the technique is creating a child process by the *CreateProcess* WinAPI function. Then there are two possibilities:

1.   A child process debugs the parent one. The parent process does all TestApplication algorithms in this case. This approach is described in this article: `www.codeproject.com/Articles/30815/ An-Anti-Reverse-Engineering-Guide#SelfDebugging`.

2.   A parent process debugs the child one. The child process does a work of TestApplication in this case.

We will consider an implementation of the second case.

Listing 3-17 demonstrates the self-debugging technique.

Listing 3-17. The SelfDebugging.cpp Application

```cpp
#include <stdint.h>
#include <windows.h>
#include <string>

using namespace std;

static const uint16_t MAX_LIFE = 20;
static uint16_t gLife = MAX_LIFE;

void DebugSelf()
{
        wstring cmdChild(GetCommandLine());
        cmdChild.append(L" x");

        PROCESS_INFORMATION pi;
        STARTUPINFO si;
        ZeroMemory(&pi, sizeof(PROCESS_INFORMATION));
        ZeroMemory(&si, sizeof(STARTUPINFO));
        GetStartupInfo(&si);

        CreateProcess(NULL, (LPWSTR)cmdChild.c_str(), NULL, NULL, FALSE,
                DEBUG_PROCESS | CREATE_NEW_CONSOLE, NULL, NULL, &si, &pi);

        DEBUG_EVENT de;
        ZeroMemory(&de, sizeof(DEBUG_EVENT));

        for (;;)
        {
                if (!WaitForDebugEvent(&de, INFINITE))
                        return;

                ContinueDebugEvent(de.dwProcessId,
                        de.dwThreadId,
                        DBG_CONTINUE);
        }
}
```

```
int main(int argc, char* argv[])
{
        if (argc == 1)
        {
                DebugSelf();
        }
        SHORT result = 0;

        while (gLife > 0)
        {
                result = GetAsyncKeyState(0x31);
                if (result != 0xFFFF8001)
                        --gLife;
                else
                        ++gLife;

                printf("life = %u\n", gLife);
                Sleep(1000);
        }

        printf("stop\n");
        return 0;
}
```

Figure 3-28 demonstrates the relationship between the parent and child processes.

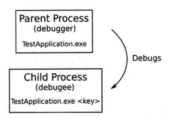

Figure 3-28. *The relationship between the parent and child processes*

TestAplication starts in two steps. The first step happens when you launch the application without any command-line parameters. You can do this by clicking the application icon. In this case, we come in the positive branch of the following *if* condition:

```
if (argc == 1)
{
        DebugSelf();
}
```

When you launch an application without command-line arguments, it has one argument that matches the executable file name. Thus, we do the *DebugSelf* call. This function has the following algorithm:

1. Get the command-line arguments of the current process and append the "x" parameter to them. This parameter informs the child process that it was launched from the parent one:

    ```
    wstring cmdChild(GetCommandLine());
    cmdChild.append(L" x");
    ```

2. Create a child process with the *CreateProcess* call. We pass the *DEBUG_PROCESS* flag to the function. This means that we debug the created process. Also, we pass the *CREATE_NEW_CONSOLE* flag to create a separate console for the child process, so you can get output messages from it.

3. Start an infinite loop, which receives all debug events from the child process.

You can launch the SelfDebugging application and try to debug it. Neither the OllyDbg nor the WinDbg debugger can attach to it. Our example is just a demonstration of the self-debugging approach. You can easily bypass the protection that we have implemented. To do so, launch the "TestApplication.exe" executable from the command line with the second parameter:

```
TestApplication.exe x
```

The application starts normally, and you can debug it.

You should not rely on the number of command-line arguments as we did in the example. Instead, you should use an algorithm to generate the random key. Then the child process receives this key via the command line and checks its correctness.

More secure approaches against an unauthorized application launch rely on **interprocess communication** mechanisms (msdn.microsoft.com/en-us/library/windows/desktop/aa365574%28v=vs.85%29.aspx).

Register Manipulations for Debugger Detection

The antidebugging approaches that use WinAPI calls have one significant disadvantage. Finding these calls in the application code is easy. Even if we use the *CloseHandle* function and the application has 100 calls of it, we can bypass the protection in the predicted amount of time.

There are several antidebugging approaches that use CPU register manipulation. We can access these registers from our applications via the **inline assembler**. When we check debugger presence without WinAPI calls, we cannot use a symbol table to find these checks. So, it is more difficult to find them.

Let us consider the internals of the *IsDebuggerPresent* WinAPI function. Probably, we can repeat its code in our application.

These are the steps to investigate the function:

1. Launch the OllyDbg.

2. Open the "TestApplication.exe" binary, which is protected by the *IsDebuggerPresent* function.

3. Find the place where the *IsDebuggerPresent* call happens. Make a breakpoint on it and continue a process execution.

4. When the process stops by the breakpoint, press the F7 key to make a step into the *IsDebuggerPresent* function.

You will see the assembler code of the function in the disassembler subwindow of OllyDbg as Figure 3-29 shows.

```
767F377C ┌$   64:A1 180000( MOV EAX,DWORD PTR FS:[18]
767F3782 │ .  8B40 30        MOV EAX,DWORD PTR DS:[EAX+30]
767F3785 │ .  0FB640 02      MOVZX EAX,BYTE PTR DS:[EAX+2]
767F3789 └ . C3              RETN
```

Figure 3-29. *Assembler code of the* `IsDebuggerPresent` *function*

Let us consider each line this code:

1. Read a linear address of the TEB segment that matches the currently active thread into the EAX register. The FS register always points to the TEB segment. The 0x18 hexadecimal offset in the TEB segment matches to its linear address.

2. Read a linear address of the PEB segment to the EAX register. The 0x30 hexadecimal offset in the TEB segment matches the PEB linear address.

3. Read a value with the 0x2 offset from the PEB segment to the EAX register. This value matches the BeingDebugged flag, which detects the debugger presence.

4. Return from the function.

Now we will try to repeat this algorithm in TestApplication. Listing 3-18 shows the result.

Listing 3-18. Detecting a Debugger via Checking Registers

```
int main()
{
        SHORT result = 0;

        while (gLife > 0)
        {
                int res = 0;
                __asm
                {
                        mov eax, dword ptr fs:[18h]
                        mov eax, dword ptr ds:[eax+30h]
```

```
                    movzx eax, byte ptr ds:[eax+2h]
                    mov res, eax
            };
            if (res)
            {
                    printf("debugger detected!\n");
                    exit(EXIT_FAILURE);
            }
            result = GetAsyncKeyState(0x31);
            if (result != 0xFFFF8001)
                    --gLife;
            else
                    ++gLife;

            printf("life = %u\n", gLife);
            Sleep(1000);
    }
    printf("stop\n");
    return 0;
}
```

You can compare our code and Figure 3-29. They look almost the same. The difference is the last line. We store the value of the BeingDebugged in the *res* variable. Then we use it to detect a debugger.

If you copy this assembler code in several places of your application, it will be difficult to find them.

What should we do if we want to keep this code in one place? That is the right question. If something changes in the next Windows versions and our code become invalid, we should fix or remove it. It will cost a lot of effort to fix it in several places.

There are several approaches to avoid duplication of assembler code. We cannot move it to the regular C++ function. It is quite easy to find calls of any function via the symbol table. So, we should do something more sophisticated.

The first approach is to make the C++ function that has the __*forceinline* keyword. The keyword forces the compiler to insert the function body into each place where it is called. However, it works correctly when we choose the "Release" configuration of the application build.

The keyword is ignored in several cases:

- If we use the "Debug" build configuration.

- If the inline function has recursive calls.

- If the inline function calls the *alloca* WinAPI function.

The second approach is the usage of the **preprocessor macro**. The compiler inserts the body of the preprocessor macro in each place of source code where the name of macro is specified. This compiler behavior does not depend on the build configuration.

The *BeingDebugged.cpp* application in Listing 3-19 shows checking the BeingDebugged flag with the preprocessor macro.

Listing 3-19. The BeingDebugged.cpp Application

```
#define CheckDebug() \
int isDebugger = 0; \
{ \
__asm mov eax, dword ptr fs : [18h] \
__asm mov eax, dword ptr ds : [eax + 30h] \
__asm movzx eax, byte ptr ds : [eax + 2h] \
__asm mov isDebugger, eax \
} \
if (isDebugger) \
{ \
printf("debugger detected!\n"); \
exit(EXIT_FAILURE); \
}

int main()
{
        SHORT result = 0;

        while (gLife > 0)
        {
                CheckDebug()
                ...
        }
```

```
    printf("stop\n");

    return 0;
}
```

This protection looks reliable enough. Can we somehow bypass it?

The answer is yes. Instead of changing the *if* condition in each place where an application checks for a debugger, we can change the BeingDebugged flag.

This is an algorithm to do it with OllyDbg:

1. Launch the debugger.

2. Open the "TestApplication.exe" binary, which is protected by the BeingDebugged flag checking.

3. Press Alt+M to open a memory map of the process. Find the "Process Environment Block" segment.

4. Double-left-click this segment. You will see "Dump - Process Environment Block" window. Find the "BeingDebugged" flag value there.

5. Left-click the "BeingDebugged" flag to select it. Press Ctrl+E to open the "Edit data at address..." dialog.

6. Change a value in the "HEX+01" field from "01" to "00" and press the "OK" button. Figure 3-30 shows this step.

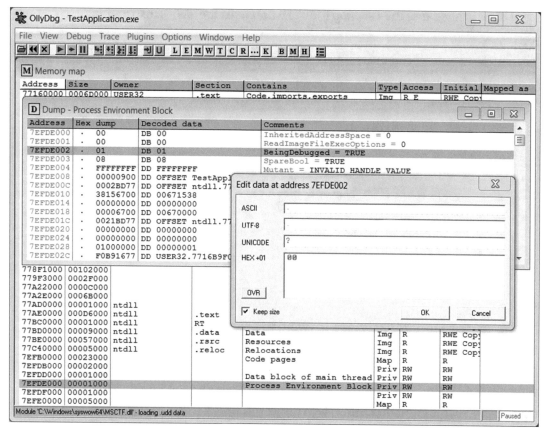

Figure 3-30. *The "Edit data at address" dialog*

Now continue with the execution of the process. The application cannot detect the debugger anymore.

This workaround looks quite simple. So, we can easily bypass protection approaches that rely on the BeingDebugged flag. Can we apply something more reliable?

As you remember, we have considered the *DebugBreak* WinAPI function. This allows us to raise an exception. Then we should check who will process it and conclude the debugger presence.

Let us investigate the internals of this function and replace it with the assembler code. For this investigation, you can follow the same approach as we applied for the *IsDebuggerPresent* function. If you do everything correctly, you will find that the *DebugBreak* function uses the *INT 3* assembler instruction only. The instruction raises the *EXCEPTION_BREAKPOINT*.

This is a version of the *IsDebug* function that uses the *INT 3* instruction:

```
BOOL IsDebug()
{
        __try
        {
                __asm int 3;
        }
        __except (GetExceptionCode() == EXCEPTION_BREAKPOINT ?
                EXCEPTION_EXECUTE_HANDLER : EXCEPTION_CONTINUE_SEARCH)
        {
                return FALSE;
        }
        return TRUE;
}
```

We can use the *__forceinline* keyword to hide calls of the *IsDebug* function. However, this keyword does not have any effect in this case. It happens because the *__try __except* handler operates in its own memory frame and it uses the *alloca* WinAPI function implicitly. It prevents the compiler from inserting the function body to the caller code. An alternative solution is to move this check to the macro:

```
#define CheckDebug() \
bool isDebugger = true; \
__try \
{ \
        __asm int 3 \
} \
__except (GetExceptionCode() == EXCEPTION_BREAKPOINT ? \
                EXCEPTION_EXECUTE_HANDLER : EXCEPTION_CONTINUE_SEARCH) \
{ \
        isDebugger = false; \
} \
if (isDebugger) \
{ \
        printf("debugger detected!\n"); \
        exit(EXIT_FAILURE); \
}
```

The *Int3.cpp* file demonstrates the TestApplication code with this protection.

You should patch the code and invert the *if* condition if you want to bypass this protection. It sounds simple, but you should find all these checks in the code.

OllyDbg provides the feature to search specific assembler instruction. You can press Ctrl+F in the disassembler subwindow and type the *INT3* value in the opened dialog. The press the "Search" button. You will get an instruction that contains the 0xCC number in its opcode. Now you should find the 0xCC byte in the whole application code. It takes a lot of time for complex applications. Also, you will get many 0xCC bytes that are not the *INT 3* instruction but something else.

Approaches Against Bots

Windows has a mechanism to restrict access to system objects (for example, processes). This mechanism is **Security Descriptors** (SD). There is an article (helgeklein.com/blog/2009/03/permissions-a-primer-or-dacl-sacl-owner-sid-and-ace-explained/?PageSpeed=noscript) that describes it in detail.

Also, you can learn more about SD from the following code examples:

- `www.cplusplus.com/forum/windows/96406`

- stackoverflow.com/questions/6185975/prevent-user-process-from-being-killed-with-end-process-from-process-explorer/10575889#10575889

They demonstrate how you can protect your application with the **Discretionary Access Control List** (DACL).

However, the SD mechanism does not protect your application if the process with administrator privileges tries to access it. Therefore, you should implement protection algorithms on your own.

The reliable protection algorithm should solve two primary tasks:

- Hiding game data from memory scanners (like Cheat Engine).

- Checking the correctness of game data to prevent their unauthorized modification.

Hiding Game Data

First, we will consider approaches to hide game data from memory scanners.

XOR Cipher

The simplest way to hide some data in the process memory is encryption. If we encrypt states of the game objects, a bot still can read them, but it cannot retrieve their actual values.

We start our consideration of encryption algorithms with the simplest one: the **XOR cipher**. Listing 3-20 demonstrates its usage.

Listing 3-20. The XORCipher.cpp Application

```cpp
#include <stdint.h>
#include <windows.h>

using namespace std;

inline uint16_t maskValue(uint16_t value)
{
        static const uint16_t MASK = 0xAAAA;
        return (value ^ MASK);
}

static const uint16_t MAX_LIFE = 20;
static uint16_t gLife = maskValue(MAX_LIFE);

int main(int argc, char* argv[])
{
        SHORT result = 0;

        while (maskValue(gLife) > 0)
        {
                result = GetAsyncKeyState(0x31);
                if (result != 0xFFFF8001)
                        gLife = maskValue(maskValue(gLife) - 1);
                else
                        gLife = maskValue(maskValue(gLife) + 1);

                printf("life = %u\n", maskValue(gLife));
                Sleep(1000);
        }
```

```
        printf("stop\n");
        return 0;
}
```

The *maskValue* function implements both encryption and decryption procedures. We use the **XOR operation** with the predefined *MASK* constant to get an encrypted value. The constant is a key of the cipher in our case. When we want to decrypt the *gLife* variable, we do the *maskValue* call again.

You can launch this application and try to find the *gLife* variable with the Cheat Engine. The scanner cannot do it anymore. However, if you know the *MASK* value, you can easily find the variable. You should calculate the encrypted value of the variable manually and search it. Then, the Cheat Engine finds the right address.

Our XOR cipher implementation is just a demonstration of this approach. You should significantly improve it before using it in real applications.

The first improvement is creating a template C++ class that encapsulates the encryption algorithm. Then you should overload the assignment and arithmetic operators for this class. This allows you to use encryption implicitly like this:

```
XORCipher<int> gLife(20);
gLife = gLife - 1;
```

The second improvement is generating a random cipher key (*MASK* value) in the constructor of the template class. This solution makes it difficult to decrypt protected values.

AES Cipher

We have considered the XOR cipher, which is quite simple to crack. You can use more sophisticated cipher algorithms to protect game data better. WinAPI provides a set of cryptographic functions (msdn.microsoft.com/en-us/library/windows/desktop/aa380252(v=vs.85).aspx). Let us consider a modern symmetric AES cipher and apply it to our test application.

Listing 3-21 demonstrates usage of the cipher:

Listing 3-21. The AESCipher.cpp Application

```cpp
#include <stdint.h>
#include <stdio.h>
#include <windows.h>
#include <string>

#pragma comment (lib, "advapi32")
#pragma comment (lib, "user32")

using namespace std;

static const uint16_t MAX_LIFE = 20;
static uint16_t gLife = 0;

HCRYPTPROV hProv;
HCRYPTKEY hKey;
HCRYPTKEY hSessionKey;

#define kAesBytes128 16

typedef struct {
    BLOBHEADER  header;
    DWORD       key_length;
    BYTE        key_bytes[kAesBytes128];
} AesBlob128;

static const BYTE gCipherBlockSize = kAesBytes128 * 2;
static BYTE gCipherBlock[gCipherBlockSize] = {0};

void CreateContex()
{
    if (!CryptAcquireContext(&hProv, NULL, NULL, PROV_RSA_AES,
    CRYPT_VERIFYCONTEXT))
    {
        printf("CryptAcquireContext() failed - error = 0x%x\n",
        GetLastError());
    }
}
```

```cpp
void CreateKey(string& key)
{
    AesBlob128 aes_blob;
    aes_blob.header.bType = PLAINTEXTKEYBLOB;
    aes_blob.header.bVersion = CUR_BLOB_VERSION;
    aes_blob.header.reserved = 0;
    aes_blob.header.aiKeyAlg = CALG_AES_128;
    aes_blob.key_length = kAesBytes128;
    memcpy(aes_blob.key_bytes, key.c_str(), kAesBytes128);

    if (!CryptImportKey(hProv,
                        reinterpret_cast<BYTE*>(&aes_blob),
                        sizeof(AesBlob128),
                        NULL,
                        0,
                        &hKey))
    {
        printf("CryptImportKey() failed - error = 0x%x\n", GetLastError());
    }
}

void Encrypt()
{
    unsigned long length = kAesBytes128;
    memset(gCipherBlock, 0, gCipherBlockSize);
    memcpy(gCipherBlock, &gLife, sizeof(gLife));

    if (!CryptEncrypt(hKey, 0, TRUE, 0, gCipherBlock, &length, gCipherBlockSize))
    {
        printf("CryptEncrypt() failed - error = 0x%x\n", GetLastError());
        return;
    }
    gLife = 0;
}
```

```
void Decrypt()
{
    unsigned long length = gCipherBlockSize;

    if (!CryptDecrypt(hKey, 0, TRUE, 0, gCipherBlock, &length))
    {
        printf("Error CryptDecrypt() failed - error = 0x%x\n",
        GetLastError());
        return;
    }
    memcpy(&gLife, gCipherBlock, sizeof(gLife));
    memset(gCipherBlock, 0, gCipherBlockSize);
}

int main(int argc, char* argv[])
{
    CreateContex();

    string key("The secret key");

    CreateKey(key);

    gLife = MAX_LIFE;

    Encrypt();

    SHORT result = 0;

    while (true)
    {
        result = GetAsyncKeyState(0x31);

        Decrypt();

        if (result != 0xFFFF8001)
            gLife = gLife - 1;
        else
            gLife = gLife + 1;

        printf("life = %u\n", gLife);
```

```
    if (gLife == 0)
        break;

    Encrypt();

    Sleep(1000);
  }
  printf("stop\n");
  return 0;
}
```

Let us consider the algorithm of the AES cipher application. These are its steps:

1. Create a context for a cryptographic algorithm by the
   CreateContex function. It does the *CryptAcquireContext* WinAPI
   call. Context is a combination of two components: key container
   and cryptographic service provider (CSP). The key container
   contains all keys that belong to a specific user. CSP is a software
   module that provides a cryptographic algorithm.

2. Append a cryptographic key to the CSP by the *CreateKey* function.
   This function takes a string with the key value as the input
   parameter. Then it creates a key BLOB structure according to the
   received string. After this, the function does the *CryptImportKey*
   WinAPI call, which transfers the BLOB to the CSP.

3. Initialize the *gLife* variable and encrypt it by the *Encrypt*
   function. It calls the *CryptEncrypt* WinAPI internally. We store
   the encrypted value in the *gCipherBlock* global array. After
   encrypting, we set *gLife* to zero, so memory scanners cannot
   find it.

4. Decrypt the *gCipherBlock* array and restore the *gLife* variable
   by the *Decrypt* function on each step of the *while* loop. This
   function calls the *CryptDecrypt* WinAPI internally. After
   decryption, we update the variable and encrypt it again. We
   interrupt the loop when the *gLife* becomes equal to zero.

What is the advantage of applying AES cipher comparing to XOR one? The steps to find an encrypted variable in the process memory are still the same for both cases:

1. Recover an encryption key.

2. Apply it to encrypt the value you want to find.

3. Search the encrypted value with a memory scanner.

XOR cipher works faster, but it is easy to crack. So, there are two options to recover the key. We can crack the cipher or search the key in the process memory. Sometimes the first option is simpler to do, other times the second one. When we apply the AES cipher, there is only one option with process memory searching. This cipher is strong; thus, it requires considerable time to crack it. To make the protection more reliable, we can generate an encryption key after each application launch and apply antidebugging techniques.

Using AES has another advantage. When we recover the key, we should repeat the cipher's algorithm. This allows us to get the encrypted value, which we can find in the process memory with a scanner. The XOR cipher is so simple that you can apply it even in your mind. However, the AES cipher has many rounds of applying XOR operation and bitwise rotation. Thus, we should write an application that does encryption for us. It requires time, and a bot developer should know how to do it.

Both of these ciphers solve the first task of data protection. They hide data from memory scanners. However, the bot still can write data to the process memory. It becomes a vulnerability in some cases.

Check Correctness of Game Data

Now, we will consider how we can protect game data from modification. The principal idea of this kind of protection is to duplicate data and compare them periodically.

When we want to change the data, we modify their copy too. If data and the copy differ, we conclude that somebody changed it in an unauthorized way. However, it is quite simple to find the copy with a memory scanner because it has the same value as original data. So, we should hide the copy. We can encrypt it, but there is a faster way. It is the **hashing**.

The hashing is something that looks similar to encryption. We take data and convert them to something. The difference is that when we encrypt data, we want to decrypt it in the future. When we hash data, we do not plan to get them back. So, hashing is a one-direction operation. This feature allows to speed up hashing algorithms.

The *HashCheck.cpp* application in Listing 3-22 demonstrates the protection of data from modification.

Listing 3-22. The HashCheck.cpp Application

```cpp
#include <stdint.h>
#include <windows.h>
#include <functional>

using namespace std;

static const uint16_t MAX_LIFE = 20;
static uint16_t gLife = MAX_LIFE;

std::hash<uint16_t> hashFunc;
static size_t gLifeHash = hashFunc(gLife);

void UpdateHash()
{
        gLifeHash = hashFunc(gLife);
}

__forceinline void CheckHash()
{
        if (gLifeHash != hashFunc(gLife))
        {
                printf("unauthorized modification detected!\n");
                exit(EXIT_FAILURE);
        }
}

int main(int argc, char* argv[])
{
        SHORT result = 0;
        while (gLife > 0)
        {
                result = GetAsyncKeyState(0x31);

                CheckHash();
```

```
            if (result != 0xFFFF8001)
                    --gLife;
            else
                    ++gLife;

            UpdateHash();

            printf("life = %u\n", gLife);
            Sleep(1000);
        }
        printf("stop\n");
        return 0;
}
```

Here we add the extra *gLifeHash* variable. It stores the hashed *gLife* value. We use the *hash* function that is provided by the STL of the C++11 standard to calculate the *gLifeHash*.

We compare the hashed and original *gLife* values in the *CheckHash* function on each *while* loop iteration. The function calculates a hash of the current *gLife* variable. If the result and the *gLifeHash* value differ, we conclude that there has been unauthorized data change.

After checking the hash, we change the *gLife* variable according to the normal algorithm. Then we update the *gLifeHash* value by the *UpdateHash* call.

You can compile and launch this application. If you modify the *gLife* variable via the Cheat Engine, the process terminates.

Bypassing such kinds of protection is possible. A bot should modify both *gLife* and *gLifeHash* values simultaneously. However, there are two obstacles here.

The first issue is choosing a proper moment when these values should be modified. If the bot changes them, the check fails when they are compared in the *CheckHash* function. So, the modification will be detected.

The second issue is a task to find the hashed value. If you know the hash algorithm, you can calculate a hash for the current *gLife* value and search for it with the Cheat Engine. In most cases, you will not know the algorithm. So, you should analyze the disassembled application code to understand it. There is another way: you can manipulate with the *if* condition of the *CheckHash* function and disable the check. However, it becomes difficult to find all *if* conditions in case the *CheckHash* function is inline or is implemented as a preprocessor macro.

The most effective way to prevent an unauthorized data modification is to store all game data on the server side. The client side receives these data for visualization of the current game state. Modification of the client-side data affects a screen picture and keeps the server-side data unchanged. Therefore, the server always knows an actual state of game objects and can force clients to accept these data as authentic.

Protection Approaches Summary

We have considered approaches to protect a game process from memory analysis. This task can be done with the WinAPI function or with CPU register manipulations.

Then we considered methods to protect from memory scanners and unauthorized memory modifications.

CHAPTER 4

Out-game Bots

We will consider out-game bots in this chapter. First, we will get a short overview of the required tools. Then, we will study the basic principles of Internet communications. We will write a sample network applications. When we become familiar with the technologies and tools, we will write a bot for the real game. At the end of the chapter, we will investigate ways to protect games from this type of bot.

Tools

Tools for out-game bot development have different requirements from those for the in-game case. Our task is not to go deep inside the internals of the launched processes. In most cases, we should repeat some major features of a game client. Thus, we do not need a language that is well integrated with WinAPI. Instead, our current focus is network communications.

Programming Language

We will use the **Python** language in this chapter. It is a scripting language with excellent features for network programming. Python has libraries (which are also known as **modules**) to support all modern network protocols and cryptographic algorithms. These two topics are the most important for our out-game bot development.

You can use any IDE to write Python scripts. I recommend that you choose **Notepad++** (notepad-plus-plus.org), which we already know from Chapter 2.

There are two options for choosing the Python version and cryptographic library. You can install the Python of the newest version, 3.6.5, and the PyCryptodome library. PyCryptodome is a fork of the PyCrypto library. It has better support for Windows. However, this fork does not have some features of PyCrypto. These features are not important for developing a final product, but we will consider them for a better understanding of the encryption topic.

© Ilya Shpigor 2018
I. Shpigor, *Practical Video Game Bots*, https://doi.org/10.1007/978-1-4842-3736-6_4

Another option is installing the older Python version 3.3.0 and the PyCrypto library. In this chapter, we will use Python features that are the same for 3.6.5 and 3.3.0 Python versions. If you choose the installation variant with PyCryptodome, you cannot launch a couple of sample scripts that we will consider here. The rest of the scripts should work well.

These are the steps to install Python 3.3.0 and the PyCrypto library:

1. Download the Python 3.3.0 release from the official website (`https://www.python.org/ftp/python/3.3.0/python-3.3.0.msi`).

2. Install it in the default installation path *C:\Python33*.

3. Download the unofficial build of the PyCrypto library (`http://www.voidspace.org.uk/python/pycrypto-2.6.1/pycrypto-2.6.1.win32-py3.3.msi`).

4. Install the library. During the installation, the Python should be found automatically.

These are the instructions to install Python 3.6.5 and the PyCryptodome library:

1. Download the latest Python release from the official website (`https://www.python.org/downloads/release/python-365`).

2. Install it in the default installation path *C:\Program Files\Python36*.

3. Download the *get-pip.py* script from the website (bootstrap.pypa.io/get-pip.py). This script installs the **pip** tool. This tool manages Python modules on your computer.

4. Launch the *get-pip.py* script from the command line:

    ```
    get-pip.py --user
    ```

    When the script finishes, it shows a message with a pip installation path. For my case, the path is *C:\Users\ilya.shpigor\AppData\Roaming\Python\Python36\Scripts*.

5. Go to the installation path and launch the pip tool:

    ```
    pip install --user pycryptodome
    ```

The last steps are similar for both installation variants. You should check that the Python path was added to the *PATH* environment variable. These are the steps to do it:

1. Open "Control Panel" ➤ "System" ➤ "Advanced system setting" and press the "Environment Variables" button. You will see the "Environment Variables" dialog, which has two lists.

2. Find the "PATH" variable in the "System variables" list. Choose the variable by left-clicking.

3. Press the "Edit" button. You will see the full list of the system variables.

4. Add the Python installation path to this list if it is absent.

Now you are ready to launch Python scripts that use cryptographic algorithms.

The Python language is cross-platform. It means that all samples of this chapter should work correctly on Windows, Linux, and macOS systems.

Network Analyzer

Wireshark (`www.wireshark.org`) is one of the most famous network packet analyzers. It allows you to capture traffic on the specified network adapter, inspect it with a user-friendly interface, filter some packets, and store your results on a disk drive. Also, Wireshark supports decryption of many widespread protocols. This tool is open source, and you can get it for free on the official website.

Windows Configuration

In this chapter, we will write several network applications. When you launch one of them, it should communicate with another app that works on another computer. Thus, you should have a minimum of two computers for testing. Another option is to use a VM. In this case, one application should work on your host OS and another inside the VM (i.e., on guest OS).

However, most modern OSs have a feature for testing network applications locally. There is a special network interface that is known as loopback. Applications that work on the same computer can communicate via loopback, and they behave almost in the same way as in a real network.

The loopback interface is disabled in the Windows by default. You should enable it if you want to run our sample scripts. These are the steps to do it:

1. Launch the Device Manager. You can open it via the Control Panel or by typing "Device Manager" in the Start menu.

2. Choose the root item of the devices tree in the Device Manager window.

3. Choose the "Action" ➤ "Add legacy hardware" item of the window menu. You will see the "Add Hardware" dialog.

4. Press the "Next" button on the first page of the dialog.

5. Choose the "Install the hardware that I manually select from a list (Advanced)" option in the dialog. Press the "Next" button.

6. Choose the "Network adapters" item in the "Common hardware types" list. Press the "Next" button.

7. Choose the "Microsoft" manufacturer and the "Microsoft Loopback Adapter" option. Press the "Next" button two times.

8. When installation process finishes, you should press the "Finish" button.

After installation of the loopback interface, it is essential to activate it. These are the steps to do it:

1. Open the "Network and Sharing Center" window. You can do it via the Start menu.

2. Click the "Change adapter settings" option on the left side of the window. The "Network Connections" window will open.

3. Right-click the "Microsoft Loopback Adapter" icon. Choose the "Enable" option.

Now the loopback interface is ready to use.

Internet Protocols

We have considered an architecture of a typical online game application in Chapter 1. It has two sides: a game client communicates with a server via a network (the Internet in most cases). We already know that the application calls WinAPI functions and asks the OS to send data. Then, the OS transfers data to the network adapter via a device driver. Now the question is, exactly what happens when the device driver transfers game data? Let us investigate this question.

Communication Tasks

If you want to understand the solutions offered by a certain technology, the reasonable approach is to consider the tasks that these solutions solve. Let us imagine that we are developers and we get a requirement to transfer game data from the client to the server via some network.

We have two connected **network hosts** like Figure 4-1 shows.

Game Client   Game Server

Figure 4-1. *Game client and server connected via the network*

The first straightforward idea is to implement the whole algorithm of data transferring in the game client application. First, we prepare a data array that contains states of game objects (for example, coordinates, health points, etc.). This array is known as the **network packet**. When it is ready, we pass the packet to the network adapter. Then the adapter sends the packet.

Wait a moment. What happens if we have three hosts that are connected to one local network? Figure 4-2 shows this case.

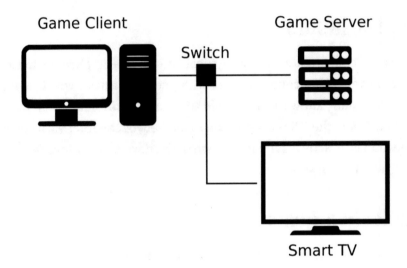

Figure 4-2. *The network of three hosts*

In this case, we use a **network switch** to connect the game client and server. Then we plug in the Smart TV to this switch. It will be enough, for now, to consider a switch as a device to connect several network cables.

Now we get a new task. We should somehow distinguish hosts and send game data to the server but not to the TV. You can say that it does not matter if the TV receives some unnecessary packets. It can just drop them. This is the right idea as long as we have such a small network. But what happens if we have hundreds of hosts? If everybody sends traffic to everybody, the network hangs because of too-high loading. Cables and network adapters have limited bandwidth, so we should use these resources reasonably.

We can solve our issue if we assign unique identifiers (or addresses) to each of our hosts. We reach the first solution that was created by real network engineers. A **MAC address** is a unique identifier of the network adapter (or another transmitting device). The manufacturer assigns this address at the device production step. It should be unique and unchangeable. Now, our application always appends a MAC address of the destination host to the transmitted packet. This feature allows the switch device to route traffic on the right port only because it knows which devices are connected to which ports.

When the server receives the packet, it wants to confirm that the data are correct. So, when we send the data, we should also specify a MAC address of the sender host. Thus, the receiver knows who has sent the packet and can answer to it.

Let us imagine that our network became bigger. For example, we have two buildings. Each building has its own local network of three hosts. Then we connect these networks via one host as Figure 4-3 shows.

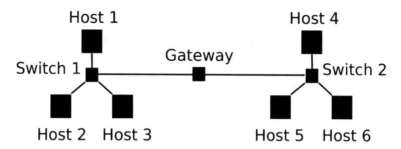

Figure 4-3. *Two local networks are connected via a gateway*

Potentially, we can have dozens of hosts total in both networks. If we still follow the MAC addressing approach, we face an issue. Each host should know about all the other hosts from the other networks if it wants to communicate with them.

The straightforward solution is to store a list of all available hosts. We should copy this list to any computer that is connected to our network. When a new host appears, we should update the list everywhere. This solution is inconvenient to maintain.

Another approach is implementing a mechanism to discover available hosts. For example, our computer sends a request to all the other network nodes. Everybody who receives it should send their own MAC address back. This mechanism exists, and it is known as **Address Resolution Protocol** (ARP). ARP works a way that's a little bit more complicated. It allows specifying the host that we want to find. Then, only this host sends own MAC address back.

What is a protocol in terms of networks? It is some kind of agreement about data format. For example, our application sends game data. Should we keep the source and destination MAC addresses at the beginning of the packet or at the end? If we choose the beginning, the receiver should follow this decision too. Also, a protocol can define what network hosts should do in case of errors. For example, a server receives only half of the packet that a client sends. It can ask the client to repeat his transmission. Thus, the client should know the format of the special message that reports about the error that happened. The protocol specification covers all similar questions.

Let us return to our network. It is evident that we have a lot of data duplication because all hosts know each other. It will be much simpler if they know hosts of the same network only. If somebody wants to communicate with nodes of another network, it should ask a host that is between two networks to route a packet. This special host is named **router** or **gateway**. You can find it in Figure 4-3.

We reached the point where we need something more flexible than MAC addresses. If we want to route traffic between networks, it will be convenient to have a mechanism to assign specific addresses to the hosts. This mechanism should allow assigning ranges of the addresses for all hosts that belong to one network. Thus, when a gateway receives a packet, it can quickly calculate the destination address range and route a packet to the corresponding local network. These addresses, which we can assign to hosts, are known as IP addresses.

Now our game application and server communicate well even they are members of a big network. But what happens if we want to launch a chat application on the same computer where the game client works? Both chat and game applications should send and receive network packets. If the OS receives a network packet, its IP and MAC addresses match to the current host. However, we do not have information to route the packet to the correct application inside the computer. We should add some kind of unique identifiers to solve this issue. These identifiers are named **ports**.

The network packet should contain ports of both sender and receiver applications. Then, the OS transfers this packet correctly. The sender port is required because the receiver should be able to respond on the received packet.

You will notice that the implementation of our game application becomes very complicated. It should prepare a network packet that contains states of game objects, MAC addresses, IP addresses, and ports. Also, it will be good to append a checksum, which helps the server to verify the correctness of the received data. Do not forget about the server side. It should have the same algorithms to encode and decode both kinds of addresses, ports, game data, and checksum.

These algorithms look universal. Any application (for example, chat clients or web browsers) can use them to transfer its own data. Each network host should have these algorithms somewhere. The best solution is moving these algorithms to OS libraries. Now we come to the term "protocol stack." This is an implementation of a set of network protocols. The word "stack" appears because one protocol depends on another. Therefore, we have a hierarchical structure of them.

Some protocols have a lower **layer** than others. This means that they provide basic features that high-layer protocols use. For example, we have the IEEE 802.3 protocol, which defines how to transmit data via a twisted pair, and the IEEE 802.11 protocol for wireless connections (WiFi). Protocols of higher layers should have a possibility to use both connection types in the same way. So, there are several possible implementations available in each protocol layer. We can choose an appropriate implementation depending on our environment and requirements. When we have such a wide variety of implementations, it is quite important to define the responsibility of each protocol layer strictly. The **Open Systems Interconnection** (OSI) model is the standard that defines this responsibility.

We have considered the most important solutions that were made in the development of modern network communications. Now we have enough knowledge to investigate a real protocol stack, which is used everywhere on the Internet nowadays.

TCP/IP Stack

You can be surprised now. Why are we going to consider some TCP/IP stack? The Internet should use the "OSI stack." Two international committees (ISO and CCITT) have developed the OSI model over several years, and they made a well-designed standard that covers all possible network user requirements.

Some network developers and companies have tried to apply the OSI model in practice and implemented protocols for each its layers. However, all these projects failed. The main reason for this result is a significant redundancy of the OSI model. The functionalities of several layers overlap. Thus, network packets should contain duplicated data. Moreover, different layers of the protocol stack should share the same algorithms and execute them at runtime. Software developers should spend more effort and time to implement solutions according to the OSI model. Therefore, these solutions become more expensive.

Meanwhile, two researchers, Robert Kahn and Vinton Cerf, had developed the TCP/IP stack. They had finished their work before the OSI model was done. Robert and Vinton focused on solving the practical task of transferring data in the ARPANET. Probably, this is a reason why their solution is more effective and easier for implementation. Afterward, the IEEE committee published it as an open standard in 1974, while the OSI model was released only in 1984.

Then, big companies and small groups of developers started to implement their own versions of the TCP/IP stack for the OSs that were used at that time. This stack is relatively simple, and even one developer can implement it in a reasonable time. The solution became a de facto standard for the Internet in the short term because almost every host that was connected to the network had some version of it.

What is a difference between the OSI model and the TCP/IP stack? The TCP/IP stack follows the OSI model principle of splitting protocol responsibilities by layers, but it reduces the number of them. If the OSI model defines seven layers, the TCP/IP stack has only four. Table 4-1 shows how these layers correlate.

It is important to note that the TCP/IP stack does not consider network technologies at the hardware level. The OSI model covers them at its physical layer. This difference appears because the TCP/IP stack was designed as a hardware-independent solution. You can get comprehensive information about TCP/IP stack in the "The TCP/IP Guide" (`www.tcpipguide.com/free/index.htm`).

Table 4-1. *The Layers of the TCP/IP Stack and OSI Model*

TCP/IP Stack	OSI Model
Application	Application
	Presentation
	Session
Transport	Transport
Internet	Network
Link	Data link
	Physical

We will consider all layers of the TCP/IP stack in a real packet. Let us investigate it with the Wireshark analyzer. You should download and install the analyzer. Then download a sample of captured traffic from the Wiki page (wiki.wireshark.org/Sample Captures?action=AttachFile&do=get&target=http.cap). You can get the *http.cap* file with example traffic. Now, launch Wireshark and open the file. You can do this by pressing Ctrl+O. When you do this, the analyzer window should look like Figure 4-4 shows.

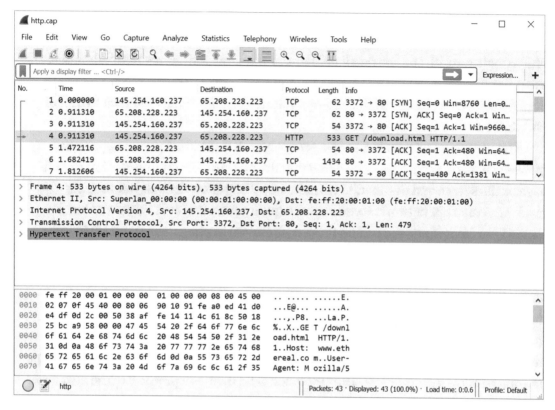

Figure 4-4. *IP packets in the Wireshark window*

The window has three parts. The upper one contains a list of captured packets. You can navigate through it and choose the packet that you want to analyze. When you do this, in the middle part of the window Wireshark shows you headers of all the protocols that this packet contains. Now if you choose one of these headers, in the bottom part of the window the analyzer highlights the corresponding bytes of the packet. You can get more details about the Wireshark interface in the official documentation (`www.wireshark.org/docs/wsug_html_chunked/ChUseMainWindowSection.html`).

We will consider packet number 4 in the captured list. It is a typical web browser request to load some page from the Internet. According to Table 4-1, protocols of the link layer is a bottom level of the TCP/IP stack. These protocols respond for packet transmission in the local networks. As you remember, if two hosts communicate in the local network, they should know each other's MAC addresses. It will be enough for a switch device to route a packet to the right receiver.

The packet sender uses the **Ethernet II** link layer protocol. You can find the corresponding header in the Wireshark window. If you expand this header (click the triangle near it), you see that it contains destination and source MAC addresses. Also, there is a type field of two bytes. It defines a protocol of the next layer, which is transferred as the payload of the Ethernet frame. The type equals **Internet Protocol Version 4** or IPv4 (0x0800) in our case.

The IPv4 protocol matches the **Internet layer**. It responds for routing packets between networks. We have considered that the most important information for this layer is the source and destination IP addresses. They allow the gateway to route packets to the right network. If you expand the "Internet Protocol Version 4" header in the Wireshark window, you find these addresses. Also, there are several fields that assist the task of routing packets. For example, there is a "Time to live" value. It defines the maximum time in which a packet can be transferred in the network. If this time is exceeded, the gateway drops this packet. The "Identification" and "Fragment offset" fields store information for the fragmentation mechanism. It allows splitting large packets into pieces (also known as fragments) and transferring them through the network. This mechanism is required because most of the networks have a limit for the maximum allowed packet size. The "Protocol" field defines a protocol of the next layer. For our case, it is **Transmission Control Protocol** (TCP).

The **transport layer** establishes a connection between processes that work on communicating hosts. The most important information for this connection is the port numbers, which identify the sender and receiver processes. You can expand the "Transmission Control Protocol" header in the Wireshark window and see the values of "Source Port" (equals 3372) and "Destination Port" (equals 80). Also, there are "Sequence number" and "Acknowledgment number" fields. These fields contain counters that are used to establish and terminate a connection between the processes. Also, the receiver uses these counters to detect if some packet was lost.

Nowadays, we have two protocols of the transport layer that are most widely used on the Internet. These are TCP and the **User Datagram Protocol** (UDP). The primary difference between them is the reliability of data transfer. The TCP protocol has a mechanism to check if all sent packets reach the receiver. If the receiver loses some packets, it asks the sender to retransmit them. The UDP protocol does not have this mechanism. The receiver does not check the sequence of the incoming packets, so it ignores the lost ones.

Why do we want to use such an unreliable protocol as UDP? The TCP protocol has one significant drawback. The mechanism of detecting lost packets leads to a considerable overhead. Let us assume that we transfer a video stream. If we lose one video frame, it does not matter. We can continue showing the video from the frame that comes after the lost one. However, if we use the TCP protocol for this transfer, our application asks the sender to resend the lost video frame. So, the sender does it instead of sending the next frame. In this case, we will see how our video hangs for a very short moment because the player application does not have the next video frame. If we use the UDP protocol, we avoid hanging. It is very probable that a user does not even notice the lost frame.

The topmost layer of the TCP/IP stack is the application layer. The stack does not restrict its data format. So, communicating applications can choose their order to store data in the packet.

Our example packet has **Hypertext Transfer Protocol** (HTTP) on the application layer. You can see in the Wireshark window that this protocol keeps data in the plaintext format. You can read it without any decryption and assume its meaning. In our case, the host asks the web server with the "`www.ethereal.com`" **Uniform Resource Locator** (URL) or web address to send back the "download.html" page. The URL is some kind of alias for the IP address. It was invented to simplify usage of the **World Wide Web** (WWW) because now users can remember website names instead of thier IP addresses.

Packet Analysis

Now, we have a basic understanding of Internet protocols. Let us consider a way to capture the traffic between two applications and analyze it. It is the first step of developing any out-game bot.

Test Application

We start considering approaches to traffic analysis by writing a simple client-server application that transfers raw bytes. The application consists of two parts: a receiver and a sender. They both work on the same host. Thanks to the loopback interface, they can communicate with each other. Wireshark allows us to capture their traffic.

Before we implement the application, we should consider one important resource of OS, which is named **network socket** or socket. As you remember, TCP and UDP headers have source and destination ports. They allow distinguishing sender and receiver applications of the communicating hosts.

Let us assume that we launch a game and chat client on our host. What happens if both applications want to use the same port for communication with their servers? Potentially, each application can choose any port. You can suggest reserving port numbers for specific applications for resolving such port conflicts. This solution was already applied. The port numbers from 0 to 1023 are officially reserved for particular cases (for example, port 80 is reserved for HTTP traffic), and you should not use them in your applications. However, we have the port range from 1024 to 65535, which is not reserved.

It is evident that somebody should manage the port assignment among applications. OS responds to this task. When an application wants to use some port, it asks OS to provide a socket. The socket is an abstraction for communication endpoint. This abstraction contains the IP address, port number, and connection state. Usually, applications do not share sockets, so an application owns the socket and releases it when it is not required anymore.

There are several types of sockets that depend on the protocol features. We will consider these types further when we will apply sockets in our test applications.

Our first test application transfers a single data packet via the TCP protocol. It consists of two Python scripts: *TestTcpReceiver.py* (see Listing 4-1) and *TestTcpSender.py* (see Listing 4-2). They work according to the following algorithm:

1. The *TestTcpReceiver.py* script starts first. It opens the TCP socket, which is bound to the 24000 port and localhost address (127.0.0.1 by default). Sockets of such configuration are known as **server TCP sockets**.

2. The *TestTcpReceiver.py* script expects the packet, which should come to its socket. We would say that it **listens** to port number 24000 for connections.

3. The *TestTcpSender.py* starts second. It opens the TCP socket but does not bind it to a specific IP address and port. This kind of socket is known as **client TCP socket**.

4. The *TestTcpSender.py* connects to the receiver socket, which has the 127.0.0.1 address and the 24000 port number. Then it sends the data packet. In this case, OS decides which IP address and port should be assigned to the sender. It means that *TestTcpSender.py* cannot choose it. After sending the packet, the script releases the socket.

5. *TestTcpReceiver.py* detects a new connection from the sender. It accepts the connection, receives the packet, prints its data, and releases the socket.

We have considered the algorithm of application work. It looks very straightforward, but OS hides several steps of establishing and terminating a TCP connection. We will see these steps in the captured traffic.

Listing 4-1. The `TestTcpReceiver.py` Script

```
import socket

def main():
  s = socket.socket(socket.AF_INET, socket.SOCK_STREAM, 0)
  s.bind(("127.0.0.1", 24000))
  s.listen(1)
  conn, addr = s.accept()
  data = conn.recv(1024, socket.MSG_WAITALL)
  print(data)
  s.close()

if __name__ == '__main__':
  main()
```

The *TestTcpReceiver.py* script uses the *socket* module, which provides access to the corresponding OS resources. Let us consider the *main* function step by step.

The first action is a call of the *socket* function, which is provided by the *socket* module. It creates a new socket object. The function has three parameters:

- The address family, which can be equal to *AF_INET* (IPv4), *AF_INET6* (IPv6), or *AF_UNIX* (local communication).

- The socket type: SOCK_STREAM (TCP), SOCK_DGRAM (UDP), or SOCK_RAW (no protocol specified).

- The protocol number. This is used when several protocols match the combination of the address family and socket type parameters. This parameter equals 0 in most cases.

We create the socket, which uses the IPv4 and TCP protocols.

The next step of our script is to bind a socket to the specific address and port. When this is done, we call the *listen* method to start listening to the socket for a new connection. The function has only one parameter, which defines the maximum number of the allowed connections. The *TestTcpReceiver.py* script stops execution at this point because the *listen* call does not return control until somebody connects to the socket.

When the *TestTcpSender.py* script tries to reach us, we accept this connection with the *accept* call. This call returns two values: a connection object (which is *conn* in our case) and the sender address (*addr*). The address value is a pair of the IP address and port.

We use a *recv* method of the *conn* object to read data of the received packet from the socket. Then we print them to the console with the *print* function.

The last step is releasing the socket via the *close* call. This call returns the resource to the OS. Now, another application can listen to the 24000 port.

Listing 4-2 demonstrates the implementation of the *TestTcpSender.py* script.

Listing 4-2. The TestTcpSender.py Script

```
import socket

def main():
    s = socket.socket(socket.AF_INET, socket.SOCK_STREAM, 0)
    s.settimeout(2)
    s.connect(("127.0.0.1", 24000))
```

```
    s.send(bytes([44, 55, 66]))
    s.close()

if __name__ == '__main__':
    main()
```

Here we create a similar socket object, which uses IPv4 and TCP protocols. Then we set the timeout for establishing a TCP connection via the *settimeout* method. If the receiver does not accept a connection during the timeout, the sender cancels it.

The next step is establishing a connection via the *connect* method call. It has one parameter, which is a pair of IP address and port. In Python, we use round brackets to make a pair of values. The *connect* method returns control when the connection is established successfully. At this moment, we are ready to transfer the packet. We do this with the *send* method. In our case, we send three bytes. Then, we release the socket with the *close* method.

Before starting the application, you should clarify an IP address of your loopback interface. These are the steps to do it:

1. Open the "Network Connections" window.

2. Right-click the "Microsoft Loopback Adapter" icon. Choose the "Status" option.

3. Press the "Details..." button. You will see the "Network Connection Details" window, which shows the IPv4 address.

Change the addresses in both scripts. In the *TestTcpReceiver.py* script, you should fix the *bind* method call. In the *TestTcpSender.py* script, the *connect* call should be changed.

I recommend that you launch our scripts from the Command Prompt application. It allows you to see the console output. If you start the receiver script first and the sender after, the receiver prints the transferred three bytes.

Packet Capture

Now we apply the Wireshark analyzer to capture the traffic of our test application. These are the steps to do it:

1. Launch the Wireshark. You will see a list of active network interfaces in its window as Figure 4-5 shows.

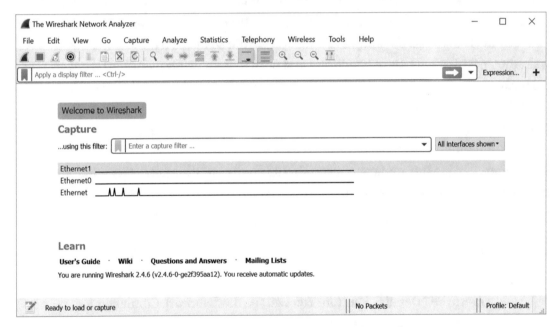

Figure 4-5. *A list of active network adapters in the Wireshark window*

2. Double-click a name of the loopback interface in the list. You can clarify this name in the "Network Connections" window (it is available from the "Network and Sharing Center"). After this action, Wireshark starts to capture all traffic that is passed via the selected interface.

3. Launch the *TestTcpReceiver.py* script.

4. Launch the *TestTcpSender.py* script.

5. You will see the captured packets in the Wireshark window as Figure 4-6 shows.

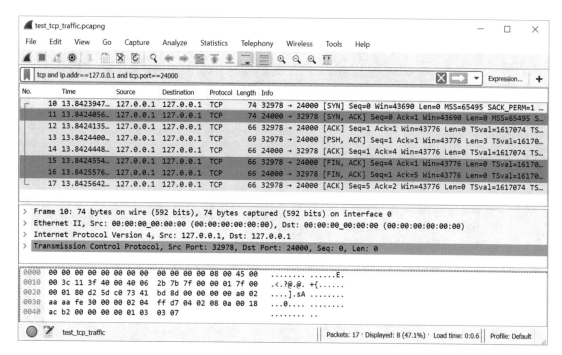

Figure 4-6. *Captured packets of the test application*

OS or some other applications can use the interface that you are monitoring. In this case, you will see their packets in the list. The Wireshark provides a feature for filtering them.

There is the line below the top panel with icons. It has the "Apply a display filter ..." text when it is empty. Here you can type the filter rules. When you do it, you should press the arrow icon near the "Expression..." button to apply the filter. Then in the list, you will see only packets that fit the inserted rules.

We apply the following filter to get only packets of our test application:

```
tcp and ip.addr==127.0.0.1 and tcp.port==24000
```

This filter contains three conditions. The first condition, which equals "tcp", excludes all non-TCP packets from the list. The next one, the "ip.addr==127.0.0.1" condition, selects the packets that have the specified IP address as the source or destination. The last, the "tcp.port==24000" condition, specifies the source or destination TCP port.

There are two options to specify the filter rules. The first option is to type a text (for example, the one we considered previously). Another option is using the "Display Filter Expression" dialog (Figure 4-7 shows it). You can open this dialog by pressing the "Expression..." button.

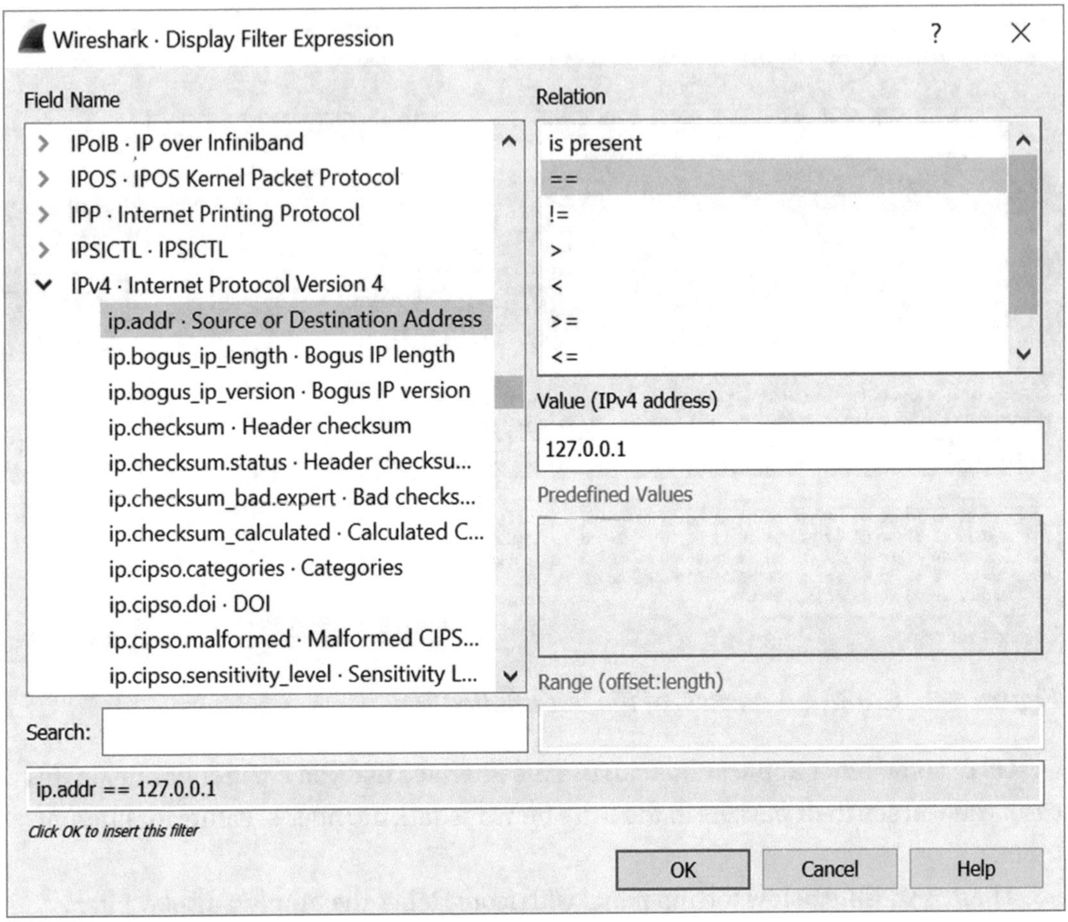

Figure 4-7. The Display Filter Expression dialog

The dialog has a list (with a "Field Name" caption) of all supported protocols and fields of their headers. The "Relation" list has comparison operators, which you can apply to the selected field. Below this list, there is a "Value" line, where you can type a value to compare. At the bottom of the dialog, you can see the green line with a text of the resulting filter. If you make a mistake in the filter rule, this line becomes red.

The filter mechanism is a powerful tool to simplify packet analysis. You should apply it any time when you use Wireshark. It will speed up your work significantly.

Let us come back to the captured packets of our test application (Figure 4-6). You might ask why we have eight packets here despite the fact that we send only one packet.

The data transfer happens in the packet number 13 on the screenshot. Packets 10, 11, and 12, which come before, respond by establishing the TCP connection. This process is known as the **three-way handshake**. Here are its steps:

1. The client (*TestTcpSender.py* script) sends the first packet (number 10) to the server. This packet has the SYN flag set in its TCP header. This means that the client wants to establish a TCP connection and sends own sequence number (seq), which equals 0, to the server. You can apply the following Wireshark filter to find SYN packets:

   ```
   tcp.flags.syn==1 and tcp.seq==0 and tcp.ack==0
   ```

2. The server (*TestTcpReceiver.py* script) answers with packet number 11, which has the SYN and ACK flags set. It has the acknowledgment number (ack), which equals the received client's seq plus one. This ack confirms client's seq. Also, the packet contains the seq number of the server (equals 0).
   The filter to find this server response in the log is

   ```
   tcp.flags.syn==1 and tcp.flags.ack==1 and tcp.seq==0
   and tcp.ack==1
   ```

3. The client answers with packet number 12, which has the ACK flag. The ack number of the packet (equals 1) confirms the server's seq. After this step, both client and server confirmed their seq numbers and can communicate with each other.
   The filter for the client answer looks like this:

   ```
   tcp.flags.syn==0 and tcp.flags.ack==1 and tcp.flags.push==0
   and tcp.seq==1 and tcp.ack==1
   ```

You can consider client and server states during the connection establishment in the article www.tcpipguide.com/free/t_ TCPConnectionEstablishmentProcessTheThreeWayHandsh-3.htm.

You can notice that we check the PUSH flag in our last filter. This flag signals that the corresponding packet contains an actual user data. You can apply the following filter to see only this kind of packet:

```
tcp.flags.push==1
```

To see data that our application transfers, you should choose the packet with the PUSH flag set (number 13). Then click the "Data" item in the header list. After this action, the corresponding bytes of the packet become highlighted in the bottom part of the Wireshark window as Figure 4-8 shows.

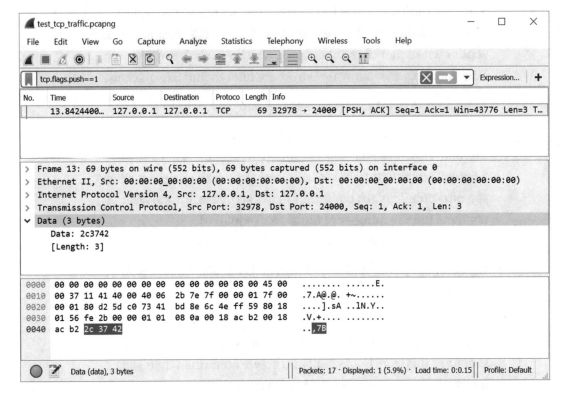

Figure 4-8. The captured data packet

We can see that the client transfers three bytes in hexadecimal: 2C, 37, and 42. They match to the decimal numbers 44, 55, and 66, respectively. You can clarify in the *TestTcpSender.py* script that it sends exactly these three numbers.

You can notice in Figure 4-6 that the following packet (number 14) has the ack number equal to four. What does it mean? When the connection is established, the seq and ack numbers are used to confirm a byte number, which the server receives from the client. Thus, when the server gets data, it answers with the packet, which has the following ack:

```
ack = client seq + data length
```

In our case, this formula looks as follows:

ack = 1 + 3 = 4

You can always check the client's seq number for this formula in packets with the
PUSH flag (number 13 in our case).

Figure 4-9 demonstrates a series of the transferred PUSH packets from the client.
You can see increasing seq and ack numbers during this communication. Each server
confirmation has an ack, which is calculated according to our formula.

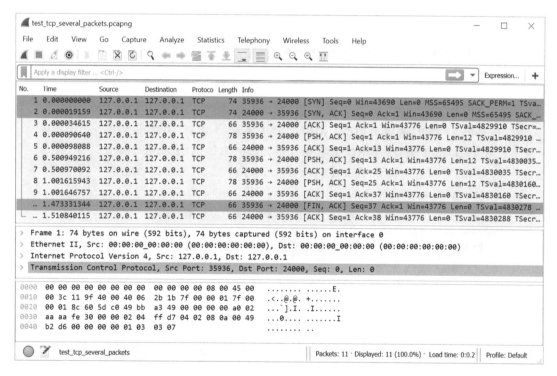

Figure 4-9. *The series of TCP packets*

You can notice that packets that our client sends have destination port number
24000. Their source port equals 35936 in Figure 4-9, and it equals 32978 in Figure 4-6. As
you remember, an OS reassigns the port for the TCP client each time it establishes a new
connection. The port number is chosen randomly, and we cannot predict its value. Thus,
if you analyze TCP packets in a Wireshark log, it is better to filter them by the destination
port instead of the source one.

Let us come back to Figure 4-6, where we transferred one packet with data. After the server's confirmation (packet number 14), we have three packets (numbers 15, 16, 17) to terminate the TCP connection. This termination has the following steps:

1. The client sends packet number 15, which has the FIN flag set. This means that the host wants to close the connection. In our case, this packet has the ACK flag too. It is the acknowledgment for the previously received server's packet (number 14), which has the seq equal to 1.
    The filter to find this packet in the log is

    ```
    tcp.flags.fin==1 and tcp.dstport==24000
    ```

2. The server responds with packet number 16, which has the ACK and FIN flags set. The ACK flag means that the server confirms the client's FIN request to close the connection. The ack number of the packet equals the client's seq plus one (it is five in our case). The FIN flag means that the server asks the client to close the connection on his side.
    You can find this packet in the log with the following filter:

    ```
    tcp.flags.fin==1 and tcp.dstport==32978
    ```

3. The client responds with packet number 17 with the ACK flag set. This means that the client confirms the closing communication. This packet has a seq number that equals the last received server's ack.
    The filter for this case looks as follows:

    ```
    tcp.flags.ack==1 and tcp.seq==5 and tcp.dstport==24000
    ```

You may notice that we should consider the seq number in our filter to find the last client's ACK packet.

More information about TCP connection termination is available in the article www.tcpipguide.com/free/t_TCPConnectionTermination-2.htm.

UDP Connection

We have considered the test application that transfers data via the TCP protocol. We know how to capture this traffic and analyze it. However, some games can use the UDP protocol for communication.

Let us apply the UDP protocol instead of TCP in our second test application and consider this case. Now, the app has the following algorithm:

1. The *TestUdpReceiver.py* script (see Listing 4-3) starts first. It opens the UDP socket, which is bound to the 24000 port and localhost address. Despite the TCP socket, it can behave as a server and client (i.e., both sides can initiate a connection).

2. The *TestUdpReceiver.py* script expects the packet from the sender.

3. The *TestUdpSender.py* (see Listing 4-4) starts second. It opens the UDP socket and binds it to the 24001 port and localhost address. This step is not mandatory. OS can assign a random port to the UDP packet sender. However, it can be useful if we decide to transfer data in both directions with the same pair of sockets.

4. The *TestUdpSender.py* sends the data packet. Then it releases the socket.

5. The *TestUdpReceiver.py* receives the packet, prints its contents, and releases the socket.

You can see that the algorithm of the modified test application becomes simpler than it was for the TCP protocol case. We should not establish and terminate the connection. All that we do is just send one packet with data.

Listing 4-3. The TestUdpReceiver.py Script

```python
import socket

def main():
  s = socket.socket(socket.AF_INET, socket.SOCK_DGRAM, 0)
  s.bind(("127.0.0.1", 24000))
  data, addr = s.recvfrom(1024, socket.MSG_WAITALL)
```

```
    print(data)
    s.close()

if __name__ == '__main__':
    main()
```

The *TestUdpReceiver.py* script has the same steps as the *TestTcpReceiver.py* one except for listening to the socket and accepting an incoming connection. Now we specify the *SOCK_DGRAM* socket type to apply the UDP protocol. We use the *recvfrom* method of the socket object to receive the data. Despite the *recv* method, which we have used for the TCP connection, it returns a pair of values: received data and sender IP address. The address can be useful if we want to respond. You may notice that we do not call the accept method now. This means that the *recvfrom* method is only one way to get the sender address. If you do not plan to answer for the received packet, you can still use the *recv* method.

Listing 4-4. The TestUdpSender.py Script

```
import socket

def main():
    s = socket.socket(socket.AF_INET, socket.SOCK_DGRAM, 0)
    s.bind(("127.0.0.1", 24001))
    s.sendto(bytes([44, 55, 66]), ("127.0.0.1", 24000))
    s.close()

if __name__ == '__main__':
    main()
```

In the *TestUdpSender.py script,* we apply the UDP protocol too with the *SOCK_DGRAM* socket type. Now we do not need any timeout, which is set by the *settimeout* method. This happens because we do not expect any confirmation from the receiver that the connection was established or that our packet passes well. Instead, we send data and close the socket.

You can launch Wireshark, start capturing a traffic on the loopback interface, and then launch the *TestUdpReceiver.py* and *TestUdpSender.py* scripts. Figure 4-10 shows what you should get.

You can apply the following filter to see the traffic of our test application only:

```
udp.port==24000
```

Now we have only one packet, which contains three bytes of data: 2C, 37, and 42.

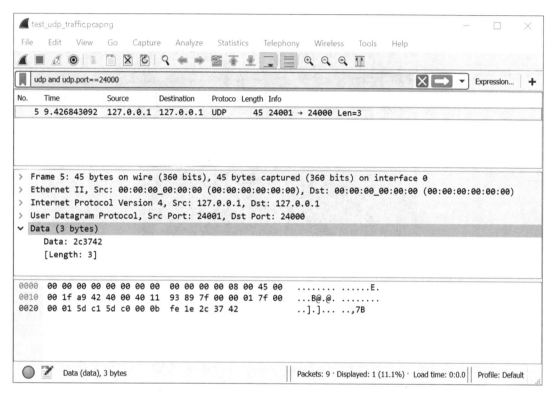

Figure 4-10. The captured UDP packet

Example with NetChess

We now have enough knowledge to write a simple out-game bot. It will make turns in the NetChess application. This application is a small chess game client and server that allows two people to play together via a local network. You can download it for free on the Sourceforge website (sourceforge.net/projects/avmnetchess). When you download the archive with the game, you should unpack it to any directory.

Let us consider the game interface in detail. Figure 4-11 shows the main window of NetChess. You can see the chessboard and pieces there. There is a menu on the top side of the window. A row of icons below the menu duplicates some of its items.

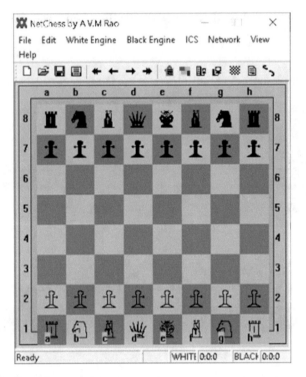

Figure 4-11. *The NetChess window*

To start playing, you should configure your application as a server. Then another player connects to you as a client, and a game begins.

The NetChess server and client can work on the same host. You can launch and connect them via the loopback interface. Please check that you configured and enabled this interface correctly.

These are the steps to launch the NetChess game:

1. Launch the *NetChess2.1.exe* binary from the *Debug* subdirectory two times. You get two NetChess processes. Choose one of them for yourself, which becomes a server. Then another is a client.

2. Switch to the NetChess server window and choose the "Network" ➤ "Server" menu item. You will see the server configuration dialog as Figure 4-12 shows.

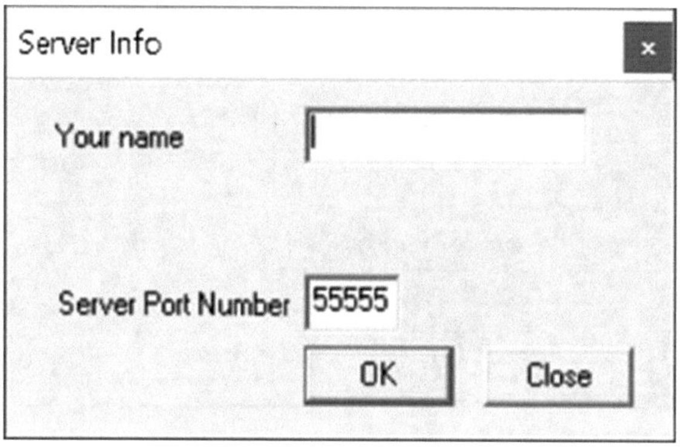

Figure 4-12. *The server configuration dialog*

3. Type a user name, who plays on the server side, in the dialog and press the "OK" button.

4. Switch to the NetChess client window and choose the "Network" ➤ "Client" menu item. You will see the client configuration dialog as Figure 4-13 shows.

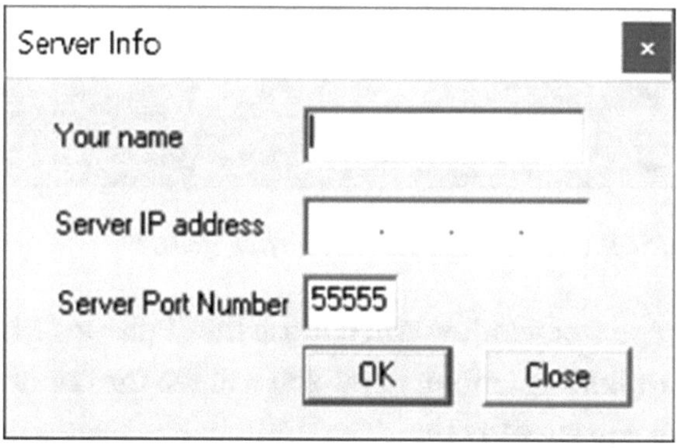

Figure 4-13. *The client configuration dialog*

5. Type a name of the client-side user and the server's IP address (which is 169.254.144.77, for example) in the dialog. Then press the "OK" button.

6. Switch to the server window. When the client tries to connect, the "Accept" dialog appears (see Figure 4-14). You should pick your side (white or black) in this dialog. Also, there is a "Toss" option, which picks your side randomly. When you are done, press the "Accept" button.

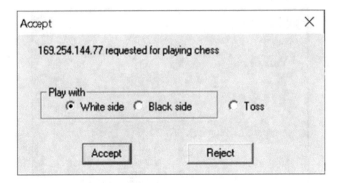

Figure 4-14. *The "Accept" dialog on the server side*

7. Switch to the client window. You will see a confirmation of a successful connection to the server. This message contains a name and side of your opponent (see Figure 4-15).

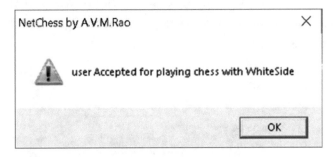

Figure 4-15. *The dialog with connection confirmation*

8. Switch to the server window and choose the "Edit" ➤ "Manual Edit" ➤ "Start Editing" menu item. You will see the confirmation dialog where you should press "Yes" button. It activates the mode that allows starting a game clock.

9. Switch to the client window and confirm activation of the "Manual Edit" mode in the dialog. You should press the "Yes" button there.

10. Switch to the server window. You will see the notification that the client has confirmed the "Manual Edit" mode. Close it with an "OK" button click. Then choose the "Edit" ➤ "Manual Edit" ➤ "Pause clock" menu item.

Now, the game clock starts, and the white side can take the first turn. To do this, you should drag and drop a piece to a new square on the chessboard.

Bot Overview

Our out-game bot should connect to the game server. Thus, it replaces the game client completely.

There are several options for how the bot can choose its turns. I suggest the most straightforward solution because now we are considering communication with the game server but not advanced chess algorithms. The bot will copy the player's turns like a mirror until it cannot do so. This task sounds easy, but it requires investigation of the traffic between the server and client.

You can find the source files of the NetChess game on the Internet. If you read them, you can quickly understand the application protocol. We will not follow this way. Let us assume that NetChess is a proprietary game, and its source code is not available to us. All that we have is captured traffic between the server and client.

NetChess Traffic Analysis

We have considered how to start a game with the NetChess client and server. So, we are ready to gather their traffic for analysis. Before we do it, let us consider a couple of questions.

How can we distinguish the traffic of the NetChess application in our Wireshark log? If we use a real network interface instead of the loopback one, we get packets that were sent and received by all launched applications at the moment. For the NetChess case, we can distinguish its traffic by the port number. When we start the server side, we should specify the port number to bind. It is 55555 by default. Thus, we can apply the following Wireshark filter to get game packets only:

```
tcp.port==55555
```

The next question is how we should gather the NetChess traffic. The most straightforward way is to launch Wireshark, capture the loopback interface, and play several games with NetChess client and server. In this case, we lose valuable information that can help a lot with understanding the traffic. When we get packets of several games, we cannot match these packets to the player's actions. For example, which packet contains information about the first turn of the white side? We get dozens of them in the log and cannot find a moment when the game has started. Therefore, we should check our Wireshark log after each action and monitor the transferred packets that match this action.

Now let us launch Wireshark, along with the NetChess server and client. The analyzer should capture the loopback interface. Then, we do the following actions:

1. Start the NetChess server ("Network" ➤ "Server"). After this action, we do not get any packets in the Wireshark log. This happens because the server opens a socket without sending something.

2. Connect a client to the server ("Network" ➤ "Client"). You will get three-step handshake packets that establish a typical TCP connection, as Figure 4-16 shows.

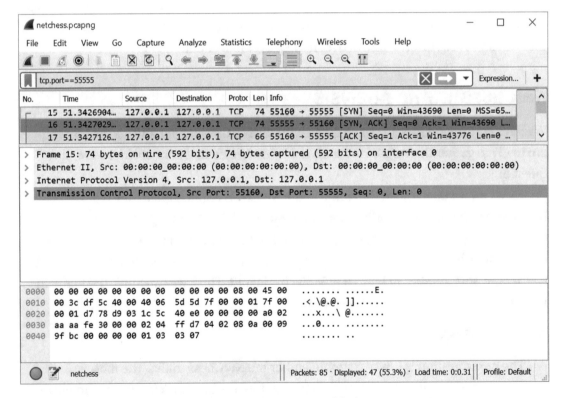

Figure 4-16. *The NetChess server and client establish a connection*

3. The server accepts client's connection. After this action, you will get two packets from the server. The client sends responses with acknowledgments (see Figure 4-17). Then it sends two packets with data.

Let us stop at this point and consider two packets from the server. The first one (number 22 in Figure 4-17) has the following data:

`0f 00 00 00`

If you restart the NetChess application and establish the connection again, you get the same data. Probably, it means that the server accepts the client's connection. To check our assumption, we should try to reject the connection on the server side. If you do so, you see the following server response:

`01 00 00 00`

We can conclude that our assumption is correct. The first 0f byte matches the case when the connection is accepted. Otherwise, this byte equals 01.

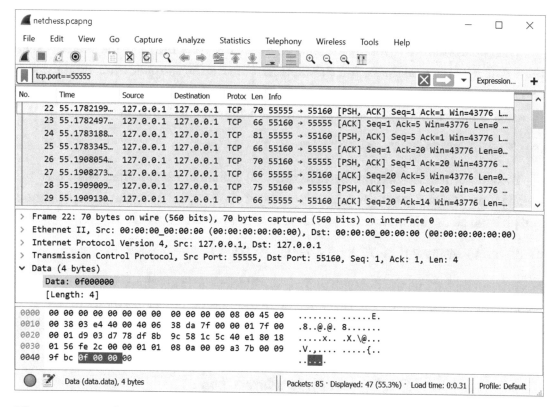

Figure 4-17. *The NetChess server accepts the connection*

The second packet from the server (number 24) contains the following bytes:

```
0b 02 46 6d e7 5a 73 72 76 5f 75 73 65 72 00
```

These bytes match the case when the server user chooses the white side and the "srv_user" name. Wireshark can decode this data partially. You can see in Figure 4-18 that the bytes from the 7th to the 15th match the username.

```
0000   00 00 00 00 00 00 00 00   00 00 00 00 08 00 45 00    ........  ......E.
0010   00 43 fe c5 40 00 40 06   3d ed 7f 00 00 01 7f 00    .C..@.@.  =.......
0020   00 01 d9 03 aa 17 57 1f   de fc 91 d6 17 9c 80 18    ......W.  ........
0030   01 56 fe 37 00 00 01 01   08 0a 00 1e 2e 9c 00 1e    .V.7....  ........
0040   2e 9c 0b 02 46 6d e7 5a   73 72 76 5f 75 73 65 72    ....Fm.Z  srv_user
0050   00                                                   .
```

Figure 4-18. Wireshark decodes data of the second packet from the server

What do the first six bytes mean? You can repeat our trick and force the server to send these data again several times. You should restart the NetChess application, establish the connection, and pick the same username and the white side for the server player.

After restarting the application, I get the following data in this packet:

```
0b 02 99 b3 ee 5a 73 72 76 5f 75 73 65 72 00
```

You can see that the first two bytes (0b and 02) remain the same. This means that they contain a color of a side that the server player chooses. Let us restart the application and pick the black side on the server. The data of this packet changes:

```
0b 01 ba 45 e8 5a 73 72 76 5f 75 73 65 72 00
```

You can repeat this test but with picking the black side. Every time, you will get the second byte equaling to 01. We can conclude that it stores a side of the server player as Table 4-2 shows. Thanks to this information, our bot can determine the color for its side.

Table 4-2. Encoding a Color of the Side That the Server Player Chose

Byte	Side
01	Black
02	White

The next two packets, which contain application data, come from the client. The first of these packets (number 26) has the following payload:

```
09 00 00 00
```

If we try to change a server player name or side, these bytes remain the same. We can assume that this is a constant response from the client.

The next packet (number 28) has the following bytes:

```
0c 63 6c 5f 75 73 65 72 00
```

Wireshark decodes these bytes as a name of the client player, as Figure 4-19 shows. There is the first byte "0c" only, which does not have a clear meaning. We can check that it always keeps the same value after restarting the application. Thus, our bot can treat it as the constant.

```
0000  00 00 00 00 00 00 00 00  00 00 00 00 08 00 45 00   ........ ......E.
0010  00 3d 37 ac 40 00 40 06  05 0d 7f 00 00 01 7f 00   .=7.@.@. ........
0020  00 01 aa 17 d9 03 91 d6  17 a0 57 1f df 0b 80 18   ........ ..W.....
0030  01 56 fe 31 00 00 01 01  08 0a 00 1e 2e a1 00 1e   .V.1.... ........
0040  2e a1 0c 63 6c 5f 75 73  65 72 00                  ...cl_us er.
```

Figure 4-19. *Wireshark decodes data of the second packet from the client*

Let us continue preparing the NetChess application for starting the game. The next step is enabling the "Manual Edit" mode on the server ("Edit" ➤ "Manual Edit" ➤ "Start Editing"). After this action, the server sends two packets to the client.

The first packet (number 41 in Figure 4-20) has the following data:

```
0a 00 00 00
```

It is probable that the 0a byte matches the code of the server's request.

This is data of the next packet (number 43):

```
13 73 72 76 5f 75 73 65 72 00
```

We already know that the bytes from the 2nd to the 9th match the "srv_user" string. The first byte (13) is a constant and our bot can ignore it.

When the client accepts the "Manual Edit" mode, it sends two packets (number 45 and 47) with the following data:

01 00 00 00

17

Our bot should repeat them without any changes when it receives the corresponding request from the server.

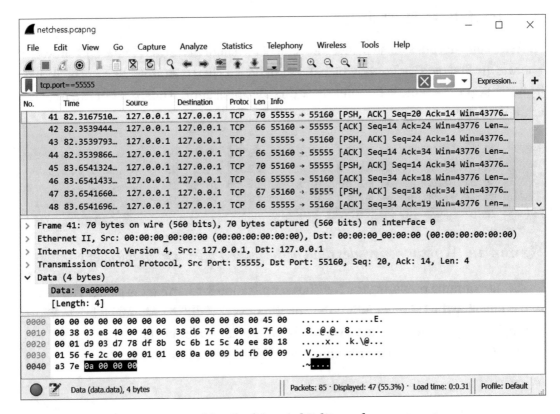

Figure 4-20. *The server enables the Manual Edit mode*

The last step to start a game is launching the clock. When the server does this action, it sends two packets (number 54 and 56 in Figure 4-21) with the following data:

02 00 00 00

22 00

The client does not respond to these packets, so our bot can ignore them.

All further packets (from number 58) contain the players' turns. The white side (the server in our case) moves first. After each turn, we capture two packets with corresponding data.

The first "e2-e4" turn of the white side matches two packets with the following data:

```
07 00 00 00
00 00 06 04 04 04 00
```

If you continue doing turns, you see that the data of the first packet remains the same. We can conclude that it is constant. So, if our bot receives data with the first byte equal to 07, the next packet contains details of the opponent's turn.

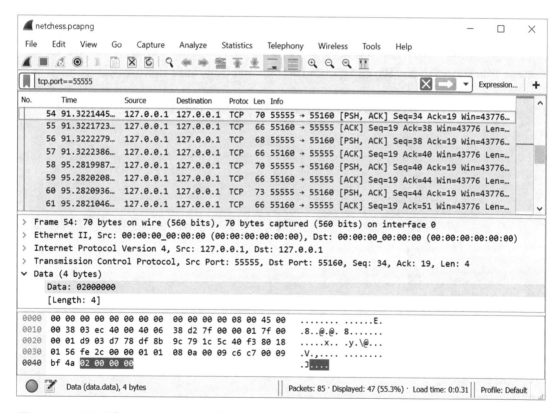

Figure 4-21. *The server starts the game clock*

Now comes the most crucial question: how can we decode the turn data? Let us think about the chessboard. Each square is labeled by a letter (a to h) and number (1 to 8). It is evident that each turn contains the current and the target squares of the moving piece.

The data of our packet with the turn information contains four nonzeroed bytes. You can do several more turns and see that the zeroed bytes do not change. This means that the current and target squares of a piece are encoded in these four bytes. Probably, two bytes define one square.

Let us assume that the current position of a piece comes first. It means that the "e2" square matches the 06 04 bytes. Then the "e4" square matches the 04 04 bytes. The letters of these two squares are the same. Thus, we assume that the second 04 byte in these pairs matches the "e" letter.

Now you should do the turn on a chessboard column with another letter to check our assumption. If you do the "d2-d4" turn, you will get the following packet:

```
00 00 06 03 04 03 00
```

It means that the 03 byte matches the "d" letter. It is logical to assume that the letter codes come successively. We can gather them in one table (see Table 4-3).

Table 4-3. *The Codes of Squares' Letters*

Byte	Letter
00	a
01	b
02	c
03	d
04	e
05	f
06	g
07	h

We start to fill the left column of Table 4-3 from the 04 and 03 values, which we already know. Then, we continue to fill the cells above 03 with the values 02, 01, 00. In the same way, we fill the values below 04.

We can do a similar table for the square numbers. We already know that the code 06 matches number 2 and the number 4 is 04. You can put these values in the table and continue filling the rest of the cells. You will get the same values as in Table 4-4.

You can test our assumptions by moving pieces around the chessboard. These assumptions should be correct.

Now, we know everything about the game protocol that is required to implement our bot.

Table 4-4. *The Codes of Squares' Numbers*

Byte	Number
07	1
06	2
05	3
04	4
03	5
02	6
01	7
00	8

Bot Implementation

The first task that our bot should solve is starting the game as a client. We know all packets that the server sends to the client and vice versa. Let us implement the script that answers to the server's packets correctly and starts the game. Listing 4-5 demonstrates this script.

Listing 4-5. The StartGameBot.py Script

```
import socket

def main():
  s = socket.socket(socket.AF_INET, socket.SOCK_STREAM, 0)
  s.settimeout(60)
  s.connect(("127.0.0.1", 55555))

  # recv - server confirmation
  s.recv(1024, socket.MSG_WAITALL)
  s.recv(1024, socket.MSG_WAITALL)
```

```python
    # send - client username
    s.send(bytes([0x09, 0, 0, 0]))
    s.send(bytes([0x0C, 0x63, 0x6C, 0x5F, 0x75, 0x73, 0x65, 0x72, 0x00]))

    # recv - manual edit mode
    s.recv(1024, socket.MSG_WAITALL)
    s.recv(1024, socket.MSG_WAITALL)

    # send - client confirmation for manual edit mode
    s.send(bytes([0x01, 0, 0, 0]))
    s.send(bytes([0x17]))

    # recv - launch the game clock
    s.recv(1024, socket.MSG_WAITALL)
    s.recv(1024, socket.MSG_WAITALL)

    s.close()

if __name__ == '__main__':
    main()
```

The *StartGameBot.py* script has lines that contain comments instead of code. They start with the number sign (#).

The first three lines of the *main* function in Listing 4-5 establish a TCP connection. You can see that we set a timeout for 60 seconds. This is a time during which the *recv* calls wait for the server packet. In other words, it is a time for a human player to make his turn.

Then we do two *recv* calls, which receive the server confirmation about a successful connection establishing. We are not interested in a username and the side of the server player. Thus, we do not assign the received data to any variables.

You might ask why the human player side is not important for our bot. To answer this question, let us ask another one. Can our bot play on either side? No, it cannot. We are implementing the "mirror" bot, which repeats player's turns. Thus, it can make its turn only after a human player. Therefore, our bot can play the black side only.

After receiving the server confirmation, the bot sends its name. It is "cl_user", which equals the "63 6C 5F 75 73 65 72" byte array. Before the name, there is a constant 0C byte.

The next step is receiving the server's request to enable the "Manual Edit" mode. When the packet comes, the bot sends the confirmation back.

The last step is activating the game clocks by the server. The corresponding packets do not require an answer.

You may ask whether it is possible to skip uninteresting packets from the server and not call the *recv* method for them. In theory, our bot needs packets with information about player's turns only. So, it can ignore all other stuff. However, the bot should know the moments when it should take its own turns. Let us assume that we stop the bot until one of these moments.

Now the question becomes, what is the moment when the bot should wake up and do his turn? This time depends on the human player: how quickly does he configure the server side? One time it can take 15 seconds and another time up to one minute. It means that we cannot predict when our bot should wake up. Therefore, the primary purpose of receiving all of the server's packets is to get the right timings when a game starts. The critical point here is to receive the first player's turn. If the bot loses it, it cannot react appropriately.

We have done the part of our bot that starts the game. The next step is implementing an algorithm to repeat the player's turns in a mirrored manner. How can we calculate the right piece to move and its new position? Let us consider several examples of "mirrored" turns (see Table 4-5).

Table 4-5. *The Mirrored Turns*

Turn	Bytes	Mirrored Turn	Bytes
e2 - e4	00 00 06 04 04 04 00	e7 - e5	00 00 01 04 03 04 00
d2 - d4	00 00 06 03 04 03 00	d7 - d5	00 00 01 03 03 03 00
b1 - c3	00 00 07 01 05 02 00	b8 - c6	00 00 00 01 02 02 00

The first turn in this table is the "e2-e4" move of the white pawn. The mirrored turn of the black pawn is "e7-e5". Different white and black pawns make the following pair of turns. The third turn is a white knight move, "b1-c3". When you reach the mirrored turn of the black knight, you should already notice several repeating patterns.

The first pattern relates to letters of the squares. The squares of the mirrored turns have the same letters as the original turns. This rule works for start and end positions of any piece.

The second pattern defines the square numbers. Just have a look at the following pairs of numbers:

- 6 and 1

- 4 and 3

- 7 and 0

- 5 and 2

How can you get a number from the right side if you know the left one? You should subtract it from the 7; then, you get the number from the right side.

Now, we can implement the algorithm that calculates the mirrored turns. Listing 4-6 demonstrates it.

Listing 4-6. The Algorithm to Do Mirrored Turns

```
# process turns
while(1):
  # recv - server turn
  s.recv(1024, socket.MSG_WAITALL)
  data = s.recv(1024, socket.MSG_WAITALL)
  print(data)

  start_num = 7 - data[2]
  end_num = 7 - data[4]

  # send - client turn
  s.send(bytes([0x07, 0, 0, 0]))
  s.send(bytes([0, 0, start_num, data[3], end_num, data[5], 0x00]))
```

Here we have the infinite *while* loop. In this loop, we receive a packet with the turn of the server player and store it in the *data* variable. Then we print it to the console with the *print* function. We calculate the number of the start square for our piece and store it in the *start_num* variable. The third byte (it has the index 2) of the received data matches the start position of player's piece. Similarly, we calculate a number for the destination square and store it in the *end_num* variable. Then we put the calculated numbers and the original letters (bytes with indexes 3 and 5 of the received data) into the packet and send it back to the server.

You can find the final implementation of the bot in the *MirrorBot.py* script, which is provided with this book. It contains steps to start a game with the server and the considered algorithm for making mirrored turns.

These are the steps to test the bot:

1. Launch the NetChess application.

2. Configure it in the server mode.

3. Launch the *MirrorBot.py* script.

4. Enable the "Manual Edit" mode on the server.

5. Launch the game clock.

6. Make your turn.

The bot will repeat your turns until it cannot. When you do a turn that the bot cannot repeat, it does nothing.

Assessing the Bot

We can estimate the effectiveness of our out-game bot if we consider its advantages and disadvantages.

The bot has the following benefits:

*   It receives full and precise information about the game state.

*   It can do all actions that the original client can do without any limitations.

The bot has the following disadvantages:

*   It costs a lot of effort to analyze the game protocol.

*   It is easy to protect a game against this bot by encrypting the traffic between the server and client.

*   Minor changes in the protocol lead to bot detection. Also, these changes can break the bot because the server rejects packets of the deprecated format.

We can generalize these points to most out-game bots. The conclusion is that these bots work reliably and can automate a game process well as long as the server does not change its protocol. When this happens, your game account will be banned in most cases. Also, you should spend significant effort and time in developing these bots.

Protection Approaches

In the previous section, we have considered the NetChess game, which is a simple application for two users who play in a local network. Modern online games have thousands of players. All of them connect to the servers via the Internet. However, if you want to make a bot for a game of this kind, you should investigate its protocol first as we did it for NetChess.

NetChess does not have any protection against out-game bots. This is a reason why we have been able to understand its protocol so quickly. If you try to investigate the traffic of a modern online game, you face obstacles. It is probable that you cannot find matching between player actions and bytes of captured packets. The same actions change bytes with different offsets and without any apparent regularity. If you get this situation, you should know that the game has protection. The most reliable and widely used approach to protect traffic against analysis is encryption.

We have considered a couple of encryption approaches in Chapter 3. They relate to a process memory protection. Now we will consider cryptographic algorithms and ways to apply them to the network traffic.

Cryptographic System

Before we start considering practical examples, let us answer the question of what a **cryptosystem** is: it is a suite of algorithms to achieve confidentiality of information. Generally, a cryptosystem has three algorithms for the following purposes:

1. Key generating.

2. Encryption.

3. Decryption.

The **cipher** term is used to refer to encryption and decryption algorithms only. The first algorithm in the list creates a **secret key** that fits the requirements of the cipher.

How do ciphers work? Let us assume that we have some information (for example, a message) that we want to protect from unauthorized reading. This information is known as **plaintext**. We pass the plaintext to the encryption algorithm together with the secret key. This key defines an output of the encryption algorithm. This output is known as **ciphertext**. Now if somebody wants to get the plaintext back, he should pass the ciphertext and key to the decryption algorithm. This means that our encrypted information is available only for receivers who know the secret key.

We have considered only general ideas about a typical cryptosystem. Real ones can have additional encryption and decryption steps and key management features.

Test Application

We will demonstrate encryption algorithms with simple sender and receiver scripts that communicate via UDP protocol. We have considered this application in the "Packet Analysis" section. Now we change the packet data from three bytes to the "Hello world!" string.

Listing 4-7 shows a modified sender script.

Listing 4-7. The TestStringUdpSender.py Script

```python
import socket

def main():
    s = socket.socket(socket.AF_INET, socket.SOCK_DGRAM, 0)
    s.bind(("127.0.0.1", 24001))
    data = bytes("Hello world!", "utf-8")
    s.sendto(data, ("127.0.0.1", 24000))
    s.close()

if __name__ == '__main__':
    main()
```

Now we send a *data* variable, which contains a byte array with letter codes in the UTF-8 encoding. You can launch the *TestUdpReceiver.py* script from the "Packet Analysis" section and the *TestStringUdpSender.py*. When the receiver gets the packet, it prints the following line to the console:

```
b'Hello world!'
```

The symbol "b" before the string means that this is a sequence of bytes. Each of them has a value from 0 to 255.

Figure 4-22 shows the sent packet in the Wireshark.

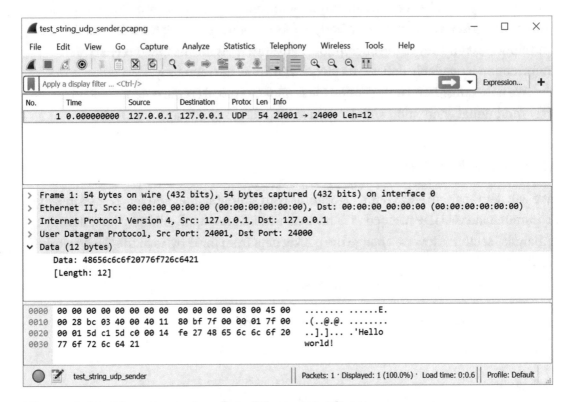

Figure 4-22. *The captured packet of the test application*

You can see that Wireshark decodes the "Hello world!" string correctly and we can read it. Now we will apply encryption algorithms to hide this string.

XOR Cipher

The simplest cryptosystem is the XOR cipher. We have considered it in Chapter 3 for hiding application variables from the memory scanners. We can apply it to encrypting the data of network packets.

The PyCrypto library implements the XOR cipher, so we can use the existing algorithm instead of implementing it on our own.

> The PyCryptodome library does not have the XOR cipher. If you have installed this library instead of PyCrypto, you cannot launch the scripts of this subsection.

Listing 4-8 demonstrates the encryption and decryption of the string.

Listing 4-8. The XorTest.py Script

```python
from Crypto.Cipher import XOR

def main():
    key = b"The secret key"

    # Encryption
    encryption_suite = XOR.new(key)
    cipher_text = encryption_suite.encrypt(b"Hello world!")
    print(cipher_text)

    # Decryption
    decryption_suite = XOR.new(key)
    plain_text = decryption_suite.decrypt(cipher_text)
    print(plain_text)

if __name__ == '__main__':
    main()
```

The first line of the *XorTest.py* script imports the XOR module, which implements the cipher. To use it, we should prepare the secret key. It is "The secret key" string in our case. Then we create an object of the *XORCipher* class with the *new* function (which takes an encryption key as the input parameter). We store this object in the *encryption_ suite* variable. It has the *encrypt* method, which applies the cipher to the passed byte array. We save the ciphertext in the *cipher_text* variable and print it to the console.

The console output should look like this:

```
b'\x1c\r\tL\x1cE\x14\x1d\x17\x18DJ'
```

The next part of the *main* function decrypts the ciphertext back. We create a *dencryption_suite* object in the same way as the *encryption_suite* one. This object decrypts the *cipher_text* string back. When this is done, we print the result to the console. It should match the "Hello world!" plaintext.

If you look at the *XorTest.py* script, you may ask whether it is possible to reuse the same cipher object for encryption and decryption. The answer is no. Classes of PyCrypto library have an internal state that depends on the last performed operation. It means that each action affects the following ones. If you encrypt two strings one after another with the same object, you should decrypt them in the same order. Otherwise, you get a wrong result. The most reliable way to use these objects is applying them to a single encryption or decryption only.

Now let us apply the XOR cipher to our UDP sender and receiver. Listing 4-9 demonstrates the modified sender script.

Listing 4-9. The XorUdpSender.py Script

```python
import socket
from Crypto.Cipher import XOR

def main():
    s = socket.socket(socket.AF_INET, socket.SOCK_DGRAM, 0)
    s.bind(("127.0.0.1", 24001))

    key = b"The secret key"
    encryption_suite = XOR.new(key)
    cipher_text = encryption_suite.encrypt(b"Hello world!")

    s.sendto(cipher_text, ("127.0.0.1", 24000))
    s.close()

if __name__ == '__main__':
    main()
```

In the *XorUdpSender.py* script, we encrypt the "Hello world!" string and send it via the UDP protocol. The *XorUdpReceiver.py* script in Listing 4-10 receives and decrypts the string.

Listing 4-10. The XorUdpReceiver.py Script

```python
import socket
from Crypto.Cipher import XOR

def main():
    s = socket.socket(socket.AF_INET, socket.SOCK_DGRAM, 0)
    s.bind(("127.0.0.1", 24000))
    data, addr = s.recvfrom(1024, socket.MSG_WAITALL)
```

```
key = b"The secret key"
decryption_suite = XOR.new(key)
plain_text = decryption_suite.decrypt(data)
print(plain_text)

s.close()
if __name__ == '__main__':
  main()
```

If you launch the receiver and sender scripts, the result of their execution looks the same as it was before. *XorUdpReceiver.py* prints the received string to the console:

```
b'Hello world!'
```

However, if you capture the transferred packet with Wireshark, you notice the difference. Figure 4-23 shows how this packet looks.

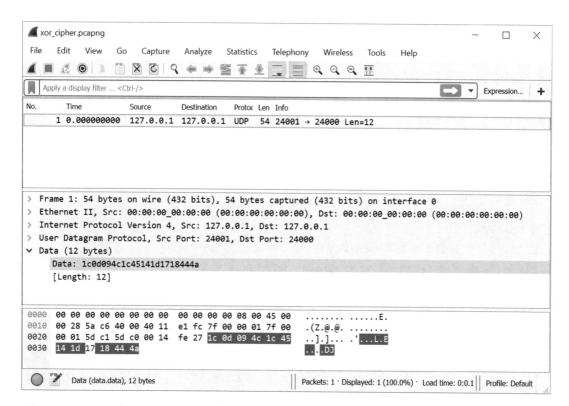

Figure 4-23. *The captured packet, which is encrypted by the XOR cipher*

You can see that now Wireshark cannot decode the string. If somebody captures it, he should manually do the XOR decryption. This operation requires the encryption key.

You can decide that the XOR cipher is a good option for your application. It is simple to use, and it works quickly. Actually, this is a bad option because we can break this cipher easily.

The cipher is based on the "exclusive or" logical operator. Let us assume that we encrypt the plaintext A with the secret key K. Then we get the ciphertext B:

A ⊕ K = B

If we perform "exclusive or" with the A and B, we will get the K:

A ⊕ B = K

This means that we can restore the secret key if we know both plaintext and ciphertext. The *XorCrack.py* script in Listing 4-11 recovers the secret key.

Listing 4-11. The XorCrack.py Script

```python
from Crypto.Cipher import XOR

def main():
  key = b"The secret key"

  # Encryption
  encryption_suite = XOR.new(key)
  cipher_text = encryption_suite.encrypt(b"Hello world!")
  print(cipher_text)

  # Decryption
  decryption_suite = XOR.new(key)
  plain_text = decryption_suite.decrypt(cipher_text)
  print(plain_text)

  # Crack
  crack_suite = XOR.new(plain_text)
  key = crack_suite.encrypt(cipher_text)
  print(key)

if __name__ == '__main__':
  main()
```

When you launch this script, you get the following console output:

```
b'\x1c\r\tL\x1cE\x14\x1d\x17\x18DJ'
b'Hello world!'
b'The secret k'
```

The first line is the ciphertext. Then comes the plaintext. The last line is the recovered key.

Why do we get a part of the key but not the whole one? When we apply the cipher, the "exclusive or" operator is applied to each letter of the plaintext and the corresponding byte of the key. If the string is shorter, the unused bytes of the key are skipped. Otherwise, the key's bytes are applied cyclically.

There is another question. How does the considered feature of the "exclusive or" operator help us to decrypt a real packet? We have a ciphertext only and do not know the key. Getting the plaintext is our primary goal. To get the key, we should apply the same encryption suite to the string that we already know. Then we will have both original and encrypted strings and can get the key.

Let us assume that we register in an online game. It asks player details (name, e-mail, password). All these data we know. When we fill the registration form and press the "OK" button, we should capture all packets that the application is sending to the server at that moment. Our data is present in these packets. Now, we should perform the "exclusive or" operator to the player details, which we know, and the data from the captured packets. It requires time to check all combinations, but finally, we will find the key.

We can conclude that the XOR cipher has some advantages, but it does not provide reliable protection for real applications.

Triple DES Cipher

The next cipher that we will consider is **Triple DES** (3DES). It applies the **Data Encryption Standard** (DES) algorithm three times to encrypt the plaintext. IBM developed DES in 1975. Today, DES cipher has become insecure because it uses short secret keys of 56 bits in length. Modern computers allow enumerating all possible keys of this length (2^{56} total) in several days. The 3DES algorithm solves the issue of DES by triple-extending the key up to 168 bits.

You might ask why we need to apply DES three times. Why can't we perform it two times and get the 112-bit key, which should be enough for modern requirements? We expect that a 112-bit key, which "double" DES encryption provides, requires enumerating 2^{112} possible combinations by an **attacker** (a person who cracks the cipher). This assumption is wrong because of the **meet-in-the-middle attack**. When we apply this attack, we reduce the number of possible keys for enumerating to 2^{57}. This number is still very low for providing reliable encryption. However, the 3DES algorithm forces an attacker to enumerate 2^{112} possible combinations, even if he applies the meet-in-the-middle approach.

The DES cipher was designed to be suitable for hardware implementation. Nowadays, there are many devices that support DES at the hardware level. It is quite easy to apply the 3DES cipher on these devices. Back-compatibility with legacy solutions is the main reason that 3DES is still used. However, there are newer and more secure ciphers that work faster than DES and 3DES.

The PyCrypto and PyCryptodome libraries provide both DES and 3DES ciphers. Here we will consider 3DES only.

The *3DesTest.py* script in Listing 4-12 applies 3DES to encrypt and decrypt the string:

Listing 4-12. The 3DesTest.py Script

```
from Crypto.Cipher import DES3
from Crypto import Random

def main():
  key = b"The secret key a"
  iv = Random.new().read(DES3.block_size)

  # Encryption
  encryption_suite = DES3.new(key, DES3.MODE_CBC, iv)
  cipher_text = encryption_suite.encrypt(b"Hello world!")
  print(cipher_text)

  # Decryption
  decryption_suite = DES3.new(key, DES3.MODE_CBC, iv)
  plain_text = decryption_suite.decrypt(cipher_text)
  print(plain_text)

if __name__ == '__main__':
  main()
```

In this script, we import *DES3* and *Random* modules of the PyCrypto library. The first module provides the *DES3Cipher* class, which implements the cipher. The *Random* module provides a generator of random bytes. We should use it instead of the standard *random* module here. The *random* is unsafe for cryptography purposes.

Why do we need an array of random bytes to apply 3DES? 3DES is a block cipher. It splits a plaintext into blocks and encrypts them one by one using the secret key. However, if we apply this step only, the cipher stays unsafe. This happens because an attacker can get matching between blocks of plaintext and ciphertext. Thus, he can determine the content of encrypted blocks easily. We can prevent this vulnerability if we mix each plaintext block with the previous encrypted one. This approach is known as **Cipher Block Chaining** (CBC). Now comes the issue of the first block. Which data should we apply to mix it? This data should be generated randomly, and they are known as the **Initialization Vector** (IV).

In our script, we create a file-like object with the *new* function of the *Random* module. Then we call the *read* method of this object. It returns an array of randomly generated bytes that has the specified length. This length equals the block size (*DES3.block_size*) in our case. We store this array in the *iv* variable. We can mix it with the first block of the plaintext.

You will notice that we extend the secret key by two extra symbols to get the 16-byte size. When you use the 3DES cipher, you should choose a key of 16 or 24 bytes in length.

When the IV and key are prepared, we create the *encryption_suite* object of the *DES3Cipher* class by the *new* function of *DES3* module. This function has three input parameters:

- Encryption key.

- Mode of mixing blocks.

- IV (if the selected mode requires it).

In our case, we use the *DES3.MODE_CBC* mode. However, there are several alternative modes that mix the blocks. You can choose any of them.

The mode and IV should be the same for both cipher objects: those that encrypt and those that decrypt data.

The *DES3Cipher* class provides the same *encrypt* and *decrypt* methods as the *XORCipher* one.

If you launch the *3DesTest.py* script, you see a similar console output:

```
b'\xdc\xce\xf1^_\x95[\x16K\x93\x9a\xb8\x01\xf3\x1b\xcb'
b'Hello world!    '
```

You will notice that we have appended four extra spaces to the "Hello world!" plaintext. This is required because a length of input data should be a multiple of eight bytes when we apply the CBC mode.

Now, we will rewrite the UDP sender and receiver scripts to use the 3DES cipher. Listing 4-13 demonstrates the implementation of the sender.

Listing 4-13. The 3DesUdpSender.py Script

```
import socket
from Crypto.Cipher import DES3
from Crypto import Random

def main():
  s = socket.socket(socket.AF_INET, socket.SOCK_DGRAM, 0)
  s.bind(("127.0.0.1", 24001))

  key = b"The secret key a"
  iv = Random.new().read(DES3.block_size)
  encryption_suite = DES3.new(key, DES3.MODE_CBC, iv)
  cipher_text = iv + encryption_suite.encrypt(b"Hello world!    ")

  s.sendto(cipher_text, ("127.0.0.1", 24000))
  s.close()

if __name__ == '__main__':
  main()
```

You can see that the *3DesUdpSender.py* script encrypts the source string in the same way as *3DesTest.py* does. There is only one difference. Now we insert the IV together with the ciphertext in the packet data.

Why do we do this? As you will remember, both IV and key are required for decryption. We can store the predefined key on both the sender side and the receiver side, but we cannot do the same for IV. It should be unique and randomly generated for each encryption operation. Reusing the same IV several times compromises the cipher, and makes it easier for an attacker to crack it. So, the receiver should have a way to get IV. The simplest way is to transfer it together with the ciphertext.

You may ask whether it is safe to transfer IV. The answer is yes. The primary goal of IV is to add some extra randomness to the encrypted data. It allows us to get different results each time when we encrypt the same plaintext. Often, IV is considered as a mandatory part of the encrypted data. Thus, we can transfer it.

Listing 4-14 shows the implementation of the receiver.

Listing 4-14. The 3DesUdpReceiver.py Script

```
import socket
from Crypto.Cipher import DES3

def main():
  s = socket.socket(socket.AF_INET, socket.SOCK_DGRAM, 0)
  s.bind(("127.0.0.1", 24000))
  data, addr = s.recvfrom(1024, socket.MSG_WAITALL)

  key = b"The secret key a"
  decryption_suite =  (key, DES3.MODE_CBC, data[0:DES3.block_size])
  plain_text = decryption_suite.decrypt(data[DES3.block_size:])
  print(plain_text)

  s.close()

if __name__ == '__main__':
  main()
```

You can see that we pass the first block of the received data (bytes from 0 to *DES3. block_size*) to the *new* function as the IV value. This function constructs the object that we use to decrypt the rest bytes of the data.

If you launch the *3DesUdpReceiver.py* script first and then *3DesUdpSender.py*, the receiver decrypts the transferred string correctly.

The 3DES cipher is safe for use in your applications. However, you should consider its features before deciding to apply it. You should have a strong reason to prefer 3DES instead of modern ciphers, which work faster.

AES Cipher

The AES cipher was created in 1998 by two Belgian cryptographers, Vincent Rijmen and Joan Daemen. It has replaced the DES cipher as the US government standard.

AES solves several issues of the DES cipher. First of all, it allows the use of longer keys (128, 192, and 256 bits). This feature comes because sizes of blocks and a key can differ in this cipher. We can choose any allowed key length, and it does not lead to encryption or decryption overhead as happens for the 3DES cipher. This is one of the reasons AES works faster.

Both PyCrypto and PyCryptodome libraries provide the AES cipher. The interface of using it looks the same as the one for 3DES.

Listing 4-15 demonstrates the usage of the AES cipher.

Listing 4-15. The AesTest.py Script

```python
from Crypto.Cipher import AES
from Crypto import Random

def main():
    key = b"The secret key a"
    iv = Random.new().read(AES.block_size)

    # Encryption
    encryption_suite = AES.new(key, AES.MODE_CBC, iv)
    cipher_text = encryption_suite.encrypt(b"Hello world!")
    print(cipher_text)

    # Decryption
    decryption_suite = AES.new(key, AES.MODE_CBC, iv)
    plain_text = decryption_suite.decrypt(cipher_text)
    print(plain_text)

if __name__ == '__main__':
    main()
```

You can compare this script with the *3DesTest.py* one. They look very similar. The *new* function of the *AES* module constructs the *encryption_suite* object of the *AESCipher* class. This function has three input parameters: a key, mode of mixing blocks, and IV. The AES cipher supports the same modes as 3DES.

If you launch the Aes*Test.py* script, you will see a similar console output:

```
b'\xed\xd5\x19]\x04\xba\xc5\x05^s\x18t\xa3\xb59x'
b'Hello world!    '
```

The *AesUdpSender.py* script in Listing 4-16 encrypts data with the AES cipher and sends it.

Listing 4-16. The AesUdpSender.py Script

```python
import socket
from Crypto.Cipher import AES
from Crypto import Random

def main():
  s = socket.socket(socket.AF_INET, socket.SOCK_DGRAM, 0)
  s.bind(("127.0.0.1", 24001))

  key = b"The secret key a"
  iv = Random.new().read(AES.block_size)
  encryption_suite = AES.new(key, AES.MODE_CBC, iv)
  cipher_text = iv + encryption_suite.encrypt(b"Hello world!")

  s.sendto(cipher_text, ("127.0.0.1", 24000))
  s.close()

if __name__ == '__main__':
  main()
```

Here we transfer the IV value at the beginning of a packet's data as we did with the *3DesUdpSender.py* script. All steps of encrypting and sending the packet are the same as for the 3DES cipher case.

The *AesUdpReceiver.py* script (see Listing 4-17) decrypts the received packet.

Listing 4-17. The AesUdpReceiver.py Script

```python
import socket
from Crypto.Cipher import AES

def main():
    s = socket.socket(socket.AF_INET, socket.SOCK_DGRAM, 0)
    s.bind(("127.0.0.1", 24000))
    data, addr = s.recvfrom(1024, socket.MSG_WAITALL)

    key = b"The secret key a"
    decryption_suite = AES.new(key, AES.MODE_CBC, data[0:AES.block_size])
    plain_text = decryption_suite.decrypt(data[AES.block_size:])
    print(plain_text)

    s.close()

if __name__ == '__main__':
    main()
```

This script has the same algorithm as the *3DesUdpReceiver.py* one.

You can test the considered receiver and sender scripts to check how they work.

When you choose a symmetric cipher for your application, you should prefer AES over 3DES. The only case when it does make sense to apply 3DES is when providing back compatibility with legacy solutions.

You may ask how we can crack the symmetric cipher when we analyze game traffic. If the game uses strong ciphers like 3DES or AES, we should enumerate possible keys and try them one after another. In the worst case, we should check all possible keys. This is known as **brute-force attack**. However, there are approaches that allow reducing the number of possible keys. They are specific for each cipher and depend on encryption mode, implementation details, and quality of the chosen secret key.

There is another question. If we apply the brute-force attack, how do we distinguish the right key? We do not know the plaintext in most cases.

The first possibility to solve this issue is an analysis of a game process memory. You can read the parameters of the game objects (for example, health points of the player character). Then you can assume that server sends this parameter to the client. Thus, you expect to get a right value from the packet data if the checked encryption key is correct.

Another approach is to apply a statistical test for the decrypted data. If the checked key is correct, the data should be more ordered. Otherwise, you get set of random bytes without any regularity.

RSA Cipher

All considered ciphers (XOR, 3DES, and AES) are symmetric. It means that we should keep a secret key on both sender and receiver sides. This feature can lead you to one idea. Why should we crack the cipher? Instead, we can investigate memory of the client process and find the key there. Then we can import this key to our bot and communicate with the server. The idea is right. The task of searching the secret key in a process memory should be much simpler than decrypting the captured traffic.

Then comes another question. Is it possible to protect a secret key of a game client? The best solution here is to avoid permanently storing the key on the client side. However, the server cannot just send the key at the beginning of communicating. If an attacker captures it, he decrypts all further traffic easily. The asymmetric encryption helps in this case. It provides a mechanism to distribute the key safely.

We will consider the RSA cipher here. Its core idea is applying a one-way mathematical function to encrypt plaintext. The secret key is an input parameter of this function. To crack the cipher, you should solve a mathematical equation and find the key from the known function and ciphertext. However, the primary feature of one-way functions is high complexity to invert them. It means that you cannot calculate the secret key in a reasonable amount of time.

You might ask how it is possible to decrypt the ciphertext, which was encrypted by a one-way function. Let us assume that we encrypt a plaintext with the secret key. We have applied some one-way function. We send our ciphertext to the receiver. He does not know the secret key and cannot decrypt the message. However, we can give him a hint, how to solve the mathematical equation and calculate the key. Thus, we come to concept of two keys: the secret key and the hint. In this case, the secret key is named public key. The hint is a private key.

How does an asymmetric cipher work? When we want to receive an encrypted message, we calculate a pair of public and private keys. Then we send a public key to the receiver. He encrypts his message and sends us ciphertext. We have a public key (which is the hint for mathematical equation calculation) and decrypt the message. As you see from this scheme, it does not matter if the attacker captures the public key and encrypted message. He does not have the private key to decrypt it.

Both PyCrypto and PyCryptodome libraries provide the AES cipher. However, some of unsecure cipher's features are not available in PyCryptodome.

Listing 4-18 demonstrates usage of the RSA cipher for encrypting the string.

Listing 4-18. The RsaTest.py Script

```python
from Crypto.PublicKey import RSA
from Crypto import Random

def main():
    key = RSA.generate(1024, Random.new().read)

    # Encryption
    cipher_text = key.encrypt(b"Hello world!", 32)
    print(cipher_text)

    # Decryption
    plain_text = key.decrypt(cipher_text)
    print(plain_text)

if __name__ == '__main__':
    main()
```

The *RsaTest.py* script does not work if you use the PyCryptodome library.

Here we import two modules: *RSA* and *Random*. The *RSA* module provides functions to manage and apply public and private keys.

We call the *generate* function of the *RSA* module to create an object of the *_RSAobj* class. It has the *key* name. This object contains a pair of public and private keys. The function has one mandatory input parameter, which is a length of keys (1024 in our case). The second optional parameter is a function to generate random numbers.

Key size for RSA cipher means the length of modulus, which is a parameter of the one-way mathematical function. This parameter is used to calculate public and private keys. Thus, the size of actual keys matches the magnitude of modulus length.

When we get the *key* object, we call its *encrypt* and *decrypt* methods to perform corresponding operations.

You may ask where the public and private keys are in our example. Both encryption and decryption operations happen in the same process, so we do not need to share the public key with somebody else. However, the *key* object provides functions to export both keys.

We have considered the usage of RSA cipher only. Nobody uses the cipher in this way because it is vulnerable to the **chosen-plaintext attack**. Combination of the RSA cipher together with the **Optimal Asymmetric Encryption Padding** (OAEP) algorithm allows avoiding this vulnerability. This combination is known as the RSAES-OAEP scheme. Also, there are several other algorithms that can enhance the RSA cipher.

Listing 4-19 demonstrates how to apply the OAEP algorithm for encrypting the string.

Listing 4-19. The RsaOaepTest.py Script

```python
from Crypto.PublicKey import RSA
from Crypto.Cipher import PKCS1_OAEP
from Crypto import Random

def main():
  key = RSA.generate(1024, Random.new().read)

  # Encryption
  encryption_suite = PKCS1_OAEP.new(key)
  cipher_text = encryption_suite.encrypt(b"Hello world!")
  print(cipher_text)

  # Decryption
  decryption_suite = PKCS1_OAEP.new(key)
  plain_text = decryption_suite.decrypt(cipher_text)
  print(plain_text)

if __name__ == '__main__':
  main()
```

You can see that now we have two extra steps. We create two objects of the *PKCS1OAEP_Cipher* class with the *new* function of the *PKCS1_OAEP* module. This function receives an object of the *_RSAobj* class as a mandatory input parameter. The first created object has the name *encryption_suite* and performs encryption. The second object is *decryption_suite*, and it decrypts our string.

Now we will apply the RSA cipher for our test application, which sends the UDP packet. First of all, we should modify the application algorithm. This algorithm was trivial for symmetric cipher cases. We encrypt plaintext on the sender side, transfer the packet, and decrypt it on the receiver side.

When we apply RSA cipher, an extra step appears. We should transfer a packet with the public key of the receiver side. The sender requires this key to encrypt plaintext. Let us consider the modified application algorithm step by step:

1. The "sender" script starts first. It binds to a UDP socket and waits for a packet with the public key.

2. The "receiver" script starts. It binds to UDP socket for sending packets. Then it generates a pair of public and private keys.

3. The "receiver" sends its own public key.

4. The "sender" receives the public key and applies it to encrypt the plaintext with the RSA-OAEP scheme.

5. The "sender" sends the packet with the ciphertext.

6. The "receiver" script receives the ciphertext and decrypts it with the RSA-OAEP scheme.

Listing 4-20 demonstrates the "sender" side of the considered algorithm.

Listing 4-20. The RsaUdpSender.py Script

```python
import socket
from Crypto.PublicKey import RSA
from Crypto.Cipher import PKCS1_OAEP

def main():
  s = socket.socket(socket.AF_INET, socket.SOCK_DGRAM, 0)
  s.bind(("127.0.0.1", 24001))
```

```
public_key, addr = s.recvfrom(1024, socket.MSG_WAITALL)

key = RSA.importKey(public_key)
cipher = PKCS1_OAEP.new(key)
cipher_text = cipher.encrypt(b"Hello world!")

s.sendto(cipher_text, ("127.0.0.1", 24000))
s.close()

if __name__ == '__main__':
  main()
```

Here we use the *importKey* function of the *RSA* module to create the *key* object of the *_RSAobj* class. The input parameter of this function is a public key in the byte array format. We get it in the UDP packet from the "receiver" side. Then we use the *key* object to construct an object of the *PKCS1OAEP_Cipher* class. It encrypts our string, and we send it to the receiver.

Listing 4-21 demonstrates the implementation of the "receiver" side.

Listing 4-21. The RsaUdpReceiver.py Script

```
import socket
from Crypto.PublicKey import RSA
from Crypto.Cipher import PKCS1_OAEP
from Crypto import Random

def main():
  s = socket.socket(socket.AF_INET, socket.SOCK_DGRAM, 0)
  s.bind(("127.0.0.1", 24000))

  key = RSA.generate(1024, Random.new().read)
  public_key = key.publickey().exportKey()

  s.sendto(public_key, ("127.0.0.1", 24001))

  data, addr = s.recvfrom(1024, socket.MSG_WAITALL)

  cipher = PKCS1_OAEP.new(key)
  plain_text = cipher.decrypt(data)
  print(plain_text)
```

```
   s.close()

if __name__ == '__main__':
   main()
```

The new step in this script, which we have not considered yet, is exporting a public key. We do it in two phases after generating a pair of public and private keys. The first step is a call of the *publickey* method of the *key* object. This call creates a *public_key* object of the same *RSAobj* class, which contains the public key only. This object has the *exportKey* method, which returns a public key in the byte array format. The *key* object has this method too. If you call it, you get the private key.

When we extract the public key, we send it in a UDP packet without any encryption. If the attacker captures it, he cannot use it to decrypt our ciphertext. Then we wait for a packet from the *RsaUdpSender.py* script with the ciphertext. We decrypt it with the constructed *cipher* object of the *PKCS1OAEP_Cipher* class, which applies the RSAES-OAEP scheme.

You can launch the *RsaUdpSender.py* script first and the *RsaUdpReceiver.py* afterward to see how they work.

The RSA algorithm has one serious drawback compared to symmetric ciphers. It works much slower. Why does this happen? The symmetric ciphers use logical XOR or bit-shift operations. CPU performs them very quickly because it has logical blocks to do one operation of this kind in one clock tick. The RSA algorithm uses mathematical functions: modular exponentiation for encryption and Euler's totient function calculation for decryption. They are heavy for CPU because they require many clock ticks to perform.

The **session key** solves this issue of massive calculations. The idea is to generate a key for the symmetric encryption during one communication (i.e., session) between a client and server. The RSA algorithm allows us to transfer this key safely. Then, both client and server switch to the symmetric cipher and apply it to all further traffic until their connection is terminated.

You can easily modify our *RsaUdpSender.py* and *RsaUdpReceiver.py* scripts to transfer a session key (AES, for example) instead of the "Hello world!" string.

Now we reach our goal to avoid storing the encryption key on the game client side permanently.

Detecting Out-game Bots

We have considered cryptographic algorithms to protect game traffic. A bot developer should spend a lot of time capturing network packets and analyzing them. Let us assume that he succeeded and wrote a bot for our game. What can we do in this case?

Actually, the task of detecting out-game bots is much simpler than detecting clickers and in-game bots. All that we should do is to react when we receive incorrect traffic on the server side.

Let us consider the simplest case. We use a symmetric cipher and store the key in the game client permanently. The bot imports this key and communicates with the server. However, we should have a mechanism to update all game clients regularly. A typical update fixes software bugs and adds new game features. One of these updates can change the encryption key without any notifications for the user. At the same time, we change the server key accordingly. Now if the bot tries to communicate with the server using the old key, we can easily detect it.

The bot developer can react to this issue and import the new key to his bot. However, we can detect and ban all players who use an old version of the bot that sends wrong packets on the server. In most cases, players buy a bot and use it without a deep understanding of its internals. Thus, this approach works well, and only a few users of the bot will avoid detection.

If our game uses an asymmetric cipher, we still can apply the same detection approach. There are several options for managing encryption keys. Let us assume that a server stores the client's public key permanently. At the beginning of communication, the client sends its own public key to the server. Then, the server compares this key with the predefined one. If the keys differ, the server concludes that there is a bot. If the keys match, the server sends its own public key to the client, and their communication continues. When we update the game client, we change its key pair and the predefined client's public key on the server side. Thus, any bot that uses the deprecated pair of keys will be blocked because the server rejects its public key.

There is an alternative approach if you do not want to change the encryption key. You can make minor changes in the game protocol periodically. It can be changing the order of game parameters in the packet or increasing some special version counters. Then, you can check the received packets on the server and detect if they have the deprecated format.

CHAPTER 5

Extra Techniques

This chapter considers advanced approaches for game bot development. These approaches focus on bypassing protections that block clicker and in-game types of bots. The first approach is emulation of the standard keyboard and mouse devices. The second approach is the interception of calls of a game process to the WinAPI libraries.

Input Device Emulation

Now we will consider how to emulate input devices like keyboard and mouse. The purpose of this feature is avoiding a game's protection algorithms. When we emulate a device, it looks like a real keyboard or mouse to the OS. In this case, the game application has no chance to distinguish bot and player actions.

Input Device Emulation Tools

First of all, we should choose hardware that will emulate input devices. To make the right choice, let us consider hardware features that are important for our purpose:

- The device should be low in cost.

- The IDE and compiler should be available for free.

- The IDE should provide libraries for emulation input devices.

- There should be an active user community and good documentation.

The Arduino board has all of these features. This hardware is the best option to start learning embedded development.

© Ilya Shpigor 2018
I. Shpigor, *Practical Video Game Bots*, https://doi.org/10.1007/978-1-4842-3736-6_5

The next question is which version of the Arduino board we should buy. Arduino IDE provides libraries to emulate keyboard and mouse devices (`www.arduino.cc/reference/en/language/functions/usb/keyboard`). According to documentation, some boards do not support these libraries. So, appropriate board versions for us are Leonardo, Micro, and Due. When you get a board, you should connect it to a computer via a USB cable. Now the hardware is ready to work.

The second topic (once we have found the hardware) is choosing tools for development. Arduino provides an IDE with an integrated C++ compiler and libraries for all of its products. You can download the IDE on the official website (`www.arduino.org/downloads`). Install it after downloading.

The next step is to install drivers for an Arduino board. You should launch the installer application from the Arduino IDE subdirectory. The default path for the installer is `C:\Program Files (x86)\Arduino\drivers`. The *drivers* directory contains two installer versions: `dpinst-amd64.exe` and `dpinst-x86.exe`. You should choose the first file for the 64-bit Windows version and the second one for the 32-bit version. You should connect a board to the computer during the installation process.

Here are the steps to configure Arduino IDE after installation:

1. Choose a model of your board as a target device for the compiler. This option is available in the "Tools"➤"Board:..." item of the main menu. You can get the correct name of your model from the "Tools"➤"Port:..." menu item.

2. Choose a connection port to the board via the "Tools"➤"Port:..." item of the main menu.

Now Arduino IDE is prepared, and you can start to program.

We will use the AutoIt language to communicate with Arduino board from a Windows side. You need **CommAPI** scripts (`www.autoitscript.com/wiki/CommAPI`), which provide access to the WinAPI communications functions.

Keyboard Emulation

There are two possible architectures of bots that emulate input devices.

The first solution implements all algorithms in an application for the Arduino board. When you upload it to the device, a bot is ready to work. It starts automatically each time you connect the board to a computer.

CHAPTER 5   EXTRA TECHNIQUES

This architecture is the best choice if you develop a "blind" clicker bot. It can simulate user actions with fixed time delays in the infinite loop. However, the bot cannot get any information about a game state in this case. This is because the Arduino board does not have access to the WinAPI interface. So, a monitor device and memory of the game process are not available. Thus, if you develop a bot that reacts to events during the game, you should choose another approach.

The second solution consists of two parts. The first part is an application that works on the Arduino board. The only task of this application is simulating user actions. The second part is a script that works on the computer. This script contains all algorithms of the bot and makes decisions about what to do. When the bot should simulate a user action, the script sends a command to the board. Then, the Arduino application receives the command and simulates a user action.

We will consider the second variant with the Arduino application and script because it is universal and flexible.

There are several options to implement a protocol for sending commands from the script. The simplest way is to use the serial interface (www.arduino.cc/reference/en/ language/functions/communication/serial).

A bot with an input device emulation feature behaves like a typical clicker bot. It analyzes a picture of the game window and simulates keypresses. There is only one difference from a regular clicker bot. It does not call WinAPI to simulate the action; it asks the Arduino board instead.

The *keyboard.ino Arduino* application (see Listing 5-1) simulates keyboard actions according to the bytes it receives via the serial interface.

Listing 5-1. The keyboard.ino Application

```
#include <Keyboard.h>

void setup()
{
  Serial.begin(9600);
  Keyboard.begin();
}
```

```
void loop()
{
  if (Serial.available() > 0)
  {
     int incomingByte = Serial.read();
     Keyboard.write(incomingByte);
  }
}
```

Here we use a **Keyboard** library, which Arduino IDE provides. It allows us to send keystrokes to the connected computer via a Human Interface Device (**HID**)-compatible protocol. It is a standard protocol for all keyboards and mouses that have USB interface.

We include the *Keyboard.h* header at the first line of the application. The header defines a *Keyboard_* class and creates a *Keyboard* global object. This object provides access to all features of the library.

Our application has *setup* and *loop* functions. When you compile any Arduino application, the IDE adds the default *main* function implicitly. It calls the *setup* function once at startup and the *loop* function repeatedly. **Signatures** of both *setup* and *loop* functions are predefined, and you cannot change them.

We initialize both *Serial* and *Keyboard* objects in the setup function. We pass the baud rate, which equals to 9600 bit/s, to the *begin* method of the *Serial* object. This parameter defines the data transfer rate between the Arduino board and the computer. Then, we call the *begin* method of the *Keyboard* object. It starts emulating a keyboard device.

Now, the Arduino application is ready to receive commands and simulate user keypresses. The *loop* function responds for this task. It has the following algorithm:

1. Call the *available* method of the *Serial* object to check if we are receiving data via the serial port. This method returns a number of the received bytes.

2. Read the first received byte by the *read* method of the *Serial* object. The byte defines an ASCII code of the key that should be simulated.

3. Send a keystroke action to the computer with the *write* method of the *Keyboard* object.

You should press Ctrl+U in Arduino IDE to compile and upload the *keyboard.ino* application to the board.

Now we have an Arduino board that emulates the keyboard. The next step is to implement an AutoIt script. The script should control the board via the serial port. We can use CommAPI wrappers, which simplify access to serial interface via WinAPI functions. To use these wrappers, you should download and copy them to the directory of your script.

This is a list of necessary CommAPI files:

- *CommAPI.au3*
- *CommAPIConstants.au3*
- *CommAPIHelper.au3*
- *CommInterface.au3*
- *CommUtilities.au3*

Make sure that you get all these files before starting the next step.

Let us make a script that commands the Arduino board to print the "Hello world!" string. Listing 5-2 demonstrates this.

Listing 5-2. The `ControlKeyboard.au3` Script

```
#include "CommInterface.au3"

func ShowError()
        MsgBox(16, "Error", "Error " & @error)
endfunc

func OpenPort()
        local const $iPort = 7
        local const $iBaud = 9600
        local const $iParity = 0
        local const $iByteSize = 8
        local const $iStopBits = 1
```

```
        $hPort = _CommAPI_OpenCOMPort($iPort, $iBaud, $iParity, $iByteSize,
        $iStopBits)
        if @error then
                ShowError()
                return NULL
        endif

        _CommAPI_ClearCommError($hPort)
        if @error then
                ShowError()
                return NULL
        endif

        _CommAPI_PurgeComm($hPort)
        if @error then
                ShowError()
                return NULL
        endif

        return $hPort
endfunc

func SendArduino($hPort, $command)
        _CommAPI_TransmitString($hPort, $command)
        if @error then ShowError()
endfunc

func ClosePort($hPort)
        _CommAPI_ClosePort($hPort)
endfunc

$hWnd = WinGetHandle("[CLASS:Notepad]")
WinActivate($hWnd)
Sleep(200)

$hPort = OpenPort()

SendArduino($hPort, "Hello world!")

ClosePort($hPort)
```

Let us consider an algorithm of the script:

1. Switch to the Notepad window with the *WinActivate* AutoIt function.

2. Open the serial port with the *OpenPort* function.

3. Send command to the Arduino board to type the "Hello world!" string with the *SendArduino* function.

4. Close the serial port with the *ClosePort* function.

Now we will consider internals of the *OpenPort*, *SendArduino*, and *ClosePort* functions.

The *OpenPort* function opens the serial port and prepares the connected device for communication. It returns a handle to the opened port. We do three CommAPI calls here:

1. The *_CommAPI_OpenCOMPort* function opens a COM port with the specified settings. We pass settings via the input parameters of the function. The *iParity*, *iByteSize*, and *iStopBits* parameters are constant for all Arduino boards. You should pay attention to two other parameters. The *iBaud* one should match the value you pass to the *begin* method of the *Serial* object in the *keyboard.ino* application. It equals to 9600 in our case. The *iPort* parameter equals to the COM port number used to connect the Arduino board to your computer. You can check the port in the "Tools" ➤ "Port:..." item of the Arduino IDE menu. For example, value 7 of the *iPort* parameter matches to the COM7 port.

2. The *_CommAPI_ClearCommError* function retrieves information about communication errors and the current status of the connected board. The second parameter of the function returns this information. We do not use it in our case. However, it is quite important to call this function. It clears the error flag on the device. This flag (when it is active) blocks the communication.

3. The *_CommAPI_PurgeComm* function clears the input and output buffers of the board and terminates all pending read and write operations. The device becomes ready to receive commands after this call.

The *SendArduino* function is a wrapper around the *_CommAPI_TransmitString* call. It writes a string to the specified serial port handle.

The *ClosePort* function closes the serial port by the specified handle.

Also, there is the *ShowError* function. We use it if any error happens during the opening of a serial port. It shows a message with the error code.

You can connect the Arduino board with the *keyboard.ino* application, launch Notepad, and start the *ControlKeyboard.au3* script. The script types the "Hello world!" text in the Notepad window.

Keyboard Modifiers

We have implemented the *keyboard.ino* Arduino application, which simulates presses of single keys. However, it does not allow us to simulate a combination of keys (for example Ctrl+Z). Let us improve the application and get this feature.

Listing 5-3 demonstrates this.

Listing 5-3. The keyboard-combo.ino Application

```
#include <Keyboard.h>

void setup()
{
  Serial.begin(9600);
  Keyboard.begin();
}

void pressKey(char modifier, char key)
{
  Keyboard.press(modifier);
  Keyboard.write(key);
  Keyboard.release(modifier);
}

void loop()
{
  static const char PREAMBLE = 0xDC;
  static const uint8_t BUFFER_SIZE = 3;
```

```
  if (Serial.available() > 0)
  {
    char buffer[BUFFER_SIZE] = {0};
    uint8_t readBytes = Serial.readBytes(buffer, BUFFER_SIZE);

    if (readBytes != BUFFER_SIZE)
      return;

    if (buffer[0] != PREAMBLE)
      return;

    pressKey(buffer[1], buffer[2]);
  }
}
```

Here we use the *readBytes* method of the *Serial* object instead of the *read* one. It reads a sequence of bytes that the serial port receives. The method returns a number of the received bytes.

The feature of transferring several bytes instead of one allows us to extend the format of our commands. We can use a sequence of bytes instead of one.

I recommend applying the following format when each command contains three bytes:

1. The **preamble:** a predefined byte that signals about the beginning of the command. So, we can distinguish two commands and avoid mixing their bytes.

2. The code of the **key modifier**. It should be pressed together with the key when you want to get a key combination.

3. The key code.

For example, if you want to simulate the Alt+Tab key combination, here is the command for Arduino board:

```
0xDC 0x82 0xB3
```

The "0xDC" byte is a preamble. The "0x82" is a code of modifier that matches to the left Alt key. The "0xB3" is a code of the Tab key.

You can see that now the *loop* function has two *if* conditions. They interrupt the processing of the received command. The first condition validates a number of received bytes. The second one checks that the preamble has been distinguished. If both checks pass, we call the *pressKey* function. It has two parameters: the modifier and key codes. We use the *press* method of the *Keyboard* object to hold a modifier until the key is pressing. Then we do the *release* call to release the modifier.

We should adopt the control script according to the new protocol. Listing 5-4 demonstrates this.

Listing 5-4. The `ControlKeyboardCombo.au3` Script

```
#include "CommInterface.au3"

func ShowError()
        MsgBox(16, "Error", "Error " & @error)
endfunc

func OpenPort()
        ; This function is the same as one in the ControlKeyboard.au3 script
endfunc

func SendArduino($hPort, $modifier, $key)
        local $command[3] = [0xDC, $modifier, $key]

        _CommAPI_TransmitString($hPort, StringFromASCIIArray($command, 0,
        UBound($command), 1))

        if @error then ShowError()
endfunc

func ClosePort($hPort)
        _CommAPI_ClosePort($hPort)
        if @error then ShowError()
endfunc

$hPort = OpenPort()

SendArduino($hPort, 0x82, 0xB3)

ClosePort($hPort)
```

As you can see, we change the *SendArduino* function only. Now we transfer the command array to the Arduino board. It contains three bytes: the preamble, the modifier, and the key. We use the same *_CommAPI_TransmitString* function to transmit data via the serial port. However, this function accepts the string as the input parameter. So, we should convert the array with a command into the string format; the *StringFromASCIIArray* AutoIt function does it.

You can upload the new Arduino application to the board and launch the *ControlKeyboardCombo.au3* script. Then you get the Alt+Tab keystroke simulation. If you open several windows, you will see how the script switches them.

Mouse Emulation

We can emulate a mouse device with the Arduino board as we did for a keyboard. The **Mouse** library of Arduino IDE provides API for this task.

However, the primary goal of this library is providing features for developers of mouse-like devices. Thus, the library uses relative coordinates for cursor positioning. It is a serious drawback for us. We want to specify a screen point where the board should simulate a mouse click (for example). When we have relative coordinates, we should notify the board about the current cursor position. We have two options here:

1. Implement a complicated algorithm that operates with relative cursor coordinates.

2. Fix the Mouse library of the Arduino IDE.

The Arduino community already solved this issue with relative coordinates in the library. The article forum.arduino.cc/index.php?topic=94140.0 describes the patch. After the patch, you can operate with absolute cursor coordinates. However, this solution works for the old 1.0 version of Arduino IDE. In this version, both Keyboard and Mouse libraries come together as one HID module.

There is an algorithm to patch the Mouse library of the newer Arduino IDE version:

1. Get the patched *Mouse.cpp* source file, which is provided with this book.

2. Replace the original *Mouse.cpp* file in the Arduino IDE directory with the patched one. The default path of this file is *C:\Program Files (x86)\Arduino\libraries\Mouse\src*.

You can patch the *Mouse.cpp* file on your own. To do so, you should change the *_hidReportDescriptor* array as the following code snippet shows:

```
#define ABSOLUTE_MOUSE_MODE

static const uint8_t _hidReportDescriptor[] PROGMEM = {
...
#ifdef ABSOLUTE_MOUSE_MODE
    0x15, 0x01,                 //      LOGICAL_MINIMUM (1)
    0x25, 0x7F,                 //      LOGICAL_MAXIMUM (127)
    0x75, 0x08,                 //      REPORT_SIZE (8)
    0x95, 0x03,                 //      REPORT_COUNT (3)
    0x81, 0x02,                 //      INPUT (Data,Var,Abs)
#else
    0x15, 0x81,                 //      LOGICAL_MINIMUM (-127)
    0x25, 0x7f,                 //      LOGICAL_MAXIMUM (127)
    0x75, 0x08,                 //      REPORT_SIZE (8)
    0x95, 0x03,                 //      REPORT_COUNT (3)
    0x81, 0x06,                 //      INPUT (Data,Var,Rel)
#endif
```

The *_hidReportDescriptor* array is a report descriptor. It declares data that the board sends to the computer and receives from it. In other words, a report descriptor defines the communication protocol between a computer and a device. This protocol allows a computer to communicate with all HID devices in one universal way.

We made two changes in the mouse device report descriptor:

1. Change the *LOGICAL_MINIMUM* byte (with 0x15 ID) from -127 to 1. This matches the minimum value of the cursor coordinate. An absolute coordinate can be positive only.

2. Change the *INPUT* byte (with 0x81 ID) from 0x06 to 0x02. It means that we use absolute coordinates instead of the relative ones.

Also, we have added the *ABSOLUTE_MOUSE_MODE* macro. It allows switching between relative and absolute coordinates. When you define the macro, the IDE builds an application with absolute cursor coordinates.

Listing 5-5 shows the *mouse.ino* application, which simulates mouse clicks.

Listing 5-5. The mouse.ino Application

```
#include <Mouse.h>

void setup()
{
  Serial.begin(9600);
  Mouse.begin();
}

void click(signed char x, signed char y, char button)
{
  Mouse.move(x, y);
  Mouse.click(button);
}

void loop()
{
  static const char PREAMBLE = 0xDC;
  static const uint8_t BUFFER_SIZE = 4;

  if (Serial.available() > 0)
  {
    char buffer[BUFFER_SIZE] = {0};
    uint8_t readBytes = Serial.readBytes(buffer, BUFFER_SIZE);

    if (readBytes != BUFFER_SIZE)
      return;

    if (buffer[0] != PREAMBLE)
      return;

    click(buffer[1], buffer[2], buffer[3]);
  }
}
```

The application has a similar algorithm as the *keyboard-combo.ino* one. Here we include the *Mouse.h* header. It provides the *Mouse_* class and the *Mouse* global object. Then we do the *begin* call of this object to initialize it.

We simulate a mouse click in the *click* function. It happens in two steps. The first step is moving a cursor to the specified position by the *move* method of *Mouse* object. The second step is the *Mouse.click* call, which simulates a click in the current cursor position.

We receive commands from a computer in the *loop* function. The meaning of the received bytes differs from that for the *keyboard-combo.ino* application. Now, the command consists of four bytes:

1. The preamble.

2. The x coordinate of the click action.

3. The y coordinate of the click action.

4. A mouse button to click.

You may have noticed that the maximum value of both x and y coordinates equals 127 (or 0x7F in hexadecimal). This value is a maximum signed number that we can be stored in one byte. It means that maximum absolute number of cursor coordinates that you can specify is 127×127. However, a screen resolution is higher than 127×127 pixels. Thus, we should do an extra step to translate the values of the actual screen coordinates to the Arduino board scale.

The following formulas translate the coordinates:

```
Xa = 127 * X / Xres
Ya = 127 * Y / Yres
```

Table 5-1 explains the formula symbols.

Table 5-1. *Explanation of the Formula*

Symbol	Description
Xa	The x coordinate in the Arduino scale.
Ya	The y coordinate in the Arduino scale.
X	The x coordinate in the screen scale.
Y	The y coordinate in the screen scale.
Xres	The horizontal screen resolution in pixels.
Yres	The vertical screen resolution in pixels.

Let us apply this formula in an example case. Our screen resolution is 1366×768. For example, we want to simulate a mouse click on the screen point with coordinates x=250 and y=300. Then, we should pass the following coordinates to the Arduino board:

```
Xa = 127 * 250 / 1366 = 23
Ya = 127 * 300 / 768 = 49
```

This means that the command to the board looks like this:

```
0xDC 0x17 0x31 0x1
```

The 0x17 in hexadecimal equals 23 in decimal and 0x31 equals 49 similarly.

Now we can implement a script for sending serial commands to our *mouse.ino* application. Listing 5-6 demonstrates this script.

Listing 5-6. The ControlMouse.au3 Script

```
#include "CommInterface.au3"

func ShowError()
        MsgBox(16, "Error", "Error " & @error)
endfunc

func OpenPort()
        ; This function is the same as one in the ControlKeyboard.au3
          script
endfunc

func GetX($x)
        return (127 * $x / 1366)
endfunc

func GetY($y)
        return (127 * $y / 768)
endfunc

func SendArduino($hPort, $x, $y, $button)
        local $command[4] = [0xDC, GetX($x), GetY($y), $button]

        _CommAPI_TransmitString($hPort, StringFromASCIIArray($command, 0,
        UBound($command), 1))
```

```
        if @error then ShowError()
endfunc

func ClosePort($hPort)
        _CommAPI_ClosePort($hPort)
        if @error then ShowError()
endfunc

$hWnd = WinGetHandle("[CLASS:MSPaintApp]")
WinActivate($hWnd)
Sleep(200)

$hPort = OpenPort()

SendArduino($hPort, 250, 300, 1)

ClosePort($hPort)
```

The *ControlMouse.au3* script is very similar to the *ControlKeyboardCombo.au3* one. Now, the *SendArduino* function has four input parameters: the port number, the cursor coordinates, and the mouse button to click. Also, you can see two new functions: *GetX* and *GetY*. They translate the cursor coordinates to the Arduino scale.

You should fix the *GetX* and *GetY* functions according to your screen resolution.

You can upload the *mouse.ino* application to the Arduino board, and then launch the Paint application and the *ControlMouse.au3* script. The script simulates the left-click at the point with x=250, y=300 absolute coordinates in the Paint window.

Keyboard and Mouse Emulation

We know how to emulate keyboard and mouse devices with Arduino boards. You may ask now whether it is possible to emulate both devices by the single board.

The answer is yes. It is not a complicated task. The HID protocol allows the device to behave as the keyboard and mouse at the same time. The only issue that we should solve is a command format. Now each command should contain enough bytes to keep all required information for keypress or mouse click. Also, the board should distinguish the action that the script asks to simulate.

We can extend our command format and add the byte that defines a code of the simulated actions. Table 5-2 shows all actions and their codes.

Table 5-2. *Action Codes*

Code	Simulated Action
0x1	Keypress without a modifier.
0x2	Keypress with a modifier.
0x3	Mouse click.

The action code byte should come on the second position after the preamble. This byte allows the Arduino application to choose the way to interpret the following three bytes of the received command. If there is a keypress action, we apply the algorithm of the considered *keyboard-combo.ino* application. Otherwise, we repeat the behavior of the *mouse.ino*.

Listing 5-7 demonstrates the final solution:

Listing 5-7. The keyboard-mouse.ino Application

```
#include <Mouse.h>
#include <Keyboard.h>

void setup()
{
  Serial.begin(9600);
  Keyboard.begin();
  Mouse.begin();
}

void pressKey(char key)
{
  Keyboard.write(key);
}

void pressKey(char modifier, char key)
{
  Keyboard.press(modifier);
```

```
  Keyboard.write(key);
  Keyboard.release(modifier);
}

void click(signed char x, signed char y, char button)
{
  Mouse.move(x, y);
  Mouse.click(button);
}

void loop()
{
  static const char PREAMBLE = 0xDC;
  static const uint8_t BUFFER_SIZE = 5;
  enum
  {
    KEYBOARD_COMMAND = 0x1,
    KEYBOARD_MODIFIER_COMMAND = 0x2,
    MOUSE_COMMAND = 0x3
  };

  if (Serial.available() > 0)
  {
    char buffer[BUFFER_SIZE] = {0};
    uint8_t readBytes = Serial.readBytes(buffer, BUFFER_SIZE);

    if (readBytes != BUFFER_SIZE)
      return;

    if (buffer[0] != PREAMBLE)
      return;

    switch(buffer[1])
    {
      case KEYBOARD_COMMAND:
        pressKey(buffer[3]);
        break;
```

```
    case KEYBOARD_MODIFIER_COMMAND:
      pressKey(buffer[2], buffer[3]);
      break;

    case MOUSE_COMMAND:
      click(buffer[2], buffer[3], buffer[4]);
      break;
  }
 }
}
```

We added the *switch* statement to the *loop* function. It chooses the right way to simulate an action depending on the second byte of the received command.

Do not forget that all arrays in C and C++ start from the 0 index instead of 1.

You have probably noticed that we transmit extra bytes when simulating the keypress actions. In cases of keypress without a modifier, there are two unnecessary bytes. Can we optimize this behavior and pass only bytes that are required?

Yes, we can make this optimization. However, before we start to change the code, let us consider exactly what we can do. We receive the bytes via the *readBytes* method of the *Serial* object. So, we should specify the number of bytes in the expected command. However, we will not know this number until we do not receive the second byte with the action code. This means that we should use another function of Arduino API.

The *Serial* object has the *readBytesUntil* method. It returns the received bytes until it does not meet a **terminator** character. The terminator is a special byte with a predefined value that signals about the command ends. This way sounds promising. The question is which value of the terminator we should choose. If you think about this question, you will understand how it is difficult to make the right choice. The terminator is only one byte. It should be unique. So, we should guarantee that any command that we send does not contain the same value in the payload. The coordinates can be from 0x00 to 0x7F. This sounds good, but a key code can have any value from 0x00 to 0xFF. So, we cannot choose the reliable terminator character.

Another way is to use the *read* method. It reads the sequence of bytes. This approach can work if the control script makes a delay after sending each command. So, the Arduino application can distinguish them. Otherwise, we receive a stream of commands and cannot get their bounds. Thus, this approach is not reliable enough because clicker bots can simulate actions very quickly.

We can conclude that our overhead because of sending extra bytes is a payment for the reliable solution. In our case, this payment is acceptable.

The *ControlKeyboardMouse.au3* script in Listing 5-8 simulates keyboard and mouse actions via the *keyboard-mouse.ino* Arduino application.

Listing 5-8. The ControlKeyboardMouse.au3 Script

```
#include "CommInterface.au3"

func ShowError()
        MsgBox(16, "Error", "Error " & @error)
endfunc

func OpenPort()
        ; This function is the same as one in the ControlKeyboard.au3 script
endfunc

func SendArduinoKeyboard($hPort, $modifier, $key)
        if $modifier == NULL then
                local $command[5] = [0xDC, 0x1, 0xFF, $key, 0xFF]
        else
                local $command[5] = [0xDC, 0x2, $modifier, $key, 0xFF]
        endif

        _CommAPI_TransmitString($hPort, StringFromASCIIArray($command, 0,
        UBound($command), 1))

        if @error then ShowError()
endfunc

func GetX($x)
        return (127 * $x / 1366)
endfunc
```

```
func GetY($y)
      return (127 * $y / 768)
endfunc

func SendArduinoMouse($hPort, $x, $y, $button)
      local $command[5] = [0xDC, 0x3, GetX($x), GetY($y), $button]

      _CommAPI_TransmitString($hPort, StringFromASCIIArray($command, 0,
      UBound($command), 1))

      if @error then ShowError()
endfunc

func ClosePort($hPort)
      _CommAPI_ClosePort($hPort)
      if @error then ShowError()
endfunc

$hPort = OpenPort()

$hWnd = WinGetHandle("[CLASS:MSPaintApp]")
WinActivate($hWnd)
Sleep(200)

SendArduinoMouse($hPort, 250, 300, 1)

Sleep(1000)

$hWnd = WinGetHandle("[CLASS:Notepad]")
WinActivate($hWnd)
Sleep(200)

SendArduinoKeyboard($hPort, Null, 0x54) ; T
SendArduinoKeyboard($hPort, Null, 0x65) ; e
SendArduinoKeyboard($hPort, Null, 0x73) ; s
SendArduinoKeyboard($hPort, Null, 0x74) ; t

Sleep(1000)

SendArduinoKeyboard($hPort, 0x82, 0xB3) ; Alt+Tab

ClosePort($hPort)
```

Here, we implement two separate functions for sending commands to the Arduino board. The *SendArduinoKeyboard* function sends the command to simulate keystroke actions. It has the same algorithm as the *SendArduino* function of the *ControlKeyboardCombo.au3* script. However, the command format differs now. We have the second byte with an action code and the fifth byte for padding a command length to the required size. Also, if we do not need a key modifier, we transfer the third byte with the 0xFF value.

The *SendArduinoMouse* function sends the command to simulate a mouse click. We added the second byte with action code to it.

You should do the following steps to test the *ControlKeyboardMouse.au3* script:

1. Upload the *keyboard-mouse.ino* application to the Arduino board.

2. Launch the Paint application.

3. Launch the Notepad application.

4. Launch the control script.

The script simulates three actions one after each other:

1. Mouse click in the Paint window.

2. Typing the "Test" string in the Notepad window.

3. Switching windows with the Alt+Tab keystroke.

There is the question of why we use the 0xFF byte instead of the 0x0 for padding in the keypress command. The limitation comes from the *StringFromASCIIArray* AutoIt function. It treats the 0x0 byte in the input ASCII array as the end of the resulting string. So, our commands should not contain zeroed bytes.

Input Device Emulation Summary

We have considered techniques to emulate keyboard and mouse devices with the Arduino board. The AutoIt script can control the board and command it to simulate user actions.

You can combine the pixel analysis feature of AutoIt with the device emulation. It allows you to develop advanced game bots. They can bypass some anticlicker protection approaches that are based on checking the keyboard state.

OS-Level Interception Data

We have considered a way to read game process memory and extract game data from it. However, if the game has strong protection, it can be difficult to follow this approach. In this case, you can apply a technique to modify OS libraries. It allows you to shift an observation point from the game process memory to the WinAPI side, which is not controlled by game developers and cannot be protected by them.

OS-Level Interception Data Tools

We will work with WinAPI functions in this chapter. The C++ language is the best choice for this task. We will use the Visual Studio Community IDE to compile our examples. You can find more details about this IDE in Chapter 3.

There are several open source solutions that can help us with hooking WinAPI calls.

The first solution is the **DLL Wrapper Generator** (m4v3n.wordpress.com/2012/08/08/dll-wrapper-generator). We will use it to create proxy DLLs.

These are the steps to install the generator:

1. Download the scripts from the GitHub project page: github.com/mavenlin/Dll_Wrapper_Gen/archive/master.zip

2. Download and install Python 2.7 (`www.python.org/downloads`).

The second solution is **Deviare** open source hooking framework (`www.nektra.com/products/deviare-api-hook-windows`).

These are the steps to install it:

1. Download the last version of the release binaries (github.com/nektra/Deviare2/releases/download/v2.8.0/Deviare.2.8.0.zip).

2. Download the latest version of the source code (github.com/nektra/Deviare2/archive/v2.8.0.zip).

3. Unpack both archives in two different directories.

You can find a list of all available Deviare releases in the GitHub project (github.com/nektra/Deviare2/releases). Please make sure that your versions of binaries and sources match.

Test Application

We need a test application to consider WinAPI call hooking techniques. I suggest reusing the application that we implemented in the "Protection Approaches" section of Chapter 3. However, it should be slightly changed. Listing 5-9 demonstrates this.

Listing 5-9. The TestApplication.cpp Application

```cpp
#include <stdio.h>
#include <stdint.h>
#include <windows.h>
#include <string>

static const uint16_t MAX_LIFE = 20;
volatile uint16_t gLife = MAX_LIFE;

int main()
{
    SHORT result = 0;

    while (gLife > 0)
    {
        result = GetAsyncKeyState(0x31);
        if (result != 0xFFFF8001)
            --gLife;
        else
            ++gLife;

        std::string str(gLife, '#');
        TextOutA(GetDC(NULL), 0, 0, str.c_str(), str.size());

        printf("life = %u\n", gLife);
        Sleep(1000);
    }
    printf("stop\n");
    return 0;
}
```

You can build the 32-bit version of the *TestApplication.cpp* and launch it.

The general algorithm stays the same. We decrement the *gLife* variable each second if the "1" key is not pressed. Otherwise, we increment the variable. The new feature is the *TextOutA* WinAPI call. It prints the hash symbols in the upper left corner of the screen. The number of symbols matches the current *gLife* value.

Why do we change the output function? Our current goal is hooking WinAPI calls. Before, we have used the *printf* function, which is provided not by WinAPI but by the C runtime library, so it is a bad example for demonstrating the hooking techniques. Now we can capture the *gLive* value by hooking the *TextOutA* call. The last parameter of this function matches it.

If you check the WinAPI documentation, you find that the *gdi32.dll* library provides the *TextOutA* function. Please remember this fact; it is essential for our investigation.

DLL Import

Before we consider WinAPI hooking techniques, we should learn how an application interacts with DLL libraries.

When we start an application, the Windows loader reads an executable file into the process memory. A typical Windows executable file has the **PE** format. It is the standard for the file header that contains the necessary information to launch executable code. The list of required DLLs is a part of this information.

The next step of the Windows loader is searching files of all required DLLs on a disk drive. It reads these files in the process memory too. Now we face an issue. When the loader reads DLL modules, it places them on random addresses. This happens because of the Address Space Load Randomization (ASLR) mechanism (blogs.technet.microsoft. com/askperf/2008/02/06/ws2008-dynamic-link-library-loader-and-address-space-load-randomization), which makes Windows resistant to some malware types. Thus, a compiler cannot hard-code addresses of the called DLL functions in the executable module.

The **Import Table** solves this issue (sandsprite.com/CodeStuff/Understanding_ imports.html). There is some confusion between Import Table and **Thunk Table**. Let us consider them in detail.

Each element of Import Table matches to one required DLL module. The element contains a name of the module, the *OriginalFirstThunk* and *FirstThunk* pointers. The *OriginalFirstThunk* points to the first element of the array with ordinal numbers and names of the imported functions. The *FirstThunk* points to the first element of the array (also known as **Import Address Table** or IAT). The Windows loader overwrites this array with the actual addresses of the imported functions when loading a DLL. The confusion happens because both considered arrays do not contain things that we name **thunk**. The thunk is a subroutine that injects an additional calculation to another subroutine. You can find more details about *OriginalFirstThunk* and *FirstThunk* pointers in the article ntcore.com/files/inject2it.htm.

The Import Table is a part of a PE header. It contains constant metainformation about imported DLLs. This table together with PE header occupies the read-only segment of the process memory. The Thunk Table (also known as a **Jump Table**) is a part of the executable code. It contains *JMP* instructions to transfer control to the imported functions. This table occupies the *.text* segment (it is read and executable) together with application code. The Import Address Table occupies the *.idata* segment with reading and writing permissions. The *.idata* segment also contains an array that is accessible via the *OriginalFirstThunk* pointer. As you see, all three tables occupy different segments.

Some compilers generate a code that does not use the Thunk Table. It allows excluding one extra jump. So, we get a code that is slightly more optimized at runtime. The MinGW compiler generates code that uses the Thunk Table. Figure 5-1 shows how an application does the *TextOutA* call in this case.

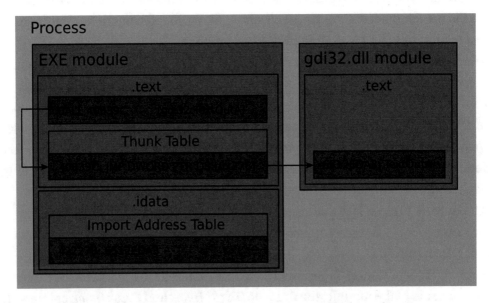

Figure 5-1. *The TextOutA call from the MinGW compiled application*

The call happens in the following steps:

1. A CPU executes the *CALL* instruction. It puts the return location to a stack and passes control to the Thunk Table element with the 40839C address.

2. The Thunk Table element contains the *JMP* instruction only. The instruction transfers control to the *TextOutA* function of the gdi32 module. It uses a record of the Import Address Table to get an actual address of the function. We can access the table via the DS segment that points to the .*idata* segment. This is a sample calculation of the Import Address Table record address:

    DS + 0x278 = 0x422000 + 0x278 = 0x422278

3. A CPU executes the *TextOutA* function. The function ends with the *RETN* instruction. It passes control to the instruction that comes next after the *CALL* in the EXE module. A CPU knows an address of this instruction because it puts the return location on the stack.

The Visual C++ compiler generates code without the Thunk Table. Figure 5-2 shows the *TextOutA* call in this case.

The call happens in the following steps:

1. A CPU executes the *CALL* instruction. We get an address of the *TextOutA* function directly from the Import Address Table record.

2. A CPU executes the *TextOutA* function. Then the *RETN* instruction passes control back to the EXE module.

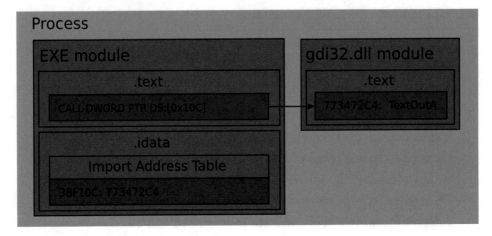

Figure 5-2. The TextOutA call from the Visual C++ compiled application

API Hooking Techniques

A game application interacts with Windows via system DLLs. For example, the DLL can print text in the game window. So, if we hook the function call that does it, we know this text. This approach reminds us of an output device capture. However, now we get data before they come to the device. Some of this data (for example, pictures, text, sounds) keeps a state of game objects.

If you launch the API Monitor tool (we considered it in Chapter 2), you get a feeling how API hooking works. The tool prints the hooked calls of a monitored application in the "Summary" subwindow. We can implement a bot that behaves similarly. Instead of printing the hooked calls, the bot should simulate player actions.

Now we will consider the most common API hooking techniques with examples.

Proxy DLL

The first approach to hook WinAPI calls is a substitution of a Windows library. We can prepare a DLL that looks like the original one for the Windows loader point of view. Thus, it loads this library into the process memory during application launching. Then, a game process interacts with the fake DLL in the same way as with the original one. This approach allows us to execute our code each time when the game process calls any function of the substituted WinAPI library. These fake libraries are known as **proxy DLLs**.

In most cases, we want to hook several specific WinAPI calls only. All other functions of the substituted library are not interesting for us. Also, you should remember about one important requirement: a game process should behave with a proxy DLL in the same manner as it does with the original library. These two reasons lead us to the idea that the proxy DLL should route function calls to the original library.

When the process makes a call to the proxy DLL, we can execute our code. It can simulate player actions or gather the state of the game objects. When this code is done, we should always call the original WinAPI function that the process asked to execute. Otherwise, it crashes (in the best case) or gets an inconsistent state (in the worst case).

So, if we do not want to hook some WinAPI function, we should make a straightforward wrapper for it. The wrapper routes a call to the original Windows library. It means that we should load this library into the process memory too. Otherwise, our wrappers cannot call the real WinAPI function.

Figure 5-3 shows how a process calls the *TextOutA* WinAPI function when we apply the proxy DLL technique.

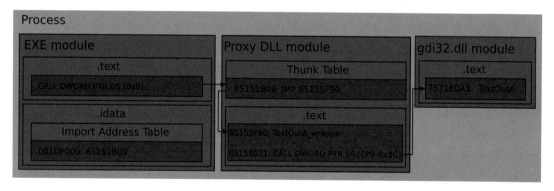

Figure 5-3. *The TextOutA call via the proxy DLL*

The call happens in the following steps:

1. The Windows loader loads the proxy DLL instead of the original *gdi32.dll* library. The loader writes the addresses of the functions that the proxy DLL exports to the Import Address Table of the EXE module.

2. The execution of the EXE module code reaches the *CALL* instruction. A CPU uses a record of the Import Address Table to get the actual function address. Now, this record contains an address of the function from a proxy DLL. So, the *CALL* instruction transfers control to the proxy DLL module.

3. The Thunk Table of the proxy DLL module receives control from the *CALL* instruction. The addresses of the exported by proxy DLL functions match the thunks in this table.

4. The *JMP* instruction of the thunk passes control to the wrapper of the *TextOutA* WinAPI function. The wrapper is in the proxy DLL module. It contains a code of our bot.

5. The *CALL* instruction of the wrapper function passes control to the original *TextOutA* function of the gdi32 module when the wrapper code is finished.

6. When the wrapper is done, it calls the original *TextOutA* function. When it is done, the *RETN* instruction transfers control back to the wrapper function.

7. The *RETN* instruction at the end of the wrapper passes control back to the EXE module.

There is one question. How does the proxy DLL know the actual addresses of the functions that the gdi32 module exports? We cannot ask the Windows loader to gather these addresses because it supposes that the proxy DLL is the real gdi32 module. Moreover, we should confuse the loader in this way. Let us consider this question in detail.

All system Windows libraries have specific predefined paths on a disk drive. The loader knows these paths and searches for the required DLLs there. The first place where the loader searches is a directory of the launched application. If the required DLL does not present there, the predefined system paths are used.

What can we do to confuse the searching DLL mechanism of the Windows loader? We cannot just substitute the system library in the Windows directory. All OS services use it. This solution can crash the whole system. However, we can force the loader to search the required library in the application directory first. Thus, we load the proxy DLL.

Now we come to the second question about loading an original library. We can solve this task in our proxy DLL manually. It can be done via the *LoadLibrary* WinAPI function. When we load the library, we should know the actual addresses of its exported functions. The *GetProcAddress* WinAPI function solves this task. So, WinAPI provides all that we need.

When we use the proxy DLL for hooking WinAPI calls, we get the following advantages:

- Generating a proxy DLL with existing open source tools is a simple task.

- We substitute a Windows library for the specific application only. All other launched applications still use the original libraries.

- Protecting an application against this approach is difficult.

These are disadvantages of the proxy DLL usage:

- You cannot substitute some of core Windows libraries (like *kernel32.dll*). This limitation appears because both *LoadLibrary* and *GetProcAddress* functions are provided by the *kernel32.dll*. They should be available at the moment when the proxy DLL loads the original library.

- It is difficult to make wrappers for some WinAPI functions because they are not documented.

Example of Proxy DLL

Now we will implement a simple bot that uses the proxy DLL technique. It keeps the *gLife* variable value greater than 10. If the value falls below 10, the bot simulates the "1" keypress. We will embed an algorithm of our bot inside the proxy DLL. So, we will now consider the steps to make this DLL.

The first step is to generate the source code of the library that contains wrappers for WinAPI functions. The DLL Wrapper Generator script solves this task.

You should do the following steps to apply the generator:

1. Copy the 32-bit version of the *gdi32.dll* library to the directory with the generator script. You can find the library in the *C:\Windows\system32* path if you have the 32-bit Windows version. Otherwise, it is located in the *C:\Windows\SysWOW64*.

2. Launch the *cmd.exe* Command Prompt application.

3. Launch the generator script via the command line:

```
python Generate_Wrapper.py gdi32.dll
```

When the script is done, you get the Visual Studio project with generated wrapper functions. The generator puts the project in the *gdi32* subdirectory.

We work with the 32-bit proxy DLL and 32-bit TestApplication to avoid confusion with versions.

The second step is implementing the bot algorithm in the generated proxy DLL. To do this, we should apply the following changes to the library:

1. Open the gdi32 Visual Studio project and answer "OK" in the "Upgrade VC++ Compiler and Libraries" dialog. Then the Visual Studio updates the project format according to the new version.

2. Fix a path to the original *gdi32.dll* library in the *gdi32.cpp* source file. You find this path on line number 10:

    ```
    mHinstDLL = LoadLibrary( "ori_gdi32.dll" );
    ```

    You should specify a path where you took the *gdi32.dll* library for the DLL Wrapper Generator script. For 64-bit Windows, it looks like this:

    ```
    mHinstDLL = LoadLibrary( "C:\\Windows\\SysWOW64\\gdi32.dll" );
    ```

3. Substitute the wrapper of the *TextOutA* function to the implementation from Listing 5-10.

Listing 5-10. The Wrapper of the TextOutA Function

```
extern "C" BOOL __stdcall TextOutA_wrapper(
    _In_ HDC      hdc,
    _In_ int      nXStart,
    _In_ int      nYStart,
    _In_ LPCSTR lpString,
    _In_ int      cchString
    )
{
```

```
    if (cchString < 10)
    {
        INPUT Input = { 0 };
        Input.type = INPUT_KEYBOARD;
        Input.ki.wVk = '1';
        SendInput(1, &Input, sizeof(INPUT));
    }

    typedef BOOL(__stdcall *pS)(HDC, int, int, LPCTSTR, int);
    pS pps = (pS)mProcs[696];
    return pps(hdc, nXStart, nYStart, lpString, cchString);
}
```

The full version of the *gdi32.cpp* source file is provided with this book.

Let us remember the code of the *TestApplication.cpp* file, which calls the *TextOutA* function. It helps us to understand better our *TextOutA_wrapper* implementation.

This is the *TextOutA* call from the test application:

```
std::string str(gLife, '#');
TextOutA(GetDC(NULL), 0, 0, str.c_str(), str.size());
```

A length of the printed string equals the *gLife* variable. We receive this length in the last parameter of the *TextOutA_wrapper* (see Listing 5-10). It is named *cchString*. We compare its value with 10. If the comparison fails, we simulate a keypress by the *SendInput* WinAPI function. Now the bot algorithm is done. Next, we call the original *TextOutA* function. To do so, we use the *mProcs* array, which contains pointers to all functions of the original *gdi32.dll* library. We fill this array in the *DllMain* function when the proxy DLL is loaded.

How do we get index 696 of the *mProcs* array to call the *TextOutA* function? Let us look to the *TextOutA_wrapper*, which the DLL Wrapper Generator made for us:

```
extern "C" __declspec(naked) void TextOutA_wrapper(){__asm{jmp
mProcs[696*4]}}
```

You see that we have the number 696 here. However, the original wrapper uses the 696*4 index of the *mProcs* array.

Why did we decide to discard the "4" multiplier? This happened because any array in the assembler is represented as a byte array. Meanwhile, each element of the *mProcs* array is a pointer to the function. The pointers have a size of four bytes (or 32 bits) for the 32-bit architecture. So, if we want to access the pointer to the function with the index 696, we should multiply this index by four. The C++ language knows a type of the *mProcs* array elements. When we access this array from the C++, we can use the actual index, 696.

Our proxy DLL library is almost done. The last step is preparing an environment for using it.

You should perform the following actions:

1. Build the 32-bit version of the proxy DLL.

2. Copy the proxy DLL named gdi32.dll to a directory of the *TestApplication.exe* executable file.

3. Add the original *gdi32.dll* system library to the *ExcludeFromKnownDLL* key register. You can do this with the standard *regedit* application. The key has the following path:

    HKEY_LOCAL_MACHINE\System\CurrentControlSet\Control\
    Session Manager\ExcludeFromKnownDlls

4. Reboot your computer. Then the register change takes effect.

Windows has a protection mechanism (support.microsoft.com/en-us/help/164501/ info-windows-nt-2000-xp-uses-knowndlls-registry-entry-to-find-dlls) that prevents malware from replacing system libraries. This mechanism stores a list of the most important libraries in the register. So, the Windows loader will load these libraries from the predefined system paths only. However, there is a special *ExcludeFromKnownDLL* register key, which allows disabling the protection. We add the *gdi32.dll* library to this exclude list. Thus, the loader uses a standard search order for this library. It starts searching from the current directory. Therefore, the proxy DLL will be loaded instead of the original library.

Now you can launch the *TestApplication.exe* file. You will see in the console that the *gLife* variable does not fall below 10.

API Patching

The second approach to hook WinAPI calls is a modification of system functions. The Windows loader loads a *gdi32.dll* library (for example) to the process memory. We can access this memory and patch functions of the *gdi32.dll* module that we want to hook. The idea of patching is inserting an assembler instruction that passes control to our code. The most appropriate place for the function to patch is at its beginning.

There are several ways to overwrite the beginning of the WinAPI function to hook it. The most common approach is inserting the control transfer assembler instructions like *JMP* or *CALL*. So, when the game process calls a WinAPI function, the added *JMP* immediately passes control to our code. When this is done, we should call the original WinAPI function to do its regular work. However, we have patched the beginning of this function, and it becomes broken. Thus, we should restore it first and then call it. Otherwise, we get recursive calls of our code, which lead to stack overflow and game process crash. When the original function finishes, we should patch its beginning again. Then we are ready to hook the next function call.

How can we patch the WinAPI function in the process memory? We have considered ways to change the process memory in the "Example with Diablo 2" section of Chapter 3. However, when we modify the Diablo 2 process memory, it is the data segment with reading and writing permissions. Now we want to change a code segment that has a read-only permission. Fortunately, WinAPI provides the *VirtualQuery* and *VirtualProtect* functions, which can switch permissions of the segments. You can find examples of their usage on the Internet (forums.codeguru.com/showthread.php?88166-HOW-TO-WRITE-CODE-SEGMENT-IN-WIN32).

There is another question. If we want to pass control to our code from the patched WinAPI function, this code should be loaded into the process memory. The game application does not load it at startup. So, we should do it at runtime. How? We can apply DLL injection techniques. You can find links to examples of these techniques in the "Example with Diablo 2" section.

Figure 5-4 shows how we hook the *TextOutA* WinAPI function with the API patching technique.

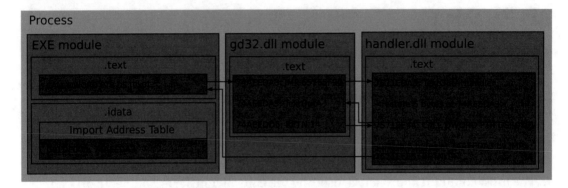

Figure 5-4. *The TextOutA call after applying the API patching*

The call happens in the following steps:

1. We inject our *handler.dll* module into the target process. When our code is loaded, it patches the beginning of the *TextOutA* WinAPI function in the *gdi32.dll* module.

2. Execution of the EXE module reaches the *CALL* instruction. A CPU uses Import Address Table to retrieve an address of the *TextOutA* function. Then, the *CALL* instruction passes control to the *gdi32.dll* module.

3. Because of our patch, the first *JMP* instruction of the *TextOutA* function passes control to the *handler.dll* module.

4. The *handler.dll* module performs our code and then calls the original *TextOutA* function.

5. The *RETN* instruction at the end of our handler function passes control back to the EXE module.

You will probably notice that the *TextOutA* function returns control to our handler function. This happens because we call it with the *CALL* instruction. That is a reason why our code returns directly to the EXE module.

When you apply the API patching technique, you get the following advantages:

-   You can hook calls from the Windows core libraries (like *kernel32.dll*).

-   There are several frameworks that automate the low-level tasks (injecting a handler module and patching WinAPI functions).

API patching approach has several disadvantages:

- The size of any hooked function should be greater than five bytes. Otherwise, we cannot patch the beginning of the function with the *JMP* instruction.

- Implementing this technique on your own is difficult. You should pay attention to avoid infinite recursive calls.

- This technique is not reliable for multithread applications. We cannot hook the target WinAPI function until the handler module processes its previous call. This happens because the beginning of the function is restored at this moment.

Example of API Patching

Now we will develop a bot that uses the API patching technique. The algorithm of the bot is the same as we have applied for considering the proxy DLL approach. We will use the Deviare hooking framework for this task.

First of all, let us review features of Deviare. The framework distribution contains several sample applications. They demonstrate typical use cases of Deviare. There is one sample application named **CTest**. It hooks WinAPI calls and logs them in the text file. We will take it as a basis for our bot. The application implements mechanisms for patching WinAPI functions and loading the handler module to the target process memory. All that we should do is to add the algorithm of our bot to this application.

Let us launch the CTest with the TestApplication and check how they work together. You should do the following steps:

1. Download the release binaries (github.com/nektra/Deviare2/ releases/download/v2.8.0/Deviare.2.8.0.zip) of the Deviare framework. Unpack this archive to the *deviare-bin* directory.

2. Copy the *TestApplication.exe* file to the *deviare-bin* directory.

3. Open the *ctest.hooks.xml* file in the *deviare-bin* directory. The file
   contains configuration for the CTest application. Here we should add
   the WinAPI functions that we want to hook. Append the *TextOutA*
   function into this list between the *<hooks>* and *</hooks>* tags:

```
<hook name="TextOutA">gdi32.dll!TextOutA</hook>
```

4. Launch the CTest application with the following command-line
   parameters:

```
CTest.exe exec TestApplication.exe -log=out.txt
```

The *exec* parameter means that CTest launches the specified executable file and
attaches to it. The *-log* parameter allows us to specify the log file. You can use the
standard *cmd.exe* Windows utility to launch an application with parameters.

After launching, you see two windows: CTest and TestApplication. The *gLife*
variable is decreasing until 0 in the TestApplication window. When it happens, you can
stop the CTest application by the Ctrl+C keypress.

The *out.txt* log file stores all hooked calls that the TestApplication did. If you open
the file, you find the following lines:

```
CNktDvEngine::CreateHook (gdi32.dll!TextOutA) => 00000000
...
21442072: Hook state change [2500]: gdi32.dll!TextOutA -> Activating
...
21442306: LoadLibrary [2500]: C:\Windows\System32\gdi32.dll / Mod=00000003
...
21442852: Hook state change [2500]: gdi32.dll!TextOutA -> Active
```

This means that the CTest patches *TextOutA* WinAPI function and installs a hook for
it successfully. You can scroll down the file and find details about each hooked *TextOutA*
call. This is an example:

```
21442852: Hook called [2500/2816 - 1]: gdi32.dll!TextOutA (PreCall)
    [KT:15.600100ms / UT:0.000000ms / CC:42258224]
21442852:   Parameters:
            HDC hdc [0x002DFA60] "1795229328" (unsigned dword)
            long x [0x002DFA64] "0" (signed dword)
            long y [0x002DFA68] "0" (signed dword)
```

```
                LPCSTR lpString [0x002DFA6C] "#" (ansi-string)
                long c [0x002DFA70] "19" (signed dword)
21442852:   Custom parameters:
21442852:   Stack trace:
21442852:      1) TestApplication.exe + 0x00014A91
21442852:      2) TestApplication.exe + 0x0001537E
21442852:      3) TestApplication.exe + 0x000151E0
21442852:      4) TestApplication.exe + 0x0001507D
```

You see that Deviare retrieves information about the types and values of the function parameters. This is enough for our bot. Also, Deviare detects the exact time of the hooked call and the full stack trace. Sometimes we want to process only calls that were done from the specific places of the target process. In this case, the stack state can help us to distinguish the right call.

Now we are ready to adopt the CTest for our purposes. We want to implement the following algorithm: when we hook the *TextOutA* call, we simulate the "1" keypress in case the *gLife* variable is below 10.

You should open the Visual Studio project of the CTest application in the Deviare sources (github.com/nektra/Deviare2/archive/v2.8.0.zip). It has the *Samples\C\Test\ CTest.sln* path.

The *MySpyMgr.cpp* file contains the algorithm for processing hooked functions. You should find the *CMySpyMgr::OnFunctionCalled* method in this file. Deviare calls this method before passing control to the hooked WinAPI function. It contains calls to the *LogPrint* function, which prints gathered information to the log file.

We implement an algorithm of our bot in the *CMySpyMgr::OnFunctionCalled* method. I suggest making a separate function for this algorithm and then calling it from the *CmySpyMgr::OnFunctionCalled*.

Our function should process the last parameter of the *TextOutA* WinAPI function. As you remember, this parameter contains a string length that matches the *gLife* value.

Listing 5-11 demonstrates the *ProcessParam* function, which implements the bot algorithm:

Listing 5-11. The ProcessParam Function

```
VOID ProcessParam(__in Deviare2::INktParam *lpParam)
{
    CComBSTR cBstrTypeName, cBstrName;
```

```
lpParam->get_Name(&cBstrName);

unsigned long val = 0;
HRESULT hRes = lpParam->get_ULongVal(&val);
if (FAILED(hRes))
    return;

wprintf(L"ProcessParam() - name = %s value = %u\n", (BSTR)cBstrName,
(unsigned int)(val));

if (val < 10)
{
    INPUT Input = { 0 };
    Input.type = INPUT_KEYBOARD;
    Input.ki.wVk = '1';
    SendInput( 1, &Input, sizeof( INPUT ) );
}
}
```

These are the steps of our algorithm:

1. Read a parameter value with the *get_ULongVal* method. If this read fails, we return from the *ProcessParam* function.

2. Print a name of the parameter and its value. We need this step for debugging.

3. Check the parameter value. Simulate the "1" keypress if the value is less than 10.

Now we should add a call of the *ProcessParam* function from the *CMySpyMgr::OnFunctionCalled* method. You can find these lines in the method:

```
if (sCmdLineParams.bAsyncCallbacks == FALSE &&
    SUCCEEDED(callInfo->Params(&cParameters)))
{
    LogPrint(L"  Parameters:\n");
```

You can find this " Parameters:" output in the log file. This means that the CTest application analyzes the parameters of the hooked function in this place of the code. So, we should call our *ProcessParam* function here:

```
if (sCmdLineParams.bAsyncCallbacks == FALSE &&
    SUCCEEDED(callInfo->Params(&cParameters)))
{
    if (SUCCEEDED(cParameters->GetAt(4, &cParam)))
        ProcessParam(cParam);

    LogPrint(L"  Parameters:\n");
```

We check the presence of the required parameter with the *if* condition and *GetAt* method. If the check succeeds, we call the ProcessParam function.

The first argument of the *GetAt* method is a parameter number of the hooked function.

Do not forget that the count of function parameters starts from 0.

The second argument of the *GetAt* is an object to store the retrieved parameter. You can find the resulting *MySpyMgr.cpp* file in the code bundle of this book.

Now we build the patched version of the CTest application. You can find the resulting executable file in the *bin* directory of the Deviare source tree.

These are the steps to launch CTest and TestApplication together:

1. Copy the resulting *CTest.exe* file to the *deviare-bin* directory.
   As you remember, we store the Deviare binaries there.

2. Copy the *TestApplication.exe* file to the *deviare-bin* directory.

3. Launch the CTest application:

   ```
   CTest.exe exec TestApplication.exe -log=out.txt
   ```

You will see windows of CTest and TestApplication, as Figure 5-5 shows.

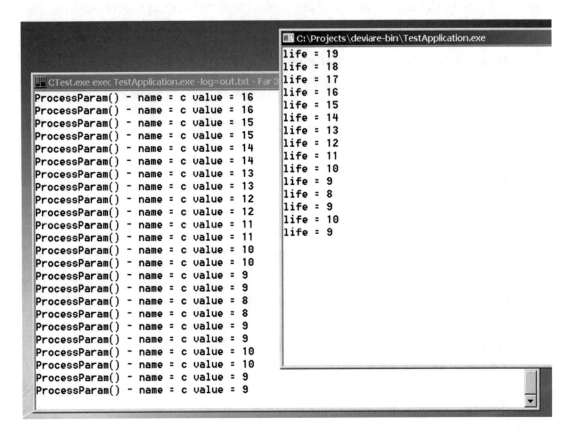

Figure 5-5. *API hooking with the Deviare framework*

We can monitor a current *gLife* value in the TestApplication window. The CTest console prints the same value that was read from the hooked *TextOutA* function parameter. If the *gLife* variable falls below 10, our bot presses the "1" key and increases it.

OS-Level Interception Data Summary

We have considered two powerful approaches to capture game data on the OS-level. They allow you to get the same precise information about a state of the game objects as analysis of game process memory. However, the OS-level data capture has several advantages:

1. Most of the well known antidebugging techniques do not help in this case.

2. It is much simpler to write several hooks for WinAPI calls of game application than to analyze its memory.

3. It is difficult to detect the OS-level data capture for game protection systems.

Also, WinAPI hooking can help with debugging and game process memory analysis a lot. It provides some extra information that can confirm or refute your assumptions about game internals.

You can learn about other hooking approaches in this article: www.woodmann.com/yates/SystemHooking/apispy.htm.

Index

A

Address Resolution Protocol (ARP), 215
AES Cipher, 199
  AesTest.py script, 264–265
  AesUdpReceiver.py script, 266
  AesUdpSender.py script, 265
  approach, 267
  brute-force attack, 266
  PyCrypto and PyCryptodome
    libraries, 264
Application Programming Interface (API)
    hooking techniques
  API patching
    advantages, 310
    algorithm, 314
    CTest and TestApplication, 311, 315
    Deviare framework, 316
    disadvantages, 311
    GetAt method, 315
    MySpyMgr.cpp file, 313
    out.txt log file, 312
    ProcessParam function, 313, 315
    steps, 310
    TextOutA WinAPI
      function, 309, 312
    VirtualQuery and VirtualProtect
      functions, 309
    WinAPI, 309
  monitor tool, 302

  Monitor v2, 19
  proxy DLL, 302
AutoHotKey language, 18
AutoIt analysis functions
  co-ordinate modes, 38
  hexadecimal representation, 39
  pixels changing, 42
  programming languages, 18
  specific pixel, 38
  StretchBlt function, 44

B

Bots
  community classification, 7
  comparison
    community and developer, 13
    compiler execution, 14
    in-game, 13
    input device, 15
    memory, 14
    network, 14
    OS libraries, 15
    out-game, 13
    output device, 14
    parameters, 13
  data embedding, 12
  developer classification, 9
  game application, 3
  in-game bot, 7

© Ilya Shpigor 2018
I. Shpigor, *Practical Video Game Bots*, https://doi.org/10.1007/978-1-4842-3736-6

Printed in the United States
By Bookmasters